עולם התפלות

•

THE WORLD OF PRAYER

עולם התפלות

THE WORLD OF PRAYER

VOLUME I

COMMENTARY AND TRANSLATION
OF THE
SABBATH AND FESTIVAL PRAYERS

•

by

RABBI DR. ELIE MUNK

PARIS

PHILIPP FELDHEIM, INC.
NEW YORK

ISBN 0 87306 171 3

(2-volume set: 0 87306 170 5)

PHILIPP FELDHEIM, Inc.
96 East Broadway
New York, NY 10002

FELDHEIM PUBLISHERS Ltd
POB 6525
Jerusalem, Israel

Printed in Israel

TABLE OF CONTENTS

PREFACE

Modern man has lost the capacity to pray. Rare, indeed, are the individuals who can free their souls from the paralysing apathy of our days, from the heavy burden of our daily sorrow, from the disastrous spell of Rationalism and materialistic thought, to pray with deep devotion for the realisation of the ultimate purpose in life. Prayer has lost all meaning to the mass of our people. The worshipper is conscious neither of the comforting and purifying power of prayer nor of its elevating and ennobling effects, for prayer fell victim to a culture estranged from G-d and became degraded to an act of mere habit.

Yet despite this the modern world, more than in any preceding epoch feels the necessity to learn anew how to pray. The fiasco which humanity has experienced in the total collapse of its culture is not the only cause which impels it to return to the Omniscience which towers far above human reason. Far higher and more ardent rises the call for help from the countless many who are driven to the brink of despair by the distress of the time, to implore the support and the mercy of the G-d of their fathers, from whom they have become estranged. They seek G-d and want to be shown the road to Him. This road, however, can be found through prayer only. For prayer in its deepest essence is the ladder which leads from Earth to Heaven. It is therefore not surprising that a desire for the path to the "Gates of Prayer" is being expressed more emphatically and urgently today from all sides. But how can we find our G-d in the prayers of our people?

Vague philosophizing about the nature and idea, origin and form of expression of the prayers is of little help. A more direct method of approach is required. Whoever has succeeded in penetrating the external shell of the formal prayer to its innermost core, will comprehend the world of thought and feeling hidden deep in its central sphere. In this manner only, which the authors of the prayers outlined with their clear, prophetic vision, will a man be enabled to find his G-d. For even the still, mystical absorption in prayer, which seeks the blissful experience of Union with G-d, cannot neglect the need of searching into the ultimate meaning and content of that prayer in order to be filled and pervaded by it so deeply and so totally, that the soul, surrendered in longing love of G-d, finds again its Creator.

The present commentary endeavors to assist the searcher in the realization of this goal. It tries to reveal the fundamental concepts and emotional valuations which the wise authors adopted as the bases of our prayers and thus bring them nearer to our understanding. The commentary adheres strictly to traditional sources and loses itself neither in speculative theories nor in homiletic interpretations. Special emphasis is laid upon the links between the individual parts and logical sequence of the prayers and their inner structure. The historical continuity of the Prayer-Book is examined and a running commentary on the meaning and terminology is given. Three introductory chapters on the *Prayer Times, The Sequences Of The Prayers* and the meaning of *The Blessings* head the commentary. The basic ideas developed in these Introductory Chapters are of fundamental importance and frequently referred to in the commentary. In this connection may it be pointed out, that a genuine inquiry cannot close its eyes to the recognition of the decisive importance of certain Kabbalistic trends of thought for a real understanding of the concept of prayer.

The explanations of Rabbi S. R. Hirsch are quoted, often literally. The interpretations of other authors also are frequently used. It was not considered to be within the scope of this commentary to give a thematic or linguistic explanation of the psalms or other passages from Bible and Talmud which occur in the Prayer-Book; in such cases merely the reason of their being included in the respective portions of the order of prayer has been given. Nor was it considered to be within the framework of this book to add general reflections on the origin and nature of the prayers nor to give explanatory remarks on the details of religious precepts relating to them.

* * *

I consider it a great privelege to see my book, "Die Welt der Gebete," translated and published in English. The political upheavals which have taken place since it was first published in 1933 justify a new edition in a language which, at present, is spoken by a large section of the Jewish people.

The translation of the prayer texts is taken from Rev. S. Singer's Daily Prayer Book.

The translation of the commentary itself was done by Mr. Henry Biberfeld of Montreal, Canada, in collaboration with Mr. Leonhard Oschry, to whom I wish to express my sincere gratitude for having undertaken this difficult work.

Thanks are likewise due to Mr. Philipp Feldheim, New York, who made the publication of this new edition, possible.

I finally thank Mr. Israel Kirzner and my son Jacob for their assistance in proof-reading and in technical problems.

E. M.

Paris, Summer 1953.

TRANSLATORS' INTRODUCTION

The aim of this commentary is to help the modern worshipper discover the "inner life" of our prayers. Here the daily service is not regarded as an unrelated collection of psalms, blessings and petitions arbitrarily strung together in haphazard fashion at various stages in our history. Instead, the prayers are shown to be one, single entity, the component parts of which are all harmoniously related to one another, and at the same time have their place and function in the whole. In presenting this view in popular form, the commentary of Rabbi Munk is, we believe, the first and only one of its kind.

The hasty and impatient reader may find it disappointing. No quick and easy answers are offered to the serious questions posed by our prayers. On the other hand the thoughtful reader will probably share our own experiences. At first he will be struck by the apparent novelty and strangeness of the explanations. He may even be incredulous. Gradually his feelings will change to profound satisfaction and delight. The parts will fit together one after another, while the completely logical and thoroughly consistent analysis and the support adduced from the Biblical, Rabbinic and historical sources will make the argument of the author convincing and irrefutable.

The basic ideas are given in outlined form in the introductions (although the Shemone Esre is explained in the commentary itself). The reader is, therefore, advised to turn to the introductions first. Then he will be sure to obtain a proper understanding of the rest of the commentary and all its details.

In rendering the work into English the translators were faced by many and varied difficulties. Our achievements are far from what we would have wanted them to be. Yet there was an urgent necessity to make the work accessible to the English speaking public, and this impelled us to undertake the task and to complete it. We present the result to our readers with the hope that they will "not look upon the vessel, but on its contents." (Aboth 4, 27).

H. B.
L. O.

INTRODUCTION
THE HOURS OF PRAYERS AND THEIR
SIGNIFICANCE

Each of the three prayers (the morning, afternoon and evening services) of the day, was originally instituted by one of the Patriarchs. The Sages later ordained these prayers for general observance in correspondence with the three daily sacrificial acts. This arrangement has, primarily, a psychological basis, explained by Rabbi Jehudah Halevi as follows (Kusari III, V): "The hour of prayer is the climax, the flowering and the goal, of the day of the pious; all other hours are merely preliminary to it. Thus the three periods of daily prayers are the climax of the day; just as the Sabbath is the goal of the week. Prayer is for the soul, what food is for the body. The blessing of one prayer lasts until the next, just as the strength gained from one meal lasts till the one after. The longer the interval between one prayer and the next, the more man's soul occupies itself with worldly pursuits—the more it is dulled by them, especially when one is forced to listen to words that dim the purity of the soul. During the time of prayer, however, man purges his soul from all that has contaminated it. He prepares his soul for the future."

However, the fact that the prayers are each tied to certain hours of the day, requires some further explanation. As Yabetz points out in his Siddur: — "No other hours are better fitted to turn the souls and minds of men towards G-d, than the hours of sunrise and sunset. At sunrise, Nature, as if touched by a magic word, springs to life in rejuvenated splendor. Man, refreshed by new strength and vigor, filled with the courage and will to live, takes up his appointed task once more. At sundown, on the other hand, when the veil of darkness is spread over nature and man, all that breathes entrusts its fate in the hand of the Omnipotent Creator." Thus the hours of morning and evening arouse differing moods in the heart of man. For the day

lays the terrestrial world at the foot of man. He is a free
person; his energy and initiative master the world around
him. But the night throws him, "the terrestrial lord of creation" into the chains of the earthly world. The day is the
period of independence, of activity for him. The night is
the time for him to yield, become passive, dependent. Night
and darkness are not merely natural phenomena, they are also
the metaphors most commonly used to describe states of spiritual
and physical bondage, the most complete dependence that can
beset nations and man.

"Human life then moves along the two different sec-
tors of a circle; the day-sector, its events being the product
of the free creative activity of man; and the night sector,
where man appears as the passive object of telluric and cosmic
influences. There man is the power and the world his material; here he is the material and the universe is the power
that masters and molds him." (Hirsch Ges. Schr. III p. 292).

Indeed, the morning and evening services in their entire content and scope, correspond most faithfully to these
two contrasting characters of the day and the night. The
morning prayer in its entirety, bears the imprint of gratitude
for liberation from the grasp of the night. In its first part
we offer the blessings for the rejuvenation of body and soul
(ברכות השחר); then follow the jubilating chants glorifying
the splendor of nature (פסוקי דזמרה); finally in the שמע
and its ברכות culminating in the historical reflections of
(אמת ויציב) the thankfulness for the redemption of Israel
from the dark Golus nights. Especially in this last portion
the difference in character between the morning and evening
prayers show up very clearly. The Talmud quoting Rav, says:

כל שלא אמר אמת ויציב שחרית ואמת ואמונה ערבית לא יצא ידי
חובתו שנאמר להגיד בבקר חסדך ואמונתך בלילות. (Ber. 12a).

Rashi and Tosafos explain this statement in the following way: The paragraph אמת ויציב recited in the morning,
has reference only to the *mercy* shown by G-d to our fathers in *the past* leading them out of Egypt, dividing the sea,
etc. On the other hand the evening section אמת ואמונה points
to *future* events, to the faith that G-d will keep His promise

and His *trust,* and free us from the power of tyrants and oppressors — "that He will sustain our lives and let us overcome our enemies etc."

Thus חסד the Divine mercy is the main idea underlying the morning prayer. The blessing specifically set for the morning — גומל חסדים וכו' hints at this. On the other hand אמונה, the faithfulness shown to us by G-d during all the "nights" of our lives, is the motif of the evening prayer. It finds expression in the Bracha characteristic of the night— שומר עמו ישראל לעד. (This difference is also apparent in the אהבת עולם and אהבה רבה (Cf. Commentary ad loc.).

The Kabbala with its keen grasp of essential elements has taken note of this antithesis.

According to the view of the Kabbala, the day is the time of rule of the מדת חסד the Divine love, which bestows upon man the full possession of his liberty and might so that he may strive, by perfecting himself morally, to become a replica of the Divine. The night, however, exposes man unprotected to the influence of the elements. It is the time of the Divine judgment, מדת הדין.

Rabbi Isaac explained the verse "Woe unto us for the day is waning!" (Jer. 6, 4) in the vein: "The day" — the time when mercy prevails "is waning," and the shadows of the evening—when דין will rule — are spreading. Indeed this was the hour when the Temple was stormed. The passage, Exodus XVI. 12, is to be understood in the same way "Towards evening you will eat meat, and in the morning — bread." Why meat at night? Because it is the hour of judgment in all its severity. They had wrongfully demanded meat. So they were punished for it later on: "The meat was still . . ." (Num. 11, 33). The request for bread was justified, however, so He gave them bread in the morning, as it is said: (Ps. LII, 3) חסד ה' כל היום.

However, these considerations ignore the third prayer, the מנחה of the afternoon. The simple contrast between the morning and evening times proves inadequate to take it into account. A more detailed enquiry is necessary. The prayers of the three patriarchs offer us a starting point.

According to tradition, Abraham inaugurated the morning prayer, Isaac the Mincha, Jacob the evening prayer. The earthly fate of each one of them closely corresponded to each of these three times of the day. Abraham's life was like the rising sun, that waxes ever brighter. Blessed with abundant success in all his undertakings, he stood alone facing the entire world and summoning it to the altar of the one and only G-d. Yet he was neither envied nor hated, but highly revered as נשיא אלקים.

During Isaac's life the light began to grow dimmer. The sun which had shone for his father, had passed the zenith and had begun to descend. Isolated on account of his "walking before G-d" he was greeted only with envy by his contemporaries for the Divine blessings he received. He had to withdraw into himself and his household. With his birth the ominous presage גר יהיו זרעך becomes a reality. Finally, with Jacob the shadows of night close in. His entire life was a concatenation of trials and tribulations. Only in fleeting moments did he experience the joy of life. Yet all three Patriarchs, much as their lives differed, found the way back to G-d in prayer. They left as their heritage to us the means of elevating ourselves to G-d from the most divergent times of life: — when the rays of morning rouse all to life, when the waning of the sun turns us to earnest self-contemplation, and when the night summons us to rally our thoughts towards G-d. Again it is the Zohar (פ' ויצא) which points out how Abraham's life is to be understood, i.e. as a gift of Divine mercy תתן . . . חסד לאברהם and how this Divine mercy is reflected in the morning prayer which he bequeathed to us. Isaac and Jacob, however, the course of whose lives curved downwards, were governed by the מדת הדין — the severe Divine judgment. Yet the Zohar finds a significant difference between Isaac and Jacob. Isaac's life was subjected to greater severity than Jacob. For, to have to descend from the heights we have climbed, is a harder blow to bear, than to begin life in suffering and struggle with the possibility of ultimately reaching the summit. Thus Jacob, when his days drew near to their end could speak in gratitude of the "G-d who hearkened to me in the day of distress" and of the "angel who redeemed me from all evil." We, too, when the day of distress comes upon us, turn for help to the G-d who gave succor to Jacob.

Into the gloom of Jacob's life there shot a ray of hope. In the midst of darkness, it revealed the source of radiant light. On the other hand the days of Isaac's life ended in blindness, in hopeless gloom. In like manner, the hour of sundown, the time when Isaac poured out his heart in prayer to G-d, leads on inevitably to night-time. It is the hour of the דִינָא קַשִׁיא the harsh judgment. This too, is properly reflected in the composition of the Minchah service. All the exultant hymns of praise uttered in the morning are omitted. The worshipper stands silent before G-d engrossed in earnest self-examination.

At this hour, the day draws to its close; the last rays of the descending sun linger on ; man will soon be surrendered to the obscurity of the night. At this hour the question is answered—have man's actions rendered him worthy to have the aspirations and hopes uttered in his Tefilla, realized or not. The Talmud lays great stress on the importance of the מנחה, for this prayer consists only of spiritual self-appraisal before G-d, the Judge. Once the worshipper has passed through this hour of judgement without blame or blemish, he may be certain, like Elijah on Mt. Carmel, (בַּעֲלוֹת מִנְחָה) that his prayers were granted acceptance. The night, however, the hour when Jacob approached G-d, וַיִּפְגַּע בַּמָּקוֹם already points towards the morning. It bears assurance of the existence of a merciful G-d, who in faithful solicitude, watches over sleeping mankind. So too, in all the nights of our lives, the merciful G-d is with us, עִמּוֹ אָנֹכִי בְצָרָה. This is the time of the דִינָא רַפְיָא the mild judgment. Now דִין is mitigated by חֶסֶד and the result is רַחֲמִים. To this last Divine attribute we turn in the Maariv prayer. That is why it begins with the formula . . . וְהוּא רַחוּם and why in the מַעֲרִיב we pray for G-d's faithful solicitude (אֱ' וֶאֱמוּנָה).

This insight also gives us the reason for the special characteristic of the evening prayer as תְּפִלַּת רְשׁוּת an optional prayer. For if it is true that the three prayers are derived from the three principles of the Divine rule חֶסֶד, דִין and

רחמים, then only חסד and דין are the two *basic* elements, while
רחמים is not an essential factor. It is only a regulative
principle. Love and justice are the pillars of the world structure; while רחמים is a function of חסד which takes effect
only when G-d's creatures become too weak to bear the
verdict of the Divine judgment. When G-d created the
world (as an overflow of His love, עולם חסד יבנה) the Midrash at the beginning of Genesis tells us, He originally planned
that Justice alone should rule in it. But He saw that
mankind could thus not endure , so he made the attribute of
Mercy, מדת רחמים "lead the way," and later on, He joined
to it the מדת הדין, the attribute of Justice. In the same way
the מעריב prayer which bears the imprint of רחמים is, in
principle, not obligatory. Nevertheless the Jew refused to
give up the מעריב (just as one would never want to turn
his back on the Divine mercy itself) and made it obligatory
upon himself.

However, according to many authorities (cf. Tur Orach
Chayim, par. 235) the Maariv should be recited immediately
after the Mincha prayer, for the מדת הרחמים comes as an
immediate consequence of the מדת הדין, and man should implore mercy at the very hour of judgment. (Cf. The regulations governing this matter in the commentary to Maariv
Intro.).

Thus the Jew begins his day in the morning, his heart
filled with gratitude for the vitality and the vigor which G-d's
חסד has restored to him. Just before the day dies, when his
daily work is done, man stands again before G-d to render an
account in prayer (דין). Finally when night closes in, he prays
that the merciful G-d grant him protection until the morning
(רחמים). The Divine governing principles חסד דין רחמים,
Love Justice & Mercy are thus like shining stars shedding
their light over the daily life of the Jew, making him turn
his eyes heavenward, in joyous gratitude (שחרית), in earnest
self-examination (מנחה) and in steadfast trust (מעריב).

THE INNER STRUCTURE OF THE DAILY PRAYER

The various prayers of the daily service have been culled from various authors who lived in different periods. They
were forged into an homogenous unity by a final author. This

order was accepted by the Halacha — it cannot be changed. To understand the inner structure of the daily prayer (as exemplified by the morning service) we have to turn to the Midrashic interpretation of Jacob's dream. "And behold a ladder was set on earth and its summit reached to heaven."— This, the Zohar (I, 269a) explains, is the prayer we utter on earth that reaches up to heaven; as it is said, "And thou, in heaven give ear" (II Kings 8, 39).

A ladder is the instrument of ascent; it symbolizes intensity rising to a climax. This, too, is the meaning of prayer. Its goal is G-d enthroned on high. In his prayer Jacob seeks the way to G-d, and in his dream this way is shown to him by G-d. The human mind must raise itself, step by step, above and beyond earthly bondage till, at the summit of the ladder, its meets His presence — but only after man has risen to Him — just as the angels, first ascended the heavenly ladder to bring the earthly prayers to the throne of the Almighty, and then descended.

The Midrash assigns four rungs to the heavenly ladder. Maimonides too, discovers four stages in the Biblical narrative. They indicate the four levels through which human perception must advance to the knowledge of G-d. "And behold a ladder was set on earth . . . . . .," the ladder here alludes to the relationship and connection of all earthly beings with worlds beyond their own. "Set on earth" points to the material world of sense perception and experience from which all knowledge must start. "And its summit reaching up to heaven" indicates the next level of knowledge to be attained, the world of saints and the heavenly spheres. "And behold the Angels of G-d went up and down on it" refers to the transcendental world of the Angels. The fourth and ultimate stage, the goal of human understanding and the goal of human prayer, is the one revealed at the end "And behold, G-d stood above it." (More Nevuchim, Intro.).

These "four worlds of the philosophers," as Rabbi Isaia Hurwitz, the great mediator between kabbalistical and philosophical thought, has pointed out, are none other than the "four worlds of the Kabbalah": The sphere of material phenomena — עולם העשיה (the "world of doing") ; that of the forms — עולם היצירה (the "world of shaping"); that of the active

forces — עולם הבריאה (the "world of creating"); and finally
the world of the pure ideas — עולם האצילות (the "world of
the spirit"). The quest for truth must pass through all these
four stages if it is to succeed. From our experience in the
world of sense perception, the mind extracts the immanent
laws of the perceived things, their "forms" which make them
what they are. Then it is led, by logical analysis, to seek their
causes, the forces that create these forms; finally it penetrates
to the Supreme Reason which is the innermost soul and prime
cause moving and controlling the lower worlds. The path tra-
versed by the enquiring mind, however, is the very same one
along which the thoughts of the worshipper must pass if they
are, like Jacob's thoughts, to ascend to the Divine presence of
the Creator. It is no wonder, then, that our daily Morning
Prayer, in its four main parts, reflects the ascent through the
"four worlds." These parts are: The first from the ברכות up
to ברוך שאמר, the second from ב"ש to ברכו, the third up to
גאל ישראל, and the fourth is the ש"ע.

In the first section (till ברוך שאמר), man's practical
needs, like awaking and clothing are mentioned. A blessing
for the work and welfare of the day follows. Then a description of the daily sacrifice, also a practical matter, is added.
Thus the entire beginning is devoted to the "עולם העשיה," the
world of material phenomena, the point from which the quest
for G-d must set out.

The second division, the "פסוקי דזמרה" deals with
G-d's revelations of Himself in nature and history. The splendor of nature, the magnificence of the starry sky, the beauty
of the reality of our world all proclaim the glory of G-d.
Thus our thoughts rise from the world of human activity to
the "עולם היצירה", the world of the forms and shapes which
are the background and the framework of the activities of
our daily life. Behind the עולם היצירה we can discern the
"עולם הבריאה" to which the third section for prayers is devoted, the world of the forces that dominate the creation.

There are three kinds of forces: the forces of nature,
the spiritual and moral ones, and finally those of history and
destiny. The three blessings which now follow conform to
these three forces. The first one יוצר אור reminds us of the

powers active in nature. The "Divine light" attended upon the
creation of the Universe, and through its radiation, the world
renews itself daily. Even darkness, apparently the negation
of light, is not a destructive force. It takes its turn in the
service of G-d. The second blessing אהבה רבה expresses the
idea that G-d is the ruler over the moral forces active in our
world. Yet while the forces that dominate the mechanical, determined world of nature are renewed by G-d every day, man
is free to use the moral and spiritual powers at will, and
so must rely upon himself. He can only humbly pray for
support from on High: "Enlighten our eyes through thy
Torah; make our hearts cleave to Thy commandments," that
he may come to proclaim with every fibre of his being the
unity and mastery of G-d, "שמע ישראל."

The third blessing גאל ישראל flows from the first two.
G-d alone rules over all the forces in the Universe, natural
and spiritual. He alone has the power to determine its destiny. Evidence of this is the outstanding event in Jewish history, the Exodus.

It is the realization that G-d is the source and the
master of all the forces of the cosmos that guides us to the
highest rung of the heavenly ladder, the עולם האצילות the
world of pure spirit. The worshipper enters this world at the
climactic moment of his prayer, at the ש"ע. Now he stands
in silent prayer in the presence of his G-d.

THE BERACHOTH (BLESSINGS)

We can distinguish three types of blessings. There is,
in the first place, the blessing bestowed by G-d upon His
creatures — the blessing which brings progress, increase and
prosperity in its wake. Then there are the blessings directed
towards G-d by man. They express praise, homage, gratitude.
Finally, there are the blessings that men extend to each other,
to be taken as the wish or the prayer that G-d grant the blessed one the benefit wished upon him.

The second category, the blessing of G-d by His creatures finds its expression in the ברכות, the benedictions that
form the core and climax of each and every prayer. The dictum וברכת את ה' אלקיך (Deut. VIII, 10), the precept or-

daining the ברכת המזון, has become the prototype of the great institutions of ברכות. Our Sages have woven them into the very texture of our lives and by so doing have elevated and ennobled the spirit of the Jewish people. The Divine Law, at the place quoted above, uses the ripening of the fruit of the land to direct our thoughts from the fruit to the owner of both fruit and land. This evokes the feelings of gratitude voiced in the ברכת המזון. In like manner our Sages, in their wisdom, have regarded all the variegated experience of life as the teachings of G-d and reminders of our devotion to Him. Time and again, they call upon us to look up to Him and to renew our offerings of gratitude towards Him through the medium of the ברכה. Every enjoyment, every striking phenemenon of nature, as well as each and every perform- ance of a mitzvah brings to our lips the acknowledgment, ברוך, etc.

In the second category of blessings, the Benedictions can be subdivided into three types. In the ברכת הנהנין, we ack- nowledge G-d as the sole source and Provider of sustenance, as well as of all pleasure. We thank Him and praise Him as such. Only if we recite the ברכה before we enjoy any pleasure, do we become worthy to receive that enjoyment. כל הנהנה מן העולם הזה בלא ברכה מעל "Whoever enjoys any- thing in this world without a ברכה, has committed sacrilege," for all belongs to Him, and only the ברכה gives us a claim upon the goods of this world. (Ber. 35a). The second di- vision consists of the ברכת המצות, the benedictions recited before the performance of a מצוה. Here the ברכה serves to direct and concentrate our thoughts upon the true purpose of the מצוה, viz., that we perform it because G-d has bidden us to do so to sanctify ourselves in His service, אשר קדשנו במצותיו. Finally there are the numerous general blessings of praise and devotion, of gratitude, homage and of supplica- tion. "They remind us constantly of G-d and deepen our awe of Him." (Rambam הלכות ברכות I, 4).

If the benediction, as a whole, conveys the idea that G-d is the sole source of all blessings, the word ברוך is the specific term transmitting this idea. It is to be taken as an adjective, of the same form as רחום and חנון, and to be un- derstood as מקור ברכות, the spring and source of blessings. The

Midrash has already pointed to the etymological connections between ברכה and בריכה, the spring (Gen. Rabba ch. 39). However, the recognition of G-d as the true source of blessings follows from two premises: The belief in the Divine Providence by which each one is allotted his rightful share, and the belief in the omnipotence of the Creator, by which the blessing becomes actualized and flows into the natural course of events. Hence our Sages made these two concepts the essential component of every blessing. Providence is the characteristic specifically conveyed by the Divine Name, שם הויה (Rashi to Ex. VI, 2). The Divine Omnipotence on the other hand, is expressed by the words מלך העולם, King of the Universe. It follows, then, that "every ברכה which does not contain שם ומלכות is no ברכה" (Ber. 40b). These two essential components also contain the explanation of an apparently strange inconsistency in the pattern of the benedictions. While in the first part of almost every ברכה, the second person is used in addressing G-d, ברוך אתה, in the second part there is almost invariably a change to the third person. אשר קדשנו במצותיו, הזן את העולם etc. Only when G-d is conceived and spoken to as Divine Providence, the שם הויה, may we approach him with the directness of the second person. As such He pervades the whole world and confronts us as "Thou." When, however, we turn to Him as the Almighty Ruler of the Universe, מלך העולם, He is exalted so far above us as to be utterly out of reach and incomprehensible in His Creative Omnipotence. So we resort to the indirect speech of the third person. (Ramban Ex. XV 26).

"What does G-d demand from man, but to live in awe of Him." The Rabbis have used this saying of the Torah as the basis for the vast structure of the ברכות. They have thereby shown that they saw in the Bracha — the most effective means of educating man towards the fear of G-d. (Men. 43b.). Whoever willingly allows himself to be guided by the ברכות, whoever utters the prescribed "hundred ברכות" daily and thus seizes upon every enjoyment as an occasion to thank G-d and to praise Him, and upon every wish as the occasion to turn towards G-d for its gratification, whoever does so, will be filled with an ever deepening consciousness of the exalted, and essential fear of G-d. The hundred daily ברכות have been compared to the מאת אדנים, hundred sockets of silver which supported the Sanctuary of the desert, for these blessings support and carry the sanctuary of our lives.

THE MORNING SERVICE

אדון עולם

He is Lord of the universe, who reigned ere any creature yet was formed At the time when all things were made by his desire, then was his name proclaimed King. And after all things shall have an end, he alone, the dreaded one, shall reign; Who was, who is, and who will be in glory. And he is One, and there is no second to compare to him, to consort with him: Without beginning, without end: to him belong strength and dominion. And he is my G-d—my Redeemer liveth — and a rock in my travail in time of distress; And he is my banner and my refuge, the portion of my cup on the day when I call. Into his hand I commend my spirit, when I sleep and when I wake; And with my spirit, my body also: the Lord is with me, and I will not fear.

אדון עולם The first words of homage issuing from the lips of the Jew in the morning are the ones that he utters when the day's work is done and he lies down to rest. Both when he lies down and when he rises, his eyes are directed towards the "Lord of the world." Night and Day, the cycle of events is linked by man's "turning towards G-d," and thus he gains a sense of security from the anxiety of the night and the hardships of the day.

The morning service begins with a serene song. It is a hymn of trust in G-d. The beauty of its form, the easy rhythm of its verse and the tender passion of its contents, have an invigorating effect upon spirit and soul. It strengthens in man that attitude of optimism towards life which every sunrise awakens in us. The hymn has been ascribed to the poet philosopher, Solomon Ibn Gabirol or, by more recent research, to Rav Hai Gaon. Its theme consists of the dual conception that man has of G-d, viz., His infinite exaltedness on one hand, and His intimate contact with the world

17

on the other. "The Lord of the world, who was King before any existence was created, and who exists through all eternity," is, at the same time, "my G-d, my Redeemer, my Rock and my Protector."

This synthesis of the exaltedness of G-d and His closeness to man is the essence of the Jewish belief in G-d. G-d is the highest and the nearest. The more transcendent the one aspect appears to be, the more intimate does the other become.

ה' לי "G-d is mine" — This is the vigorous expression of joyous faith, and at the same time the tender spiritual note describing the unique relationship between G-d and man. The G-d to whom our prayers rise is at the same time the personal G-d, Who looks upon us with paternal love, "Who dwells on high yet descends to look upon heaven and earth," Who "looks down from heaven to listen to the sigh of the imprisoned, to free the children of death." One cannot pray to theoretical concepts. It was Abraham who first proclaimed the Lord as the personal G-d, and applied to Him the title אדון, Master of our lives and aspirations. Abraham taught mankind to love G-d, our Father and Redeemer, to feel secure in Him, to acknowledge Him, to trust in Him, to think of Him, to pray to Him. The expression "my G-d," is utterly foreign to the polytheistic religions. On the other hand, the Jew begins his daily prayer by calling G-d by the name designating Him as a personal G-d, by the name first used by Abraham.

Thus, this hymn which serves as an introduction to the prayers in general, contains the fundamentals of Jewish monotheism out of which we derive our belief in the efficacy of prayer. It creates that exalted atmosphere of hopeful joy which makes the prayer rise all the more fervently to heaven.

ברוך וכו' על נטילת ידים *Blessed art thou, O Lord our G-d, King of the universe, who has sanctified us by thy commandments, and given us command concerning the washing of the hands.*

ברוך וכו' על נטילת ידים The blessing for the washing of the hands begins the succession of the hundred Berachoth

to be recited every day. (Cf. Intro. p. 15). This rite was the
first act performed by the priests as they began their sacred
services in the Temple each morning (Ex. XXX, 20). It has
accordingly been set at the commencement of our daily service as well. Although the actual washing of hands should
follow immediately upon waking, the Bracha is held over
to the beginning of the morning service to connect it to the
two succeeding Berachoth. In the morning men's strength of
body and soul is refreshed. He is like a being emerging
newly born from the Creator's hand. Before he does anything else, he first renders thanks to his Creator for the rejuvenation of his physical powers, in the אשר יצר, and his
spiritual powers in the אלקי נשמה. Even before this however,
he dedicates his entire being to the service of G-d by reciting
the blessing over the sanctifying ablution of his hands, נטילת
ידים. (נטל, Aramaic for נשא to raise, really means to lift,
raise, the hands from their merely physical nature to their
higher, moral destiny מגן אברהם 4, 1). Thus the washing
of the hands is a symbolic preparation for the *ensuing* service. It is in accord with the spirit of the prophetic announce-
ment, "הכון לקראתאלקיך ישראל" "Prepare thyself, Israel,
to face thy G-d" (Amos IV, 12).

ברוך אשר יצר *Blessed art thou, O Lord our G-d King
of the Universe, who hast formed man in wisdom, and created
in him many orifices and vessels. It is revealed and known
before the throne of thy glory, that if one of these be opened,
or one of these be closed, it would be impossible to exist and
to stand before thee. Blessed art thou, O Lord, who healest
all flesh and doest wondrously.*

ברוך אשר יצר . . . While the preceding benediction
was a Bracha for the performance of a מצוה, this one represents the first Bracha of Thanksgiving. It tells of the revival
of our physical energy. Later on in the פסוקי דזמרה we acknowledge and praise the activity of the free, creative Being
in the workings of nature and as revealed in the majestic harmony of the star-studded firmament. But first we
praise our Creator for the blissful feeling of bodily well-
being. The Jew recognizes the wisdom of his Creator not with
the sophistication of the scientist who scans the stupendous
display of nature with cold, detached objectivity. Instead he

is brought to sincere and humble admiration by the operations of the human body: respiration, digestion, metabolism
and excretion. To him, these are miracles of Divine wisdom
performed every day within ourselves. For the regular and
undisturbed operation of these functions we thank the Creator.

Generally, this Bracha is recited only after the discharge of the bodily functions. Still it is always to be said
at this point of the daily service, as an offering of gratitude
for our physical health. By also serving as the Bracha after
excretion, it has the effect, so typical of the Jewish view of
life, of bringing even the grossest physical act within the orbit
of religion. It has been said that the minutiae of religious
precepts attendant upon the slaughtering of an animal divert
the Shochet's mind from the crude act of slaughtering, and
direct his thoughts towards the conscientious fulfillment of
a religious duty. In the same way, it can be said that the
physical act of excretion, without which "it would be impossible to exist and to stand before Thy (G-d's) countenance"
is divested of all that is vulgar and repulsive in it by this Bracha.
In this way the religious precepts elevate all the organs of
man, the very lowest which serve purely physical ends, as
well as the noblest and most highly developed ones, to the rank
of moral and ethical agents. That such is the basic meaning
of this Bracha is evident from the Midrash (Tanchuma to
Shemini). "אשריכם ישראל! Every organ of man's body
has the function of fulfilling a מצוה. So each day, we
bless G-d, who with wisdom created man and formed multitudinous apertures and cavities in him. — חלולים חלולים has
the numerical value of 248, the number of the organs of the
human body, as well as the positive commandments of the
Torah." — ומפליא לעשות The miraculous achievement mentioned in the closing of this ברכה is none other than the
fusion of the soul with the body. This idea offers the transition to the following אלקי נשמה hence the introductory
"ברוך" is there omitted. (דרכי משה to Tur Shulchan Aruch).

The juxta-position of these two Brachoth leads us to
conclude that Judaism regards body and soul as interacting
and co-existent. It does not consider them to be a dualism
or a parallelism, a kind of harmony. Such an idea would be
incompatible with monotheism. Co-existence entails mutual in-

teraction. Here is where man's great task in life arises. In some incomprehensible way, the incorporeal spiritual soul is connected with the body. Its presence and activity depends upon the unimpaired health of the body. This view is expressed by the words רופא כל בשר ומפליא לעשות etc. (cf. Darkei Moshe loc. cit.). The recognition of this connection does away with all those "Theories of Identity" which end in a one-sided materialism or spiritualism and distort all the data of sensory perception to absurdity.

אלקי נשמה *O my G-d, the soul which thou gavest me is pure; thou didst create it, thou didst form it, thou didst breathe it into me; thou preservest it within me; and thou wilt take it from me, but wilt restore it unto me hereafter. So long as the soul is within me, I will give thanks unto thee, O Lord my G-d and G-d of my fathers, Sovereign of all works, Lord of all souls! Blessed at thou, O Lord, who restorest souls unto the dead.*

אלקי נשמה "My G-d, the soul Thou gavest me, is pure." This declaration is a clear and categorical denial of the Christian dogma of Original Sin. It is not true that the soul has been darkened by the Fall of Man, that man is inherently corrupt. The soul which G-d has given me is pure. This confession should be recited by man "upon awakening from his sleep" (Berachoth 60a). At this moment, more than at any other, man has no evil lingering in his breast. As yet, he is free of all passion, and unsullied by impure thoughts. Only through contact with the realities of life, is the heavenly purity of the soul made dim. With the dawn of the new day, however, man feels reborn. His innermost being is cleansed of all impurities. He is reconciled to his fate and his fellow men. He is filled with fresh intentions and good will. For this reason, at least so it seems to us, this paragraph retains the first person and does not follow the rule of the bracha. It is "I," the totality of each man's experience, which should bear witness to the purity of the soul. On the other hand, from this fact which we experience anew and confirm each day, we deduce the converse conclusion that man as he is formed by the hand of G-d, is essentially good and pure.

To be sure this freedom from sin was lost through the transgression of the first human beings. It must now be regained through the conquest of evil. The fact that his soul is pure, proves that he is able to achieve this. However, the goal has changed. It is no longer: *"Remain* pure," but : *Become holy,* תהיו קדשים. Holiness represents the conquest of sin. It is the victorious outcome of the struggle against evil; while טהרה, purity, is the natural state of being without blemish and sin. Thus קדושה and טהרה, the achievement of holiness and the natural state of purity, are two degrees of morality. אתה בראתה אתה יצרת אתה נפחת בי The verb "ברא" invariably designates a creatio ex nihilo (creation out of nothing) Ramban Gen. I, 1). The soul, as all other beings, has been created by G-d out of nothing. The explicit mention of this fact, seems to be directed against the Doctrine of the Emanation of the soul. — "Thou has created it, Thou has formed it." Then only, do we say — "Thou hast breathed it into me." The expressions "create," "form" and "breath in," refer, according to the מהרש"א (to Berachot 60a) to the three components of the soul, נפש, רוח, נשמה. This distinction was as current in the Greek-Arabic philosophy as it was among the Jewish religious philosophers of the Middle Ages and in the Kabbala. Plato and Aristotle, in their psychology, describe these three stages in the same terms as our religious philosophers. The lowest component is the vegetative soul, נפש, which even the plants possess. The second is the sensory soul, רוח, possessed both by man and beast. The highest is the rational soul, נשמה, given to man alone. The modern classification of the psychical functions into thinking, feeling and willing is analogous to this classical division.

ואתה משמרה בקרבי. The expression used: בקרבי "within me" is an intensive form of בי "in me," used until now. For as long as the soul is within the body, it strives to return to its heavenly source, and therefore has to be restrained and safeguarded, "משמרה" within the body. (Midrash to Ps. LXII).

המחזיר נשמות לפגרים מתים In this paragraph the fundamental doctrines of the nature, origin and attributes of the soul were first set forth. Then, at the end, the fact of the immortality and resurrection of the soul is proclaimed. We recognize "(G-d's) great trust" to revive the dead from the very fact of our daily awakening. This the Midrash infers from the verse "New are we every morning; great is Thy trust" (Lamentations III, 23). Indeed, the regular blackout and reawakening of consciousness connected with sleep is an inexplicable process, as far as science is concerned. On the other hand the Talmud sees a certain similarity between sleep and death. It says, "Sleep is one-sixtieth of death" (Berachoth 57b). Science too has made statements to this effect. "It is very probably that a certain relationship exists between the changes taking place in the tissues during fatigue and those occuring in death." Why then should the miracle of our reawakening every morning not help us to conceive the miracle of the revival of the dead body as being within the realm of possibility? Indeed the revival of the dead was one of the points at issue between our sages and the Sadducees. The latter denied the resurrection of the dead. Our sages had not only to bring proofs from Biblical verses, which the Sadducees would have disputed, but to use logical inference and analogies as well. They considered the analogy between sleep and death so conclusive that they made it the subject of a special Bracha. The formulation they gave to the blessing is such as to leave no doubt about the future resurrection of man as an individual being.

> Blessed art thou, O Lord our G-d, King of the universe, who hast given to the cock intelligence to distinguish between day and night.

> Blessed art thou, O Lord our G-d, King of the universe, who hast not made me a heathen.

> Blessed art thou, O Lord our G-d, King of the universe, who hast not made me a bondman.

> Blessed art thou, O Lord our G-d, King of the universe, who hast not made me a woman.

Women say:
> Blessed art thou, O Lord our G-d King of the universe, who hast made me according to thy will.

> Blessed art thou, O Lord our G-d King of the universe, who openest the eyes of the blind.

> Blessed art thou, O Lord our G-d King of the universe, who clothest the naked.

Blessed art thou, O Lord our G-d King of the universe, who loosest them that are bound.

Blessed art thou, O Lord our G-d King of the universe, who raisest up them that are bowed down.

Blessed art thou, O Lord our G-d King of the universe, who spreadest forth the earth above the waters.

Blessed art thou, O Lord our G-d King of the universe, who hast supplied my every want.

Blessed art thou, O Lord our G-d King of the universe, who hast made firm the steps of man.

Blessed art thou, O Lord our G-d King of the universe, who girdest Israel with might.

Blessed art thou, O Lord our G-d King of the universe, who crownest Israel with glory.

Blessed art thou, O Lord our G-d King of the universe, who givest strength to the weary.

Blessed art thou, O Lord our G-d King of the universe, who removest sleep from mine eyes and slumber from mine eyelids.

אשר נתן לשכוי. This Bracha does not refer to the crowing of the cock. According to the ראשונים it speaks of the ability of *man* to distinguish between day and night. it is evident from Job XXXVIII, 36 that שכוי means heart. This organ is regarded as the seat of the sense of discernment. "Therefore this Bracha should be recited even if one did not hear the crowing of the cock, for it is just an expression of gratitude at enjoying the benefit of light." (Rashi (Rabba Gen. Ch.14).

This Bracha fits in closely with the preceding and the following ones. They all speak of the daily renewal of the miracles of the creation which should evoke our gratitude each day. "For every breath you breathe, you should praise G-d," as the Psalmist teaches when he sings כל הנשמה תהלל י׳ (Rabba Gen. Ch. 14).

The physical hulk of the original man was shaped first, then the soul was breathed into it afterwards. So for

every day of life granted to us, we should give first thanks
for the sustenance of our bodies, אשר יצר, then, secondly,
for the regeneration of our souls, אלקי נשמה. The Bracha
for the "enjoyment of the light" comes next. The break of
day awakens new faith and fresh initiative everywhere. The
first morning that dawned over the world was, to Adam, a
message that the Divine grace for which he had fervently
hoped was granted to him. To him it meant that G-d had
given him the chance to begin life all over again, and to atone
for the transgression of the night. He greeted the first sunrise
with a cry of heartfelt gratitude. ". . . . להגיד בבקר חסדך"
"To tell in the morning Thy lovingkindness" (Psalm XCII,
3). So the daily "enjoyment of the light" also was deemed
worthy of a special blessing.

The form given to this Bracha is indeed noteworthy.
It is not "that Thou hast given us the light of day;" but
"that Thou hast given us the intelligence to distinguish between
day and night." This blessing really expresses our gratitude
for the gift of intelligence. Nevertheless, it does not refer
to intelligence in general, but to our ability to make distinctions, which, in fact, is the basis and foundation of all knowledge. "בינה," derived from "בין" is a thought process without which no "דעה," no knowledge can exist. (Aboth III,
21. Bertinoro ad loc.). It is only a preliminary stage in the
acquisition of knowledge to which our Bracha refers. This
fact fits it perfectly into the order of the succession of the
Brachoth we have outlined. The two preceding Brachoth treat
of the two constituent elements of the human being, body
and soul. They are followed by the blessing for the first independent activity of the conscious mind. For it is man's
highest bliss to become aware, upon awakening, that he retains full possession of his mental faculties. His consciousness of the change from night to day proves this to him.

שלא עשני נכרי, עבד, אשה. These three Brachoth again
are directly connected with the preceding ones. They, too,
refer to the creation and the daily regeneration of man. For,
his religious affiliation, social status, sex (as referred in these
Brachoth), no less than his physical, mental and intellectual
states, are determined by G-d. The succeeding Brachoth which

speak of man's rewards and obligations, are preceded by these
three which form the connecting link between the two groups.

The first of the three expresses our gratitude "that G-d
has not made me a gentile." It has always been difficult to be
a Jew; yet even in the darkest times our forefathers always
prayed each morning: "Blessed be Thou, O G-d, for not having
made me a gentile." This fact alone shows very clearly, how
eminently suited is such a Bracha, to keep alive the consciousness of the inspiration that is Judaism, even amidst persecution and assimilation. A people that has suffered so terribly,
eminently suited is such a Bracha, to keep alive the consciousness of its higher destiny. The knowledge that he is nearer
to G-d than the gentile who scorns and abuses him has made
the Jew strong enough to bear his fate. However, the Bracha
by no means assigns a lesser worth to the gentile. This is
amply proved by the fact that a good many of the greatest
Halachic authorities sanction the positive "שעשני ישראל" "who
has made me a Jew," rather than the negative form. The
Bracha should be understood in this form: "It expresses gratitude to G-d for having let us become Jews — for having
chosen us from all people, and having introduced us to His
service, so that we may fulfill His commands." (לבוש). This
belief in the election of Israel is as indispensible for the fulfilment of its mission, as is a man's belief in himself for
the success of any educational endeavors he may undertake.

To see, in the idea of the Chosen People, and in the
daily reiteration of the idea in this Bracha, a sign of conceit
and self-glorification, would be a gross error. Our destiny, viz.,
to be a "Kingdom of priests and a holy nation," has always
been considered a duty rather than a privilege. Moreover, the
conviction was always there, that the fulfilment of this mission
was only the prelude to the rise of all humanity to similar
ethical heights. If Israel always emphasised its Uniqueness,
and thanked G-d for this distinction, if it remained the
nation "that dwelleth in solitude and does not count itself
among the peoples," then it did so only to preserve the precious
trust of the Divine message in its purity, and to keep this
message safe from contaminations and corruptions by alien
ideas. Israel has always considered itself the "Keeper of the

Divine vineyard" and left the responsibility for the conversion of mankind to its G-d.

The interrelation of these two fundamentals of Judaism — election and universalism — is set forth in striking clarity in the עלינו prayer. In the first half, we thank G-d for "not making us like unto the peoples of the earth." In the second, almost in the same breath, we utter the wish that mankind speedily achieve universal recognition of G-d. Thus, the "Chosen People" is to preserve the idea of monotheism unadulterated, till this idea should some day become the common possession of all men. Therefore, whoever believes that he may water down or reject the idea of the election of the Jewish people, undermines one of the fundamentals of Judaism and denies the mission of our people.

שלא עשני עבד The feeling of gratitude which prompts the free men of Israel to praise their G-d does not spring from the privileges or wider freedom they enjoy. Rather does it well up, as we saw in the previous Bracha, from the joy in the special task allotted to them. The division of duties is a characteristic of Judaism. Equal rights but different duties assigned to each group! Judaism regards the welfare of the world dependent on this premise. The Messianic dynasty was assigned to the House of David, the priesthood to the House of Aaron, the Temple service to the tribe of Levi. So too, only the free-man was obligated to fulfill the totality of all the Mitzvohs. Nature has most certainly assigned different physical, emotional and mental dispositions to men and women. So the Jewish religion, too, has created a social order which grants to woman, as well as to man, the opportunity for the complete fulfilment of her natural vocation. It would be madness to accuse nature of committing an injustice; it would be equally absurd to accuse religion. The existence of a serving class of society, tolerated by Judaism, seems to conform to the innate structure of society. To this day, in spite of all the social revolutions the world has undergone, the difference between a ruling and a serving class has nowhere been eliminated. Nowhere, however, do those who serve enjoy the elaborate and effective protection provided by the Jewish Law, with its sweeping principles of true social justice. Judaism, however, does not make the value of a personality dependent

upon the amount of its responsibilities or the size of its task
but only upon the conscientious fulfilment of the duties
assigned. The priest may come forward to bless the congregation; the head of the סנהדרין may not. Does that make one
superior to the other? Nowhere does Scripture limit the promises of reward or the exhortation to justice to a specific
class of people. On the contrary, an expression inclusive of
all social orders from that of the High Priest to that of non-
Jew is invariably used. (Sifra to Leviticus XVIII, 5). This
fact is emphasised by Rabbi Meir, (Sanh. 59a) the same
Rabbi Meir who also orders the inclusion of the three blessings under discussion here (Men. 43b). In the most solemn
manner, a Rabbi of the Talmud declares: "I call heaven and
earth to witness , be a man Jew or non-Jew, man or woman,
manservant or maidservant — only according to their actions
will the spirit of holiness rest upon them." (Yalkut to Judges IV, 4).

    This concept of the moral value of the human person-
ality makes it possible for each man to be content with his lot,
and to be grateful for the "measure granted to him by G-d."
The Jewish woman, relieved by the Divine law from the obligation to observe a large portion of its precepts, can see in
this exemption a manifestation of Divine faith in the greater
strength of her moral self-discipline. The Torah assumes that
the woman has greater faith in her Jewish destiny and fears
less for temptation in her sphere of activity. So it absolved
woman from many of the practices designed to protect man.
When the Torah was given, the first appeal was made to the
faith and trust of the woman. Indeed, the Jewish mentality
has always recognized that during all the aberrations and periods of decline, it was the "בזכות נשים צדקיות," "the merit
of the righteous woman" which kept alive and safeguarded
the seeds of restoration. In Israel, the woman is honored as
the guardian of the pure and the moral. She recites the blessing, שעשני כרצונו, daily, not in humble submission to the immutable will of the Creator, — but rather in joyous gratitude
that her Maker has created her כרצונו "to his satisfaction."
(רצון *always* means a positive affirmative liking and sense of
satisfaction. cf. the formula רצה, יהי רצון etc.).

    The daily repetition of these three blessings is emi-
nently suited to renew and reinforce in us, the joy in our

destiny. Yet the Reform movement saw fit to omit them from
the prayer book. The Reformers claimed that the postulation
of the threefold barriers did not conform to the views of an
advanced culture. Yet we must recognize a most remarkable
fact. Far from being injurious to the welfare of the Jewish
people, the three Brachoth have exerted a forthright beneficial
influence upon it. In spite of these barriers — termed anti-
social and discriminatory — class-spirit and class-hatred have
never predominated in Israel. The Jew is universally recognized as possessing a highly developed social consciousness.
Nor could the difference between men and women in religious
practice impair, in the slightest degree, the honor and dignity
accorded to the Jewish woman. She has always maintained
her special position of distinction and respect in the family and
the community. Finally who can deny that the third barrier
(שלא עשני גוי), has tended to prevent rather than encourage
the development of a chauvinistic nationalism among Jews,
such as exists among people who preach the brotherhood of
all men?

Where can we look for the explanation of this strange
phenomenon? What is it that has saved the Jewish people from
the symptoms of decay, which otherwise invariably follow
upon the maintenance of such barriers?

The basic reason is to be found in the Jewish concept
of "right" which is diametrically opposed to that of other
nations. To them, right is the means of safeguarding ethics
among man. Ethics are preserved by right. In Judaism, however, right does not assign areas of *power* to the individual,
but rather refers to the allotment of appropriate spheres of
positive *duties*. However, even in the performance of diverse
duties, the prerogatives of powers may be abused. The Divine
Lawgiver has therefore entrusted the eradication of such abuse
to the free, ethical conscience of the parties concerned. Thus
for instance, the precept regarding the treatment of servants
states: אתה נוהג בו כאחוה והוא נוהג בו בעצמו בעבדות "You must
treat him as a brother, but he must conduct himself as a servant." (T. K. Behar) Right, in this way, is *complemented*
and *perfected* by ethics. צדק ומשפט — ethics and right — are
the two poles which mark the "way of G-d." As "the Lord
of Hosts is exalted by the righteousness" (of His faithful),

so their ethical conduct gives rise to a Kiddush Hashem, a sanctification of the Divine Name, וינבה ה' צבאות במשפט והאל הקדוש נקדש בצדקה.

In like manner, while "the power of the earthly kings is the love of justice (ועז מלך משפט אהב), Thou, O G-d hast founded rectitude (אתה כוננת מישרים), and hast created 'right and ethics' in Israel" (משפט וצדקה ביעקב). These admittedly high demands made upon the Jewish people have not always been met. Yet, on the other hand, so deeply was the impulse to ethical behavior rooted within the Jewish conscience, that the powers granted could never lead to the abuse and disregard of human dignity. Therefore the erected barriers could without any qualms be left to the people.

Human beings are no mere schemes. The totality of physical, mental and social activities make up the human personality, and the divergent characteristics of the individual give meaning and vitality to life. After the blessings for the Divinely assigned life-task of the individual, come the blessings for the Divinely granted benefits to man in the activities and occupations of his daily life. These benedictions, from פוקח עורים to המעביר שנה, to be recited, according to Talmudic precept (Ber. 6ob) for each action during awakening, rising and dressing, were only introduced into the prayer book in days of the גאונים. (At the same time new blessings were added, and the order altered). This innovation was due to the fact that during the performance of these acts, the hands are still unwashed. Moreover, there were many ignorant people who were not familiar with the texts of these ברכות, for the hand-written prayer books of those times were extremely scarce. These people could only fulfill their obligation by responding with אמן to the recital of these Brachoth in the synagogue. In later times, the author of the של"ה, in his Siddur recommended that the first benedictions (including those for the Torah) were to be said at home, especially by such persons who rise early to study Torah. The prayers, from יהי רצון onwards, were to be recited in the Synagogue.

These benedictions seem to have been chosen with the intention of making a series of eighteen Brachoth. (From המעביר שנה to הנותן לשכוי including the ברכת התורה). This number (18) pervades the entire morning prayer. It appears again in the eighteen verses of the יהי כבוד, in the eighteen Names of the שירת הים, in the eighteen Names of the שמע and its ברכות, in the eighteen benedictions of the Tefillah ש"ע, and finally in the eighteen Names of the ובא לציון. The eighteen-fold repetition of the four-lettered name of G-d, the Tetragrammaton makes up the Great Divine Name of seventy-two letters. This Name designates G-d as revealed by the fullest unfolding of His wonderworking might, as will be explained in detail in the comments on the Song of Moses. The Almighty presence of G-d fills the whole world with His Omnipotence — מלא כל הארץ כבודו. The prayers which reflect the cosmos in their structure (cf. introduction), are also completely pervaded by the "Great Divine Name." It must not be missing from any part of the service. Even the first section of the prayers, which merely concerns itself with the lower material world, is illumined by the radiance of the Divine Name. When the Name is put together by the eighteenfold repetition of the שם הויה, in the benedictions, homage is at the same time paid to the Name itself. This consideration governed the selection of the "ברכות השחר" in their number and position. They recount the benefits which man experiences and of which he becomes aware, as his consciousness awakens to life. They follow the chronological order of the events of the day. "On opening our eyes, we say, "Who makes the blind see." On sitting up and stretching our limbs, we say: "Who frees the bound;" on dressing ourselves — "Who dresses the naked." When we stand erect, we say: "Who lifts those who are bowed down;" When we set our feet on the ground — "Who spreads the earth over the waters." As we walk, we say: "Who makes firm the steps of man," etc.

רוקע הארץ. The Bracha to be recited when we set our feet on the firm ground, requires some explanation. The text, "Who spreads out the earth on the waters" is taken from Psalm CXXXVI. Even the obvious fact that he has firm ground under his feet, should not be taken for granted by the Jew. This fact too is a miracle, and the Jew, when he enjoys its benefit, should thank G-d *for having made it so*.

According to the historical account of the Genesis (I, 9), the "dryland," called "earth," was formed from the

waters gathered "beneath the heaven." "And G-d said, Let
the waters beneath the heaven be gathered to one place, and
let the dry land appear." It was Maimonides who pointed to
the miraculous quality of the phenomenon, viz., "The Earth,"
miraculously defying the law of gravitation, "is founded upon
the seas (waters)." והוא על ימים יסדה (Ps. XXIV, 2). It is
therefore, repeatedly emphasised in the Scripture, that G-d
set a boundary to the floods, not permitting them to overflow,
lest they inundate the dry land. גבול שמת בל יעברון בל
ישבון לכסות הארץ (Ps CIV, 9, also Jer. V, 23). Science too,
regards the regular motions of the tides, which protect the
continents, inexplicable phenomena.

This Bracha shows how our prayers utilize every opportunity to direct our thoughts to the wondrous phenomena
of creation and nature.

When we tie our shoelaces we say: "שעשה לי כל צרכי"
"Who provided me with all my needs." As Samson Raphael
Hirsch remarks, "According to the view of our Rabbis, the
putting on of the shoes is the outward sign of our being prepared to engage in self-reliant activity. By contrast, those in
the Scripture, who step upon sacred ground are commanded
to take off their shoes. This symbolizes their relinquishing all
independence, and their complete surrender to the Holy."
(Choreb §314, 12). This Bracha acknowledges, then, that all
human achievement stems only from Him; "Who provides
all my needs."

אוזר ישראל בגבורה עוטר ישראל בתפארה   These two Bra-
chas are the only ones that specifically mention Israel. They
illustrate the importance of his dress to the Jew. When tying
the belt we say: "Who girds Israel with strength!." The belt
(or tightly fitting garment) divides the upper half of the body,
the seat of the spiritual and intellectual faculties, from the
lower, the region of the organs performing physical and sensual functions. The precept (to wear a belt) is derived from a
Scriptual passage (Deut. XXIII, 15, Cf. Berachoth 25b). It
also accomplishes שלא יהא לבו רואה את הערוה "that the heart
should not see the nakedness of the organs of sensuality, and
so it keeps impure thoughts from the mind." Thus this precept serves to strengthen our control of our sensual desires.
So we thank G-d for the strength גבורה, with which he guides

Israel, for גבורה is always the strength that comes from self-control (איזהו גבור הכובש את יצרו Aboth IV, 1).

As the sensual nature of man is to be subordinated to his spirit, so are both made to serve G-d in humility. This idea receives its outward expression in the covering of the head. "Since Israel was commanded to do so,"says Bais Joseph, "so that the fear of G-d be upon them, therefore we say: He crowns Israel." The expression "To crown" is used to convey the idea that the covering of the head is an honor for us. "Thou shalt be a crown of honor — עטרת תפארת — in the hand of G-d" (Isaiah LXII, 3). So we close with עוטר ישראל בתפארה — "He crowns Israel with honor." The Jew sees in his headgear a sign of subordination to G-d, which, in contrast to the non-Jewish conception, he considers an adornment and an honor for man.

הנותן ליעף כח "Who lends strength to the tired." This Bracha is not mentioned in the Talmud. An interesting explanation for its inclusion is given by Rabbi Arye Leib Gordon in his Iyun Tefilla: "When the unending persecutions and oppressions threatened to overcome Israel's strength, the Chachmei Ashkenaz decided to offer encouragement to the despairing masses by including this Bracha. They joined it, appropiately, to the preceding two blessings, "Who girds Israel with strength," and "Who crowns Israel with honor."

המעביר שנה מעיני וכו' "Who takes the sleep from my eyes and slumber from my eyelids." This is to be said only after washing the face. For this ablution removes the last traces of drowsiness after waking (Abudraham).

With the last Bracha and the accompanying act of washing the face — complete consciousness and wakefulness are attained. However, this may not always be regarded, without any reservation, as a beneficial state. "The sleep of the G-dless is a benefit for themselves and for the world," says the Talmud (Sanhedrin 71b) for, as Rashi points out, while they are asleep, they do not sin. The day, the period of free activity, is not spent in vain only when it is devoted to the pursuit of "justice and mercy." Hence the gratitude for the removal of the bonds of sleep from our eyes, leads us to the following prayer for Divine assistance in the performance of our daily tasks.

ויהי רצון. *And may it be thy will, O Lord our G-d and G-d of our fathers, to make us familiar with thy Law, and to make us cleave to thy commandments. O lead us not unto sin, or transgression, iniquity, temptation, or shame. Let not the evil inclination have sway over us, keep us far from a bad man and a bad companion, make us cleave to the good inclination and to good works, subdue our inclination so that it may submit itself unto thee; and let us obtain this day, and every day, grace, favour, and mercy in thine eyes, and in the eyes of all who behold us; and bestow lovingkindnesses upon us. Blessed art thou, O Lord, who bestowest lovingkindness upon thy people Israel.*

ויהי רצון מלפניך We would have expected this prayer to be in the singular just like the preceding Bracha. To our surprise it abruptly changes to the plural. All the succeeding requests and supplications are made on behalf of "us," the community, rather than the individual. Here, a basic characteristic of Jewish prayer is revealed.

Said אביי (Berachoth 29b): "Always include the community in your prayers," for as Rashi explains, your prayers will in this way be rendered acceptable. All our prayers, then, are in the plural, if only their contents permit them to be so. (The second יהי רצון, coming next, is an exception to the rule. It was originally the personal invocation of Rabbi יהודה) (Berachoth 16). Even the special intercession for private fasts, has the plural, "for it is not possible that there should not be at least one other Jew, somewhere in the world, who is also fasting on this day." For similar reasons, the prayer for going on a journey, תפלת הדרך, is also kept in the plural.

This rule, to have all the prayers in the plural, and not to think of oneself only, contains an idea of highest educational value. Through it, prayer becomes a community building factor. It greatly intensifies and strengthens the feeling of mutual responsibility and the complete solidarity of the community. It guards the individual against inconsiderate selfishness. The Kabbala therefore, recommends that one should prepare oneself before each prayer by reciting the words: הרני מקבל עלי מצות עשה של ואהבת לרעך כמוך "I hereby undertake to fulfill the Divine command: Love thy neighbor as thyself."

Judaism holds that any prayer uttered for selfish interests will be rejected. Only such prayer will be answered as is broadened by pure brotherly love into a supplication for the welfare of the whole community. The following passage from the ספר חסידים (§553) is to be understood in this sense. It reads: "Many a one prays but is not heard. Because the misfortune of others did not move him, therefore he is not heard. Would he have followed the precept, "Love thy neighbor as thyself," he would have said to himself: Were I in his position, I too would have needed intercession." All our prayers, are, therefore, written in the plural. "Heal us . . . look upon our distress . . . etc." He who has no compassion, is no different from an animal, for only an animal has no pity for the suffering of its kind. Of such a person it is said: "There is no difference between man and beast." This motive explains the transition from the singular in the introductory Bracha (which is based on Psalm CXXXII, 4 and is therefore not changed), to the plural in the succeeding יהי רצון. It may be added, parenthetically, that according to the Zohar (בשלח p. 150) David, always referred to the community in his psalms, even when he uses the singular. Thus in a deeper sense, no real change of person takes place at all.

The basic idea of the יהי רצון can be summed up in the saying of the Talmud: בדרך שאדם רוצה לילך מוליכין אותו "G-d leads man in the way he chooses to follow." (מכות 10b). This view is in complete agreement with our everyday experience. Once a man has chosen a certain way of life, he follows it ever more readily and steadfastly, whether it be the right or the wrong way. Therefore, before we take up our daily work, we ask for Divine assistance in our struggle against temptation, and for encouragement in our resolve to strive for the good. . . . הבא לטהר מסייעין אותו "He who strives with pure intents will be helped" from on High (Yoma 38a).

The paragraph concludes with גומל חסדים טובים. This may fittingly be called the "Bracha of the daytime". It mentions the attribute, חסד, which we find to be the principle governing the daytime, as expressed in Psalm XCII להגיד בבקר חסדך (Cf. Intro. p.7). This Bracha expresses our gratefulness for G-d's acts of loving-kindness which are renewed every day. The addition of לעמו ישראל (which is not mentioned in the

Talmudic source), has apparently been added to balance the
Bracha of the night, שומר עמו ישראל לעד. There we acknowe-
edge that during the "night-times" of life, G-d exercises special
care and solicitude for Israel. Here we reaffirm that He,
in his mercy, supports Israel in all its struggles and endeavors.

יהי רצון. *May it be thy will, O Lord my G-d and G-d of
my fathers, to deliver me this day, and every day, from arrogant
men and from arrogance, from a bad man, from a bad companion and from a bad neighbour, and from any mishap, and
from the adversary that destroyeth; from a hard judgement,
and from a hard opponent, whether he be a son of the covenant
or be not a son of the covenant.*

יהי רצון. The personal petition which its author Rabbi Yehuda used to recite at the end of the ש"ע. It is to be said here
because this is the place "where anyone may insert additional
personal requests." (Tur) It is a prayer for protection against
harmful influences and such accidents as may occur in everyday
life. פגע רע, שטן המשחית are the unforseen incidents and obstructions in daily life. "Satan" does not designate an independent evil power, but an angel of G-d serving as executor of His
will. The effect is invariably to obstruct; however this may
well be for the good of man ultimately if, for instance, he
is about to commit a sin.

Thus "an angel of G-d" barred Balaam's way. "He
was an angel of mercy to hinder him lest he sin and die"
(*Num. XXII, 22. Rashi ad loc*). For this reason, the explanatory term רע was added to שטן, and the meaning of the
passage, is: "may G-d save us from harmful obstructions!"

לעולם. *At all times let a man fear G-d as well in private as
in public, acknowledge the truth, and speak the truth in his
heart; and let him rise early and say:*

*Sovereign of all worlds! Not because of our righteous
acts do we lay our supplications before thee, but because of
thine abundant mercies. What are we? What is our life? What
is our piety? What our righteousness? What our helpfulness?
What our strength? What our might? What shall we say*

before thee, O Lord our G-d and G-d of our fathers? Are not all the mighty men as nought before thee, the men of renown as though they had not been, the wise as if without knowledge, and the men of understanding as if without discernment? For most of their works are void, and the days of their lives are vanity before thee, and the pre-eminence of man over the beast is nought, for all is vanity.

Nevertheless we are thy people, the children of thy covenant, the children of Abraham, thy friend, to whom thou didst swear on Mount Moriah; the seed of Isaac, his only son, who was bound upon the altar; the congregation of Jacob, thy first born son, whose name thou didst call Israel and Jeshurun by reason of the love wherewith thou didst love him, and the joy wherewith thou didst rejoice in him.

It is, therefore, our duty to thank, praise and glorify thee, to bless, to sanctify and to offer praise and thanksgiving unto thy name. Happy are we! how goodly is our portion, and how pleasant is our lot, and how beautiful our heritage! Happy are we who, early and late, morning and evening, twice every day, declare :

Hear, O Israel, the Lord our G-d, the Lord is One. Blessed be His name, whose glorious kingdom is for ever and ever.

Thou wast the same ere the world was created; thou hast been the same since the world hath been created; thou art the same in this world, and thou wilt be the same in the world to come. Sanctify thy name upon them that sanctify it, yea, sanctify thy name throughout thy world; and through thy salvation let our horn be exalted and raised on high. Blessed art thou, O Lord, who sanctifiest thy name amongst the many.

Thou art the Lord our G-d in heaven and on earth, and in the highest heaven of heavens. Verily thou art the first and thou art the last, and beside thee there is no G-d. O gather them that hope for thee from the four corners of the earth. Let all the inhabitants of the world perceive and know that thou art G-d, thou alone, over all the kingdoms of the earth. Thou hast made the heavens and the earth, the sea and all that is therein; and which among those above or among those beneath, can say unto thee, What doest thou? Our Father who

*art in heaven, deal kindly with us for the sake of thy great
name by which we are called; and fulfill unto us, O Lord
our G-d, that which is written, At that time will I bring you
in, and at that time will I gather you; for I will make you
a name and a praise among all the peoples of the earth, when
I bring back your captivity before your eyes, saith the Lord.*

לעולם יהא אדם. The following prayer up to לעיניכם
אמר ה' goes back to days of persecution, when it was dangerous to utter the Shema in public. — Hence the introductory
exhortation viz. to preserve within the heart (where only
the eyes of the Omniscient can penetrate), what we were
forbidden to proclaim openly. That is why this prayer leads
to the blessing of G-d מקדש שמו ברבים "Who will have His
Name sanctified amidst the multitudes (i. e., in public)" (בית
יוסף 46).

This prayer was most probably first introduced in
the time of the neo-Persian King Yezdigird II. He forbade the
Jews of his realm to observe the Sabbath and the daily recitation of Shema (4216 i. e. 456 C. E.). A believer in the
dualistic Persian religion, he persecuted the followers of other
faiths. The Jews were singled out as the special target of his
zeal, because of their belief in *Monotheism* and creatio ex
nihilo. He had guards posted daily in the synagogues to
supervise the services, and to ensure that the שמע ישראל
was not said. "They remained at their posts until the third
or fourth hour when they knew, the time for the recitation
of the Shema was over, and then they left." (Pardes of Rashi
Chap. IV).

The purpose of the prayer (as well as of many *piutim*
written then) was to enable all to read the Shema for themselves, in private, before the beginning of the public morning
service and so elude the king's detectives. (In an emergency,
the reading of the first verse of the Shema is considered a
fulfilment of the obligation of the reading of Shema, see Ber.
13b). The Minhag of reading the Shema in the קדושה of
the מוסף services of Sabbath and holidays also dates
back to the days of Yezdigird's decrees. The Jews did
not want to give up the public recital of the Shema altogether, hence it was inserted in the מוסף. Since the

מוסף service was recited much later in the day, by the time Yezdigird's guards had long been gone from the synagogue, the Shema was included at this remote juncture of the services.

The persecution lasted only for five years. The Persian King died suddenly. "Nevertheless the Rabbinical authorities of those days, decided to retain these prayers to make known the miracle of deliverance (viz., the speedy death of the king) to all generations."

אתה הוא. The train of thought connecting the following portions is, in brief, as follows : — We pray for a speedy recognition of G-d all over the world, and for " the exaltation of our horn", i. e., the restoration of the glory of our past. We know that we cannot claim this as reward for our having led blameless lives. Instead we rely on G-d's boundless mercy. For what are we without Him? What are our lives, our loves, our righteousness and our strength, our help and our power? Are not the very greatest achievements of men, those which secure fame for him, might and wisdom, like unto nothing in G-d's eyes? "For the difference between man and beast is nothing, since all is vanity". This inordinately gloomy mood of resignation negates everything. It denies value to individual morality in life, as well as to the whole of human existence. The mood, is, however, only transitory. The Rabbis themselves frequently warned against regarding oneself as devoid of any meritorious deed. (קדושין 40b; אבות II, 18). Man was created in G-d's image and this grand revelation in itself must instill him with courage and inspire him to action. Moreover, the "sons of thy covenant, the descendants of Abraham, who loved Thee and to whom Thou didst swear on Mount Moriah are G-d's own nation. The pride flowing from the recognition of this fact makes them shake off the depressing bonds of a pessimistic outlook on life. It rouses them to lofty heights of confidence in the positive value of life.

Our noble ancestry obliges us to carry on the work begun by our forefathers, the work for which they lived and suffered. "To exalt Thy Name, to praise It and bless It, and to proclaim It at all time". Into the gloom and dejection of a seemingly endless succession of ordeals, into the annals of a history bathed in the blood and tears of generations, come the rays of hope and encouragement emanating from these ideas. Proudly and defiantly we cry out: אשרנו "Blessed are we who, early and late, in the morning and in the evening, say twice every day: "HEAR, O ISRAEL THE LORD, OUR G-D, THE LORD IS ONE." Not with sighing and despair, not by deploring our fate, not with disgruntled hearts, shall we fulfill the destiny which He has chosen for us as, Jews. Instead with gratitude and enthusiasm in our hearts, we steadfastly proclaim twice every day, our Jewish creed — even though a hostile world may jeer and curse, fight and persecute us.

This, to be sure, is all we can do — keep alive in our midst the glow of pure monotheism. We have not the power to set all mankind afire with enthusiasm for our ideals. "But Thou, O G-d, Who art everlasting and omnipresent, the Same in this world as in the world to come, sanctify Thy Name over the whole world." Hasten the coming of the age ·when all mankind will recognize that only when Thy Great Name will be the seal of authority, on law and justice, will peace and justice endure. Then "our horn" will be lifted up too, for Israel's fate is inextricably bound up with the fate of His Name in this world. When the forces of evil gain and spread, the star of Israel wanes and grows dim. When law and order dispel the gloom, then the Star of Israel ascends and grows brighter.

We pray for the Divine help only for the sake of the Divine Truth which we have the responsibility to preserve. "Not to·us O G-d, not to us, but to Thy Name give honor." (Ps. CXVI). So through all the times of persecutions and humiliations, we compress all our hopes and prayers into the one blessing which concludes this portion of the services: "Blessed be Thou, O G-d, Who sanctifies His Name among the multitudes."

אתה הוא ה' אלקינו... קבץ קויך מארבע כנפות הארץ. The next supplication, which is joined to this Benediction and which makes mention of the relevant Divine promises, prays for the gathering of all the exiles and the redemption of our land. But for this too, we do not pray because we seek greater national self-assertiveness, but for the same purpose which determined the content of the previous chapters, viz.: — That the Kingdom of Heaven be re-established on Israel's soil and lead all humanity into the service of the Almighty G-d.

ברוך *Blessed art thou, O Lord our G-d, King of the universe, who has sanctified us by thy commandments, and commanded us to occupy ourselves with the words of the Law.*

Make pleasant, therefore, we beseech thee, O Lord our G-d, the words of thy Law in our mouth and in the mouth of thy people, the house of Israel, so that we with our offspring and the offspring of thy people, the house of Israel, may all know thy name and learn thy Law. Blessed art thou, O Lord, who teachest the Law to thy people Israel.

ברוך לעסוק בדברי תורה After the blessings in which we render thanks for the gifts of our physical and spiritual sustenance which are renewed daily, and after the declaration of our unshakable faith in our national destiny, our prayers now turn to what has been, throughout our history, the centre of Israel's existence: the Torah. The Vilna Gaon, after consulting all the known ancient prayer books, has upheld this order of the prayers as the correct one. It is parallel to and reflects the train of thoughts followed in the sentence : ברוך הוא אלקינו שבראנו לכבודו creation — מן ונתן לנו תורת אמת election — העמים והבדילנו law.

The ברכת התורה, as is evident from the Talmudic source (Ber. 11b.) are not to be taken as integral parts of the morning service. Instead they are to be considered as the Blessings preliminary to the daily study of the Torah. Nevertheless they have been justifiably inserted here, at this stage of the regular daily service, for without the Torah, all the good things of life (which were the subjects of the first Brachoth) as well as our national destiny (which was the content of the prayers immediately following the Brachoth) would lose all sense and significance. It is the Torah which gives meaning and purpose to the life of the individual, and significance to the history of the nation. Therefore, we pray that our minds and souls be ready to accept the commands of the Torah למען לא ניגע לריק ולא נלד לבהלה "so that we may not toil for what is vain, and create what must inevitably perish."

The order and structure of the section of the morning
service, dealt with thus far, now reveal a most remarkable
significance. At the very beginning (from אדון עולם to
בן ברית), the individual and his daily needs occupy the center
of attention. Then (from יהי רצון to אמר ה') the fate of the
nation becomes the theme of the prayers. The immediate succession of these two parts throws the dependence of the individual and the group upon each other into bold relief. Here
the living experience of the people has created a connection
for all time. It has bound the Jew to the fate of his nation
with unbreakable ties. Then, after dwelling upon the *outward*
manifestations of individual and national life, our prayers
lead us on to the principle *underlying* the phenomena of the
world, the Torah.

The ברכות ק״ש follow along parallel lines, for they
too proceed from the physical life יוצר המאורות, to the
realization of the Jewish national destiny הבוחר בעמו ישראל
באהבה and connect this with the basic principle of the Torah
לשמע ללמוד וללמד.

The relevant sources show that the extracts from the
Torah, Mishnah and Talmud adjoining the ברכת התורה have
not been inserted here as material for study just to follow upon
the recital of the ברכת התורה. The reverse, rather, is true.
The daily duty of learning has to be fulfilled — so selections
from the different portions of the Torah have been added
here which, in turn, have to be preceded by the ברכת התורה.
Any other explanation would flagrantly contradict the spirit
of Judaism as we know it. For it is not the praise and panegyrics sung in honor of the Torah that has made it so
vitally important for the Jewish people. It is purely the
intense *study* of the holy literature by generation after generation of students that saved it from becoming antiquated
and obsolete.

There is no doubt that the obligation to study Torah
every day is in itself a precept of the Torah, although not
all authorities consider the precept to recite the ברכות, of the
same order. Nevertheless extraordinary importance is accorded to these benedictions. The ש״ע refers to this when it says
ברכת התורה צריך ליזהר בה מאד "The Blessings over the Torah
require very special care." The Tur and the Beis Yoseph ex-

plain its importance by citing the following Talmudic discussion: (נדרים 81a) Why is the Torah so seldom inherited by the sons of תלמידי חכמים? Ravina said: שלא ברכו בתורה תחלה "Because they do not utter the blessings over the Torah first." Rav Yehuda said in the name of Rav: It is written (Jer. IX) "Who is the wise man that may understand this and who is he to whom the Lord has spoken that he may explain it? Wherefore is the land perished, and laid waste like a wilderness deserted of men, so that none pass through?" This question was put to the sages but they could not answer, to the prophets but they could not answer . . . Finally G-d Himself answered, as it is written, "Then G-d said, because they have forsaken My Torah which I have set before them and have not listened to My voice, neither followed it." Is not "to listen to My voice," the same as "to follow it"? So Rabbi Yehudah in the name of Rav explained it thus : שלא ברכו בתורה תחלה "They did not first recite the blessing over the Torah." This difficult passage in the Talmud was masterfully explained by the ר"ן (Rabbenu Nissim) quoted by the Beis Yoseph: "The conclusion that the land perished because they did not recite the Blessing over the Torah follows from this reasoning: — If the cause of the destruction would have been "because they had forsaken My Torah," as the letter of the verse says, (i. e. because they did not occupy themselves with the Torah), then why were the sages unable to find the answer to the question? Would they have missed so obvious a matter? However, the fact was that they *did* occupy themselves with the Torah. So the sages and prophets knew of no reason for the destruction, but G-d Himself explained it. He looks into the innermost regions of the hearts of men; He knew that they did not recite the blessing over the Torah first. He knew that they did not consider the Torah worthy of having a special Bracha recited over it. The did not *prize* the Torah above all else. They did not study it with pure hearts and noble purpose. That is the meaning of "did not follow it"— "did not follow its aim and purpose."

This argument sets forth the idea of the ברכת התורה with proper clarity. Even more important than learning itself is the spirit in which one studies! Study that does not have the ultimate aim of recognizing the will of G-d as expressed through the Torah and of obeying it in word and deed, is not

performed "לשמה." It is therefore harmful. (Taanis 7a).
From the days of the Karaites and the followers of the New
Testament to the modern Bible critics, the Torah has always
been the object of disputation. In the light of this fact, one
must realize that the spirit in which one learns can carry seeds
of destruction, far more harmful for Judaism than disinterest
in the study of the Torah altogether. So the sages laid
strongest emphasis on the introductory Brachoth, for they are
to awaken the proper attitude in the student.

The blessings contain the acknowledgement of the
Divine origin of the Torah (in the words ברוך. . . נותן התורה);
they stress that preoccupation with the Torah is a religious
command אשר קדשנו במצותיו . . . לעסוק בד"ת, and carry the
prayer that we may "study it with pure intentions" לומדי תורתך
לשמה. Thus we approach the words of the Torah that are
to us the true Holy writ, as Jews, and in the name of G-d.

The foregoing considerations explain also why the
Brachoth as well as the succeeding selections from the Scripture, Mishnah and Talmud have been included in the Prayer
Book. "Learning" is a Mitzvah sui generis, not essentially connected with prayer. However, by an amalgamation of Torah
with עבודה (Prayer) our sages intended to demonstrate the
close connection of these two Mitzvoth. They wanted to em-
phasise, as the ברכת התורה show, that "Learning" is to be
considered an עבודה, an act of Divine Service, in the full
meaning of the phrase. They may also have desired that the
זכות (merit) of learning should precede the prayers. For the
שכינה rests upon everyone engaged in the study of the Torah,
as it is said: בכל מקום אשר אזכיר את שמי אבא אליך וברכתיך
(Ber. 6a). Moreover a covenant has been set up with all those
who study in the house of prayer, that they should never forget what they have learned (ירושלמי ברכות V).

It must appear strange, at first sight, that we should
first recite the Bracha that refers to our preoccupation with
the Torah (לעסוק), and only afterwards thank G-d for the
gift of the Torah (אשר בחר בנו). The explanation for this
is given by the בית יוסף. He points out that the first Bracha
(consisting of two parts and ending . . . ברוך המלמד תורה)
refers to the Oral law. The second, the shorter one, on the

other hand, (אשר בחר) refers to the Written Torah. It will
be shown further on, that the wording of the Bracha bears
out the opinion of the בית יוסף. However, so far, we only seem
to have shifted the question around without answering it.
Would it not be more appropriate to have the Bracha on the
Written Torah recited first, and then the one that deals with
its complement, the Oral Law?

The following historical excursus should furnish the
answer.

The authors of the first Bracha were the Amoraim,
Rabbi Yochanan and Shemuel (who added the passage beginning והערב). During the times of these sages, as Rabbi Arye
Leib Gordon has proved in his תקון תפלה from the handed-
down records of many disputations, the מינים (heretics) re-
newed their attacks against the Oral Law. The contemporary
Amoraim therefore, felt compelled to strengthen the prestige
and authority of the Oral Law by appropriate measures. While
Rav, the teacher and colleague of Shemuel, urged the intro-
duction of a Bracha on the study of Torah in general,
Shemuel composed a formula which specifically refers to the
Oral Law. R. Yochanan is even more outspoken in his de-
fense of the traditional elaboration of the scriptures than
Shemuel, with whom he shares the authorship of this Bracha.
This becomes evident from the following of his statements:
"G-d has made his covenant with Israel for the sake of the
Oral Law alone" (גיטין 60b). "The larger part of the Torah
is oral, the smaller written" (ibid.). Even the oral laws'
minutest details were revealed to Moses on Sinai (מגילה 19b).
R. Yochanan also explains the verse: כי טובים דודיך מיין (Cant.
I, 2.) "Sweeter are the words of your friendship (i.e., the Oral
Law) to me, than the wine of the written Torah." (Cf. also
ע"ז 35a). The desire to accentuate the Oral Torah, which
to the Amoraim seemed to invite attacks by the heretics, led
them to arrange the blessings on this apparently illogical order.
History, in this case as in so many others, vindicated the almost prophetic foresight of our sages, for today, as 1500
years ago, it is principally the traditional elaboration of the
Scripture which bears the brunt of attacks of the critics of
the Torah. It is therefore necessary that a bold reaffirmation
be made of its sacred, revealed character.

The fact, that the first Bracha refers to the Oral Torah is confirmed by the wording "the occupation with the *words* of the Torah," which leads on to none other than the תשבע"פ, the Oral Torah. Moreover, the דברי תורה, "the words of the Torah" are specifically understood as the oral part, the exposition of, and the commentary on the תשב"כ, the written Torah (e. g. in Meg. 19b).

The Bracha also mentions that we are "to endeavour earnestly," hinted at by the word "לעסוק" which according to the ט"ז means "to engage in the argumentation and dialectic reasoning of the Torah!" This interpretation of לעסוק is based on Sifrah XXVI 3, אם בחוקותי תלכו "If thou wilt walk in My laws" implying that G-d desires us to exert ourselves (labor) in the Torah.

True, not everyone can become a Talmid Chacham, — yet everyone has "his share" in the Torah: ותן חלקנו בתורתך. Like every great achievement, knowledge of the Torah is only assimilated by constant and assiduous effort. Ultimately, however, one experiences the pleasure that attends upon achievement. This may be the implication of the words: והערב נא . . "And make pleasurable for us, the words of Thy Torah."

"In our mouth and in the mouth of Thy people . . ." another allusion to the oral law. Cf. גיטין 60b, where R. Yochanan the author of this Bracha, deduces the essentials of the תשב"פ from the words כי על פי הדברים האלה. (Ex. XXXIV, 24). Cf. also ערובין 54b where it is shown that Torah can only be assimilated and appreciated by those who constantly have its words upon their lips.

אנחנו וצאצאינו . . . . includes the third generation (Mogen Abraham סק"א). There seems to be a definite connection between the short prayer, והערב נא, inserted here, and the Talmudic discussion, cited before, regarding the ברכת התורה. The question raised there was; why is the Torah so seldom passed on from father to son? The answer was : על שלא ברכו בתורה תחלה . . . . . This reference to our posterity causes us to mention them in our Bracha, and to utter the prayer that they too, like we, may be "לומדי תורתך לשמה."

If the knowledge of the Torah continues in the home for *three* generations, then G-d Himself vouches that henceforth the Torah will always return "to its old home." This conclusion is deduced from Isaiah LIX, 21, and again it is R. Yochanan who states the proposition (ב"מ 85a). כלנו יודעי שמך. The word יודעי refers to the most intimate knowledge of the Divine attainable by man—the knowledge which leads to the supreme love of G-d. (Cf. Kimchi and Ibn Ezra to Ps. XCI, 14 and Midrash ad loc). "The Torah in its entirety is but שמותיו של הקב"ה the teaching of the essential attributes of G-d," as the מהרש"א remarks in his novellae on ברכות 21a where the Berachoth of the Torah are derived from the verse: כי שם ה' אקרא הבו גודל לאלקינו. This explains the words יודעי שמך.

המלמד תורה. G-d Himself helps us to understand the Torah. David frequently refers to this idea especially in Ps. XCI, 14 and Midrash ad loc.). "The Torah in its entirety Torah are revealed only to those who have been enlightened by Divine revelation. "Learning needs help from Above," לאוקמי גירסא סייעתא דשמיא as the Talmud puts it (Meg. 6b). We find the same idea expressed in the ש"ע: "ומלמד לאנוש בינה."

ברוך. *Blessed art thou, O Lord our G-d, King of the universe, who hast chosen us from all nations and given us thy Law. Blessed art thou, O Lord, who givest the Law.*

אשר בחר בנו. This Bracha refers to the written Torah. According to its author R. Hamnuna it is "the ברכת התורה par excellence," for, as Rashi explains, is includes gratitude to G-d, and the praise of the Torah and Israel (Ber. 11b). The Tur provides the following background for its content: "When reciting the Bracha, one thinks of the revelation at Sinai when G-d chose us from amongst all the nations, caused us to hear His words from the midst of the fire, and gave us His holy Torah, the preserver of our lives, and G-d's precious jewel in which He found delight every day."

The place of eminence accorded this Bracha, as well as the brief comment of the Tur require further elucidation.

The Torah is regarded as G-d's personal possession; תורה קנין אחד, דכתיב ה' קנני ראשית דרכו קדם מפעליו מאז (אבות VI, 10). This means that Torah, being the essence of absolute truth, and the highest ideal of morality, is owned by G-d alone. He made it the blueprint of creation. "His precious

tool" i. e. the Torah, served as the yardstick for the creation
of the world, for its laws and orders. This Torah, G-d gave
us, ונתן לנו את תורתו, and with it, the right of way to absolute
perfection. Understood this way the Bracha, containing "the
praise of G-d," "His Torah" and (through making mention of
them as the carriers of the Torah), Israel, — brings together
all that is most praiseworthy.

However, as we have observed before, in our comments on the Bracha שלא עשני גוי, the possession of the Torah
is not to be taken as an invitation to develop pride and harbor
prejudice against others. It is instead a heavy responsibility.
אין תחלת דינו של אדם אלא על ד"ת (Sanh. 7a). If we bear in
mind that it is R. Hamnuna, who thus holds that Torah-study is
of such decisive importance, we can readily perceive that the
center of attention of our Bracha is focussed upon the obligation it lays upon us. Our privileged position as recipients of
the Torah was not conferred upon us by virtue of our possessing special racial characteristics or on account of
common national or historical experiences. Israel is the people
of religion, and the Torah alone is its constitution. With
striking clarity this fact is emphasised in the words :
אשר בחר בנו מכל העמים ונתן לנו את תורתו. Yet Israel is only
the messenger, the servant of the Lord. It is Israel's duty to
carry religion throughout the world, to bring light and salvation to all the peoples. "I, the Lord, have called upon you
for salvation, have taken you by the hand, have formed you
and given you as covenant among the nations and for a light
among the peoples; to open the eyes of the blind, and to lead
the fettered from the dungeons, from the prison those that
dwell in darkness" (Is. XLII, 6). This mission of Israel to
mankind at large is further expressed in the ברכת התורה,
although in a rather negative way, by our omissions. Why,
asks Yabetz, does the conclusion of the Bracha, נותן התורה,
lack the customary determining phrase "לעמו ישראל"? Because, he says, the Torah was given in the desert, free, as a
common possession for all men. (ילקוט Ex. XIX, 2: כל הרוצה
לקבל יבא ויקבל). Even the gentile who studies the Torah is
considered the equal of the High Priest (Sifra Leviticus
XVIII, 5).

The wealth of the Torah is inexhaustible. Whoever
occupies himself with it constantly, always finds novel and

surprising ideas in its teachings. Even today, after 2,000 years have been devoted to research in Torah, the student finds the same abundance of stimulating ideas, the same treasure of spiritual values as on the day when the Torah was revealed at Mt. Sinai:. (54b עירובין)כל זמן שאדם הוגה בהן מוצא בהן טעם Each day it seems to be a new gift to its devotee. Therefore, the Bracha concludes in the present-tense, נותן התורה (ט"ז ס"ק ה').

Everyone is to study the Torah, even if his powers of grasping and retention are weak. Whoever toils and does not give up, will finally obtain understanding as a "gift from G-d." Even the superhuman abilities of Moses were insufficient to complete the task of learning the Torah in all its connotations, during the forty days he spent on Mt. Sinai, the Talmud tells us. It was given to him, finally, as a present by G-d. This story is to serve as a stimulus for those who, on account of their limited faculties feel constrained to renounce the study of the Torah (Yerushalmi Horayoth III, 8). The first Bracha, accordingly concludes by praising G-d as המלמד תורה, and the second praises Him as נותן התורה.

Women too, even, though they are exempted from the mitzvah of studying the Torah, recite the ברכת התורה. Firstly these benedictions have become part of the service. Moreover women are required to study the precepts that concern them. (Beis Yosef, cf. also Tosafos R. H. 33a). For the same reason they also recite the words ועל תורתך שלמדתנו in the ברכת המזון.

יברכך. *The Lord bless thee, and keep thee, the Lord make his face to shine upon thee, and be gracious unto thee, the Lord turn his face unto thee, and give thee peace.*

יברכך etc. is the Blessing of the Priests ordained in Num. VI 24-26. These and the following passages culled from the sacred writings have been inserted here, so that the study of the Torah follow the recital of the Bracha without any interruption. They are selected from the three sections of the Torah: the first (יברכך) from Scripture itself, the second (אלו דברים) from the Mishnah (Peah I), the third (אלו דברים שאדם) from the Gemarah (Sabbath 127). (This consideration removes the difficulties seen by מהרש"א — cf. Berachos 11b. and מהרש"א ibid). The priestly Blessings seem to have been chosen with an eye to the passages following, which treat of the sacrificial services in the sanctuary. From the Biblical verse, וישא אהרן את ידיו אל העם וירד מעשות החטאת (Lev. IX, 22) it is inferred that the blessing followed directly after the sacrifice. However, since the ברכת התורה may be recited before daybreak, the order has been reversed.

The Priestly Blessing is considered as the consequence and the completion of the sacrifice. The benefits promised in it are a reward for the עבודה, the service. In Biblical history as well, we find that the offering—the symbol of man's surrender to G-d, was followed by a blessing from Heaven. Noah's sacrifice, the first ever to be brought to G-d, was answered by G-d blessing all mankind. So too Abraham's descendants were blessed after the עקידה, the binding of Isaac. There is also a distinct and direct relationship between the three sentences of the Priestly Blessing and the three main categories of sacrifices — חטאת, עולה, ושלמים. The חטאת obtains atonement for sins connected with the world of physical activity. It parallels the material blessing of . . . יברכך. The עולה, symbolical of the purification of the spiritual nature of man, has its reward in the spiritual blessings of יאר, the middle verse. Finally the blissful experience of peace, the reward of the concluding verse of the Blessing, has its counterpart in the שלמים, the voluntary "Peace Offering." (cf. Levit. Rabbi Ch. 7 — Tanchuma to Lev. VII, 2).

אלו דברים.*These are the things which have no fixed measure (by enactment of the Law): the corners of the field, the first fruits, the offerings brought on appearing before the Lord at the three festivals, the practice of charity and the study of the Law. — These are the things, the fruits of which a man enjoys in this world, while the stock remains for him for the world to come, viz., honouring father and mother, the practice of charity, timely attendance at the house of study morning and evening, hospitality to wayfarers, visiting the sick, dowering the bride, attending the dead to the grave, devotion in prayer, and making peace between man and his fellow; but the study of the Law leadeth to them all*

אלו דברים. The משנה and ברייתא recited here enumerate deeds of charity and kindness. Both culminate in the declaration that Torah-study is pre-eminent. No better choice

could have been made than to have the blessings over the
Torah followed by these passages. They are Torah in themselves, and they declare the supremacy of the Torah at all
times, both in this world and the next.

אלו דברים. For a detailed explanation of the two paragraphs we refer the reader to the standard commentaries
on Peah I, 1, Sabbath 127a, Kiddushin 39b).

וידבר. *And the Lord spake unto Moses, saying, Command the children of Israel, and say unto them, My oblation,
my food for my offerings made by fire, of a sweet savour unto
me, shall ye observe to offer unto me in its due season. And
thou shalt say unto them, This is the offering made by fire
which ye shall offer unto the Lord; he-lambs of the first year
without blemish, two day by day, for a continual burnt offering. The one lamb shalt thou offer in the morning, and the
other lamb shalt thou offer at even; and the tenth part of an
ephah of fine flour for a meal offering, mingled with the
fourth part of an hin of beaten oil. It is a continual burnt
offering, which was ordained in Mount Sinai for a sweet
savour, an offering made by fire unto the Lord. And the drink
offering thereof shall be the fourth part of an hin for the
one lamb, in the holy place shalt thou pour out a drink offering of strong drink unto the Lord. And the other lamb shalt
thou offer at even, as the meal offering of the morning, and
as the drink offering thereof, thou shalt offer it, an offering
made by fire, of a sweet savour unto the Lord.*

וידבר The daily recital of the chapter on the sacrifices has its origin in a Midrash (Cf. Tur, §48), G-d, it says
there, assures Abraham that sacrifices offered by Israel will
always secure atonement for the transgressions they might
commit. Then Abraham answered: "This could be so, as long
as the Sanctuary stands. What will happen to the people
once it is destroyed?" Thereupon G-d said to him, "My son,
I have already prepared for them the chapters on the sacrifice. Whenever they read these words, I shall regard them
as having actually offered the sacrifice mentioned, and I shall
forgive them all their transgressions."

The view, that the preoccupation with the laws and
practices of sacrifice will effect atonement even without the

actual performance of the act, is aired in many places in Talmud and Midrash. As Bachya (to Lev. VII, 33) points out, the daily repetition and study of the laws of sacrifice will bring out the ideas behind them. This, in turn, will intensify one's sense of duty and sharpen one's conscience.

Prayer too, like the study of the sacrificial law, is regarded as a substitute for the sacrifices themselves. "Let us replace the (sacrifical) bulls with our lips" as the prophet phrased it (Midrash Rabba to Num. II & XVIII. Gen. LXVIII).

Thought, word and deed are the three media used by G-d Himself in the education of man. Of these, deed is by far the most effective. However, when we are prevented from the actual performance of the deed or symbolic act itself— as in the case of the sacrifice—the two other activities, thought and word remain, though only as mere substitutes. The study of the sacrificial laws (מחשבה) and the word of prayer (דבור) are substitutes for the most effective of all means of education, the act itself (מעשה).

The Torah, too, alludes to this connection in Deut. XXX, 1-4. Speaking of the exile in the future it says: "For this matter (תשובה, repentance) is in your mouth and in your heart that you may do it." Why—it has been asked—does the verse not mention ובעשייתך "and by your deed," which would follow logically upon "in your mouth and heart." The answer is that this prophecy refers to the time when the "deed" of the sacrificial service could no longer be carried out. Nevertheless "the matter (i. e. the way back to G-d) is still very close to you — in your mouth (prayer), and in your mind (study), to do it (as if the deed had actually been done)." (ד"ה כבר 27b, תענית to מהרש"א). Of course, we still steadfastly hope for the eventual restoration of the sacrificial service itself, והביאנו לציון עירך ברנה ושם נעשה לפניך את קרבנות וכו'.

On the specific significance of the תמיד sacrifice see the relevant commentaries. It is a symbol of the daily rededication of the whole nation to G-d. The שמונה עשרה represents the equivalent to it in Exile. (Cf. commentary ibid.).

ושחט. *And he shall slay it on the side of the altar northward before the Lord: and Aaron's sons, the priests, shall sprinkle its blood upon the altar round about.*

ושחט. The תמיד was offered each day, morning and afternoon. Its purpose was to express man's readiness to surrender unconditionally to the will of G-d (נחת רוח לפני) not only on the Sabbaths and Holy days, when the exaltation of the festival spirit may have stimulated man to higher levels of thought and feeling, but even when he was in the midst of his every day activities. That a Jew must always be ready for self-sacrifice was the lesson thus impressed daily upon the mind of the people. "Judaism is maintained by the act of sacrifice in the morning and in the evening."

The pre-condition of all surrender is the will, the decision to conquer oneself. Abraham stands at the beginning of out history, unexcelled in the generation of sheer spiritual energy devoted towards surrender to G-d. His almost superhuman mastery of himself, the subjugation of his love as a father to his love of G-d in the עקידה stands unique. The idea that sacrifice, in its profoundest sense, signifies the conquest of one's own nature is most deeply impressed upon our minds by the sentence ושחט, for this victory over ourselves is but a "slaughtering" of the evil urge within us. (cf. Sukkah 52b לע"ל מביאו הקב"ה ליצה"ר ושוחטו. Also Pesikta חקת: ... ושחט).

איזהו מקומן. This piece (the 5th Perek of the משנה זבחים) and the next (the ברייתא דר' ישמעאל introduction to the Sifra) are included here to fulfill the duty laid down in Kiddushin 30a, viz., to study a portion from the written Torah, Mishnah and Gemarah every day. The passage on the תמיד is from the Torah, איזהו מקומן from the Mishnah, and the Braitha is considered Gemara because it holds the key to the understanding of the entire Oral Law. The obligation to study all three branches of the Torah is derived from the verse: "ושננתם לבניך" — אל תקרי ושננתם אלא ושלשתם. It is apparently the result of the conviction that wisdom cannot be attained by a narrow one-sided predilection for certain types of learning, but only by a coordinated search into as many branches of revealed knowledge as possible. (איש עשיר מתכלכל בכלן Soferim 15, 8).

The introduction of certain textual material into the prayer
book, however, also helps those not well versed in Torah study
to acquaint themselves with sources of the religious laws. This
blending of the purely intellectual exercise of learning with
the religious experience of prayer, prevents even the broad
mass of the unlearned from becoming oblivious to the Law.
For this reason, these passages at least should be understood
by everyone. It would be meaningless to recite them day after
day without understanding them (מג"א). The choice of these
two paragraphs fulfilled two purposes: — The first to provide subject matter for study and the second, to engage, in
spirit at least, in the sacrificial service. The Braitha of ר'
ישמעאל too serves the latter purpose. It is the introduction to
ת"כ, the laws of the sacrifices (Tur).

ר' ישמעאל. The Torah, as first proclaimed to Israel
and subsequently written down by Moses at the Divine be-
hest, is based upon thirteen principles. These principles revealed simultaneously with the Torah itself, make it possible to deduce the whole breadth and depth of meaning hidden in the epigrammatic brevity of the written word. These
thirteen hermeneutical principles (Middoth) are:

(1) קל וחומר. Reasoning from the lighter to the graver
case. The prototype is the punishment of Miriam by leprosy
(Num. XII, 14). R. Yishmael explains the passage as follows: "If Miriam's father had spat in front of her, she would
have been disgraced for seven days. Then, by קל וחומר, when
G-d disgraced her it should be for fourteen days. However,
the conclusion cannot contain more than the premise. So
Miriam shall be expelled from the camp for seven days."

(2) גזרה שוה. Verbal analogy. It is used whenever
tradition asserts that two legal texts containing similar expressions complement each other. (Prototype Ex. XXII, 10
שבועת השם.) "What the syllogism is in logic, the verbal analogy
is in philology."

(3) בנין אב. Regulations mentioned in the Torah in one
connection are applied to all similar cases, e. g. the permission
given to prepare such food on the Holy-day of Passover
as may be needed for the day itself, is extended to all Holy
Days. The reason for the permissibility being mentioned in

connection with the Passover, is merely that this holiday is the first of the three festivals. (For examples of בנין אב משני כתובים see Baba Kama 6a, Sifra Levit. 24, 3).

(4) כלל ופרט. A law contains a general term. Next follows the mention of a specific individual case already included in the general term. The law, then, applies to the specific individual case only. Example: since the general בהמה is followed by the specific בקר וצאן, the law is restricted to these two categories alone, (Levit. I, 2). The Scripture uses the general and specific terms to indicate that, out of the entire species only the individual categories are affected.

(5) פרט וכלל. The reverse procedure. If a specific term is followed by a collective term, then the entire species is included in the law. Example חמור או שור או שה ולכל בהמה לשמר (Ex. XXII, 9).

(6) כלל ופרט וכלל. The combination of the two foregoing principles. Two general terms enclosing a specific one, raise the latter to the rank of a collective term. All cases covered by the general term come under the purview of this law as long as they possess the essential characteristics of the specific term. A typical example: Deut. XIV, 26.

(7) כלל הצריך לפרט. When the general term depends upon the specific term that follows it for the clarification of its meaning, then the rule of כלל ופרט does not apply. And vice versa, a collective term which is needed to clarify the preceding specific term does not allow the application of the rule stated in (5), e.g. Deut. XV, 19.

(8) דבר שיצא מן הכלל. An example of this rule is Levit. VII, 20. The Torah has already specifically included the שלמים or peace offerings in the general class of sacrifices, and the laws applying to the other sacrifices apply to it as well. Here a law of sacrifice is decreed in a passage dealing with peace offerings. We conclude then, that in this law too, the other sacrifices are no different, and are governed by this law as well.

(9) יצא לטעון כענינו. Cf. Lev. XIII, 18-24.

(10) יצא לטעון שלא כענינו. Cf. Lev. XIII, 29.

(11) דבר שהיה כו' בדבר חדש. Cf. Lev. XIV, 14.

(12) a) דבר הלמד מענינו. A conclusion deduced from
the context, e.g. the laws proclaimed in the Ten Commandments, such as לא תרצח וכו' "Thou shalt not kill, commit adult-
ery, etc." all carry capital punishment for their infringement.
The conclusion follows, therefore, that the prohibition, לא תגנוב
"Thou shalt not steal" also refers to a crime punishable by
death, viz., kidnaping.

b) דבר הלמד מסופו. When an object is further described by its particulars, then the law only applies to such
objects as possess the particulars mentioned, e. g. "They
shall tear down the house, its stones, its timbers, and its
mortar," refers only to such homes as are made of all the
materials listed (Lev. XIV, 34 and 45).

(13) וכן שני כתובים וכו'. Two statements seem to
contradict one another. A third statement removes the diffi-
culty. In Ex. XX, 22 we find "From the heaven I have spoken
to you." In the same chapter, verse 20, G-d is said to have
descended on Mt. Sinai. The disagreement is explained in
Deut. IV, 36, "From the heaven He made thee hear His
voice, and on the earth He made thee see His great fire;
and thou heardst His words from the fire." For the reason
behind the insertion of the apparently irrelevant "וכן" cf.
אוצר התפלות and J. Z. Mecklenberg's תפלת ישראל.

יהי רצון. This prayer (taken from Aboth V, 20) concludes the section of the sacrifices. It is also recited at the end
of the ש"ע, which, as we have pointed out is said כנגד תמידין
instead of the daily sacrifices. In both places, the prayer is
included to keep alive the idea that both the study of the
laws of sacrifice and prayer itself are merely substitutes. True
עבודה is achieved only through the medium of the actual
sacrifices. The Vilna Gaon taking his cue from Lam. II, מלכה
ושריה בגוים אין תורה remarks that a complete understanding of
the Torah can only be attained in the Holy Land. Therefore
our petition for the rebuilding of the Sanctuary is linked
to the request ותן חלקנו בתורתך to give us our full share
of the Torah. The harmonious development of complete
Jewishness is hampered by all kinds of restrictions in the
Galuth. For the proper maturing and flowering of Judaism,
the sanctuary and sacrifical service are necessary.

עטיפת טלית והנחת תפילין.

The Mitzvah to wear the Tefillin, as the wording of the Shema paragraphs shows, does not have to be performed at any specific time of the day. Nevertheless, it is customary to wear the Tefillin only when reciting the morning prayer. This is because it seems almost impossible to maintain the perfect purity of mind and body necessary for the wearing of those sacred seals of the Divine. The wearing of the Tallith and Tefillin is *obligatory* during the recital of the שמע and ש"ע (O. CH. §25, 4).

Said Rabbi Yochanan "He who is willing to accept the yoke of the kingdom of heaven, should cleanse himself, wash his hands, put on the Tefillin and read the שמע and ש"ע. He who reads the Shema without Tefillin is to be compared to one who brings a peace-offering without a meal-offering, or a sacrifice without libations! According to עולא he bears false witness against himself. (Ber. 14b). The meaning of this statement is explained by Rabbenu Yonah (ibid.): "By placing the Tefillin on his *head,* man performs the act of submitting his *mind* and *spirit* to the Divine rule, while the subordination of his *body* and achievements to G-d, is brought out by the Tefillin on the *arm.* To recite the Shema while one is wearing the Tefillin, is therefore, considered an act of total submission to the Kingdom of G-d." If, however, one prays while not wearing the Tefillin he does not fulfill the Mitzvah properly, as the simile used by Rabbenu Yonah shows. Or else, he "bears false witness against himself," by repeating the command to wear Tefillin, appearing in the Shema (וקשרתם) without observing it.

The Mitzvah of Tzizis is partially fulfilled by means of the "small Tallis" (ארבע כנפות). It is completed by the wearing of the "large Tallis" during prayer. Only the latter tallis meets and fulfills quite literally the requirement "אשר תכסה בה" of the Torah (Deut. XXII, 12). The significance of Tzizis as the reminder for all the commandments (Num. XV, 39) is broad and comprehensive. Moreover, it is the more frequently observed Mitzvah of the two, since it is

worn on Sabbaths and Holy Days as well. Therefore, the
Tallis is donned before the Tefillin. The latter, in their turn,
are the "Sign of G-d" (Deut. VI, 8). They bear a higher
degree of holiness. The rule is that we proceed from the
lower to the higher degree in matters of holiness. For this
reason, too, the Tallis comes before the Tefillin. (For the
details of the regulations governing the Mitzvos of Tallis
and Tefillin cf. Orach Chaim §§ 8, 25).

With the donning of the Tallis and Tefillin, we have
performed the last part of the morning service that is confined within the עולם העשיה, the world of deed (matter).
In the next section, the פסוקי דזמרה, we ascend another rung
of the ladder of prayer, and enter the עולם היצירה, the world
of forms — the realm of those forces which serve to keep the
complex organism of nature moving and alive, and so give it
its final shape — its "form."

פסוקי דזמרה.

מִזְמוֹר. *A Psalm; a Song at the Dedication of the House; a Psalm of David. I will extol thee, O Lord; for thou hast drawn me up, and hast not made my foes to rejoice over me. O Lord, my G-d, I cried unto thee, and thou didst heal me. O Lord, thou broughtest up my soul from the grave, thou hast kept me alive, that I should not go down to the pit. Sing praise unto the Lord, O ye his loving ones, and give thanks to his holy name. For his anger is but for a moment; his favour is for a lifetime, weeping may tarry for the night, but joy cometh in the morning. As for me, I said in my prosperity, I shall never be moved. Thou, Lord, of thy favour hadst made my mountain to stand strong, thou didst hide thy face; I was confounded. I cried unto thee, O Lord; and unto the Lord I made supplication. What profit is there in my blood if I go down to the pit? Can the dust give thanks to thee? Can it declare thy truth? Hear, O Lord, and be gracious unto me; Lord, be thou my helper. Thou hast turned for me my mourning into dancing; thou hast loosed my sackcloth, and girded me with gladness. To the end that my glory may sing praise to thee, and not be silent, O Lord my G-d, I will give thanks unto thee for ever.*

מִזְמוֹר (Ps. XXX) Only vague answers have been given to the questions, when and why this psalm was inserted at this particular point in the Shacharis service. It is first found in 17th century Sephardic prayer books. In some Siddurim the introductory phrase has been omitted, and the prayer begins אֲרוֹמִמְךָ. There seems to have been a special reason for this procedure. It was the custom that those who entered the temple with their "First Fruits" recited the words אֲרוֹמִמְךָ in grateful homage to the Giver of the produce of the land. A similar idea may have led to the introduction of these words at the beginning of the first part of the public service. However, the thoughts expressed in this psalm seem particularly suited to form an overture to the פסוקי דזמרה. In them, G-d is praised by the jubilant homage of His creatures, by the concert of the

59

multitudinous forces and forms of nature. Yet the worshipper does not always find himself in the proper mood to join
in the joyous theme-song of the cosmos. His heart may be
burdened by sorrow and despair, emotional states that render
him numb to the feelings of utter surrender and undivided
love which evoke such hymns of praise. So at the beginning of
the service the Psalmist approaches the worshipper with words
of comfort and encouragement. He tells him of his own strange
fate. He too had fallen into sadness and despair, yet he rose
to the heights of happiness and bliss. ארוממך The assurance
of the   ever-present mercy of G-d, gives even the depressed
and unhappy the courage to join the universal chorus, למען
יזמרך כבוד.

ברוך שאמר. *Blessed be he who spoke, and the world
existed, blessed be he, blessed be he who was the maker
of the world in the beginning, blessed be he who speaketh
and doeth, blessed be he who decreeth and performeth , blessed be he who hath mercy upon the earth, blessed be he who
hath mercy upon his creatures, blessed be he who payeth
a good reward to them that fear him, blessed be who liveth
for ever, and endureth to eternity, blessed be he who redee-
meth and delivereth, blessed be his name. — Blessed art thou
O Lord our G-d, King of the universe, O G-d and merciful
Father, praised by the mouth of thy people, lauded and glorified by the tongue of thy loving ones and thy servants. We
also praise thee, O Lord our G-d, with the songs of David thy
servant; with praises and psalms we will magnify, laud and
glorify thee, and we will make mention of thy name, and proclaim thee our King, O our G-d, thou the only one, the life of
all worlds. O King, praised and glorified by thy great name
for ever and ever. Blessed art thou, O Lord, a King extolled
with praises.*

ברוך שאמר. This is the real beginning of the second
division of the Shacharis. The Bracha, ברוך שאמר, opens the
section, and the Bracha, ישתבח, concludes it. Enclosed between
the two Berachoth, this part becomes a complete and distinct
entity. When ברוך שאמר is recited, the worshipper stands,
raises the ציצית hanging over the front of his body and holds
them in his hands, "to declare that the ב"ש treats of the
Higher Regions." This behavior, as well as the remarkable

statement recorded in Kabbalist literature that the ברוך שאמר was handed down to the Men of the Great Assembly in a script that came from heaven, leads us to pay closer attention to this Bracha and thoroughly examine its content.

We find that the seven introductory benedictions (ברוך . . . etc.) interpret the seven attributes implied in the sacred Name of G-d, שם הויה, understanding of which is considered a precondition to our prayers being accepted. The Midrash to Ps. 91, 14 asks, "Why does Israel pray in this world and is not heard?" and answers, "Because it does not know the Holy Name." The exposition of the meaning of the Sacred Name is set, therefore, at the beginning of the service. Moreover, by preceding the פסוקי דזמרה, the song of G-d's many-sided activity in nature and history, these blessings proclaim that His attributes are the one ultimate, single cause of the countless patterns and of the constant succession of cosmic events.

In the succeeding explanation of the ב"ש, we follow the explanations given by the late Professor David Hoffman in his commentary on Leviticus I, 7.

The ב"ש contains those interpretations of the Holy Name which are found in the Talmud and Midrash. Instead of having the שם המיוחד, the Tetragrammaton, follow the Baruch (as in other benedictions), its different meanings are here substituted for the Name itself. In all these interpretations the verbs: היה הוה — to be, is regarded as the etymological root of the שם. This view finds its source in the verse, Ex. III, 14 where, as Rabbi Samuel Ben Meir (רשב"ם) remarks, G-d called himself אהיה (the first person future of היה), whereas Moses, in disclosing the Divine Name to the children of Israel, changed the form to the third person, and in so doing substituted a ו for the second י. In its different implications, the שם is regarded either as a Kal, a Piel or a Hiphil form.

1) The meaning of the שם הויה we encounter most frequently, is: שאמר והיה העולם viz., Creator of the world. This is the significance which Rabbi Eliezer attaches to it in the Mechilta to Ex. VI 2, אני הוא שאמרתי והיה העולם. Great emphasis is placed on the fact that it was G-d's WORD alone which called forth the creation הוא אמר ויהי. The belief

in creatio ex nihilo is further affirmed in the more explicit
ברוך עושה בראשית.

    2) The second implication of the שם הויה is that G-d
is מהוה דברו, He makes his promises come into *being.* Cf.
Mechilta to Ex. VI 2, where R. Shimon explains the Name as
נאמן, G-d always fulfills his promise of reward, even though
the recipient may no longer deserve it, even though the con-
dition upon which the promise was made to depend was not
fulfilled. (Ber. 17a, Maim. הלכות יסודי התורה X 4, Mechilta
ibid.). In like manner, the warnings of punishment are im-
plemented as well, unless the sinner mends his ways. An example of the latter is Babylon. Its destruction was foretold,
complete in every detail, in the Bible. That is why whoever
passes by the ruins of the ancient Babylon should recite the
words: ברוך אומר ועושה ברוך גוזר ומקיים.

    3) In ברוך מרחם, the שם is regarded as the מדת
הרחמים, the attribute of mercy. This interpretation is quite
common in Rabbinical literature. We cite: כל מקום שנאמר
ה' זו מדת הרחמים. Moses, before he undertook his mission to
the Israelites, asked G-d to tell him which name he should
communicate to them. The answer was: אהי' אשר אהי'. It
seems to us that this name is not to be understood in its philosophical sense(as some commentators would have it), i. e.
as expressing the immutability of the existence of G-d. It is,
indeed, difficult to see how so abstract a concept could have
brought hope and encouragement to the downtrodden slaves
in Egypt, even if we assume that they could grasp its metaphysical implications. We believe instead that the Name (which
we have interpreted above as connoting the attribute of mercy)
was to convey to the Children of Israel the message that G-d
was always with them. So too on the same occasion, G-d assured Moses of his aid in his difficult calling, using the same
term כי אהיה עמך. (Cf. Ps. 91, 14; עמו אנכי בצרה...כי ידע שמי).
To ברוך על הארץ. Cf. Rashi, Gen. I, 1 . . . הקדים. (See
also the intoduction to this commentary p. 10).

    4) ברוך משלם שכר טוב ליראיו is the fourth idea con-
veyed by the Sacred Name. Rabbi Joshua explains it in these
words (Mechilta to Ex. VI, 2): נאמן אני לשלם שכר "I can be
relied upon to pay reward." G-d's trustworthiness has to be
affirmed because reward is not always meted out in this world.

It is often safeguarded for full and certain payment in the world to come.

In this interpretation the שם הויה seems to have been understood as a future form of the verb, to be translated "Who *will be* with man in the future," or in some similar way. Only in the עולם הבא, in the lasting, *perfect* world of the future can there be an award of lasting goodness (therefore משלם שכר טוב,)), reserved for those alone who fear Him.

5) ברוך חי וקים לנצח. G-d is eternal, as the prayer אדון עולם attests. The Midrash Rabba, ad loc., discovers this meaning in the Holy Name. אמר הקב"ה למשה אמר להם אני שהייתי ואני הוא עכשיו ואני הוא לעתיד לבא. But G-d's is not the detached, indifferent existence with which certain pagan religions endowed their godheads. They considered their gods as powers of the past who might, for a fleeting moment, have made contact with the world, but have long since withdrawn to a distant realm far removed from any interest in this world. How different is our concept of G-d. To us, He is חי לעד, alive to every moment of the present; and קים לנצח, He exists for ever. Judaism affirms its faith in a free and active Providence, constantly, creatively in touch with the world, a Providence which will lead mankind on to the ultimate, inevitable goal — redemption. משלם שכר טוב וקים לנצח is only possible if חי לעד.

6) ברוך פודה ומציל. G-d is a "מהוה" in the sense that He restores new life to the lost and forsaken. It seems that פודה signifies rescue from moral decline, מציל from physical distress. The redemption from Egypt exemplifies a redemption from total destruction. When all hopes had gone from the hearts of the downcast slaves of the Pharaohs and even the last semblance of national existence had disappeared, G-d as the פודה ומציל raised Israel to undreamed of heights, to be a "kingdom of priests and a holy nation."

7) ברוך שמו is the seventh and final meaning which our sages found in the שם המפורש, the nomen proprium (proper name) of the Deity. Thus the Midrash (Bereshith Rabba 17 and Yalkut to Isaiah XLII 8) says : ה' הוא שמי שקרא לי אדם הראשון, הוא שמי שהתניתי ביני לבין עצמי הוא שמי שהתניתי ביני ובין מלאכי השרת

"הויה is the name by which I called Myself; it is the Name to which the ministering angels address their call." How a name can be applied to a Being so far exalted above human perception and experience, is a problem dealt with in the book of the Kuzari (IV, 3). The answer is that Adam acquired the right to call G-d by a specific, personal Name, because G-d revealed a specific aspect of Himself to Adam. ברוך שמו may therefore be explained in this way: Blessed be the Being whose essential nature is utterly incomprehensible to man, but Who can be called by a name which expresses the effect that the revelation of His attributes makes upon man.

Professor Hoffman ז"ל gives the following, as being the historical motive for the inclusion of the ברוך הוא: According to an ancient source quoted in the ספר היוחסין, the ברוך שאמר was chanted at the ceremony of the inauguration of the ראש גלותא, the Exilarch in Babylon. The precentor read the prayer sentence by sentence, and a choir of boys would respond with ברוך הוא to each blessing.

Having completed the recital of the sacred Names of the Deity, the ברוך שאמר now declares that G-d, the Lord, the Loving Father האל האב הרחמן is to be praised and extolled by the mouths of His faithful worshippers. However, G-d is the ruler of the entire universe. So His Great Name will be praised and glorified for all time by His creation quite apart from the adoration accorded him by human beings. With this declaration, setting forth both the importance and the limits of man's role in the universe, we come to the beginning of the פסוקי דזמרה.

Two terms for praise, הלול and שבח, predominate in this section. The first denotes the praise obviously due to G-d as Master of the Universe. שבח, on the other hand, is the praise evoked by patient, devoted research into the wonders of nature. It is heard within the narrow circle of the faithful servants of G-d, משבח בלשון חסידיו. (Cf. Malbim to Psalms CXLV, 4); while הלול is the ringing acclamation issuing from the whole nation, מהלל בפי עמו. This is the most profound meaning of the concluding Bracha: — The King whose praise is evoked by the admiration His boundless might inspires (בתשבחות).

Finally, the purpose of the פסוקי דזמרה is also suggested in the introductory Bracha by the words נגדלך ונשבחך
ונפארך. We have pointed out how this whole section of the
Shacharis seeks to proclaim that all the events in nature and
human life can be traced back to G-d. Any belief in interme-
diary powers must be eliminated before man may approach
G-d in prayer. The פס' דז' thus have the preparatory, rather
negative purpose of purifying our thoughts by expelling erroneous ideas and false dogmas. The same idea underlines
a statement in the Kabbala. There the word זמרה (in פסוקי
דזמרה) is derived from the same root as the word תזמור (לא
תזמור Lev. XXV, 5) viz. "to cut." פס' דז' would then indicate
that, in this section of the service, all impediments to prayer are
cut off. The *positive* accomplishment of the פס' דז' is then
to have G-d acknowledged as the sole source of power within
the organism of the cosmos : יחיד חי העולמים, where עולמים
has the double sense — infinity both of space and time. The
Bracha that closes the פס' דז' contains the parallel expression,
מלך אל חי העולמים.

'הודו לה' *O give thanks unto the Lord, call upon his
name; make known his doings among the peoples. Sing unto
him; tell ye of all his marvellous works. Glory ye in his holy
name, let the heart of them rejoice that seek the Lord. Search
ye for the Lord and his strength; seek ye his face evermore.
Remember his marvellous works that he hath done; his wonders, and the judgements of his mouth; O ye seed of Israel,
his servant, ye children of Jacob, his chosen ones. He is the
Lord our G-d, his judgements are in all the earth. Remember
his covenant for ever, the word which he commanded to a
thousand generations; the covenant which he made with
Abraham, and his oath unto Isaac; and confirmed the same
unto Jacob for a statute, to Israel for an everlasting covenant,
saying, Unto thee will I give the land of Canaan, as the lot
of your inheritance, when ye were but a few men in number;
yea, few, and sojourners in it; and they went about from nation
to nation, and from one kingdom to another people. He suffered no man to oppress them; yea, he rebuked kings for
their sakes; saying, Touch not mine anointed ones, and do
my prophets no harm. Sing unto the Lord, all the earth; proclaim his salvation from day to day. Recount his glory among
the nations, his marvels among all the peoples. For great is*

the Lord, and exceedingly to be praised, he is to be feared above all gods. For all the gods of the peoples are things of nought, but the Lord made the heavens. Grandeur and majesty are before him, strength and gladness are in his place. Give unto the Lord, ye families of the peoples, give unto the Lord glory and strength. Give unto the Lord the glory due unto his name; take an offering, and come before him, worship the Lord in the beauty of holiness. Tremble before him all the earth, the world also is set firm, that it cannot be moved. Let the heavens rejoice, and let the earth be glad; and let them say among the nations, The Lord reigneth. Let the sea roar, and the fulness thereof; let the plain exult, and all that is therein. Then shall the trees of the forest exult before the Lord, for he cometh to judge the earth. O give thanks unto the Lord; for he is good, for his lovingkindness endureth for ever. And say ye, Save us, O G-d of our salvation, and gather us and deliver us from the nations, to give thanks unto thy holy name, and to triumph in thy praise. Blessed be the Lord, the G-d of Israel, from everlasting even to everlasting. And all the people said, Amen, and praised the Lord.

Exalt ye the Lord our G-d, and worship at his footstool, holy is he. Exalt ye the Lord our G-d, and worship at his holy mount; for the Lord our G-d is holy. And he, being merciful, forgiveth iniquity, and destroyeth not. Yea, many a time he turneth his anger away, and doth not stir up all his wrath. Withold not thou thy mercies from me, O Lord, let thy lovingkindness and thy truth continually preserve me. Remember, O Lord, thy tender mercies and thy lovingkindnesses; for they have been ever of old. Ascribe ye strength unto G-d, his majesty is over Israel, and his strength is in the skies. O G-d, thou art to be feared out of thy holy places, the G-d of Israel, he giveth strength and power unto his people. Blessed be G-d. O G-d of venegeance, Lord, O G-d of vengeance, shine forth. Lift up thyself, thou judge of the earth, render to the proud their desert. Salvation belongeth unto the Lord, thy blessing be upon thy people. Selah. The Lord of hosts is with us; the G-d of Jacob is our stronghold. Selah. O Lord of hosts, happy is the man that trusteth in thee. Save, Lord; may the King answer us on the day when we call. Save thy people, and bless thine inheritance, feed them, and carry them for ever. Our soul waiteth for the

Lord, he is our help and our shield. For our heart shall rejoice in him, because we have trusted in his holy name. Let thy lovingkindness, O Lord, be upon us, according as we have hoped for thee. Show us thy lovingkindness, O Lord, and grant us thy salvation. Rise up for our help, and set us free for thy lovingkindness' sake. I am the Lord thy God, who brought thee up out of the land of Egypt. Open wide thy mouth, and I will fill it. Happy is the people, that is in such a case. Happy is the people, whose,G-d is the Lord. And as for me, I have trusted in thy lovingkindness; my heart shall be glad in thy salvation. I will sing unto the Lord, because he hath dealt bountifully with me.

הודו לה'. The first part of this prayer (to והלל לה') was sung for the first time when the Holy Ark was brought, amidst great rejoicing and festivity, to the עיר דוד. The text is recorded in I Chr. XVI, 8. — 36. King David, we are told, handed the words to the Sons of Asaf. The first part of the text corresponds to Ps. CV, 1-15; the second part to Ps. XCVI, 2-13 and CVI, 47-48.

According to the סדר עולם, the excerpt from הודו to אל תגעו was chanted daily as an accompaniment to the morning sacrifice during the period that the Ark was sheltered in a temporary location — a tent — where it remained until it was taken to its permanent abode — the Temple of Solomon. The second section (from שירו to והלל לה') was chanted as an accompaniment to the evening sacrifice. (The Sephardic Minhag, accordingly, places the הודו before ב"ש, as these verses are held to belong rightfully to the section dealing with the sacrifices, whereas in our prayer-books it is placed after ב"ש because it belongs to the שירי דוד עבדך).

It is very interesting to examine the two parts just mentioned to discover what inner connection, if any, they bear to the daily sacrifices which they regularly accompanied.

We find that the initial section, the morning song, is a hymn of thanksgiving for the miraculous deliverance of the Ark from the hands of the Philistines. (Cf. Rashi ad loc.). The mention of this event leads the Psalmist to digress upon the many other miraculous, Divine interventions on behalf of Israel in the past. The second part, the evensong, is, by contrast, a vision of the future. It is a שיר חדש, portraying the coming, universal recognition of the sovereignty of G-d. (Rashi). Nature itself, freed from immoral abuse, and all the peoples and races of mankind join together to offer gifts to G-d שאו מנחה ובאו לפניו, and to prostrate themselves before his Sanctuary. The concluding verses (taken from Ps. CVI) recapitulate the two main ideas — gratitude to G-d for the benefits of the past הודו .... כי טוב, and a prayer for a peaceful future הושיענו וקבצנו להודות.

We recall that in our introduction (p. 6), we pointed out that the morning service in its entire purport and content dwells upon our gratitude for favors of the past, while the evening service looks towards the future. The verse להגיד בבקר חסדך etc. provides the leitmotif for these two themes. The recital of the first section of the הודו at the morning sacrifice, and the second section during the offering of the תמיד של בין הערבים, fits into this pattern. However, in our morning service we include both sections so as to provide an appropriate transition from the sacrifice to the פס' דז'.

The succeeding verses of the הודו prayer seem at first to be a random agglomeration of Biblical verses. To closer scrunity however, they reveal an orderly and logical progression of thought. First come the verses רוממו. Even at the time when the Sanctuary, הדם רגליו, and the sacrificial services are gone, G-d will listen to the prayer of those who pay homage to להר קדשו, where His שכינה once resided. Did He not answer the prayers of Moses, Aaron, Samuel who called to Him when there was no Temple. This seems the obvious idea of the Psalm (XCIX) from which the two verses are taken. — He even accepts the prayer of those not worthy of being heard, as long as the prayer is offered from the midst of the community of worshippers. (This is the meaning of the next verse, והוא רחום יכפר עון, according to the Talmud, Taanis 8a). For G-d's mercy and faithfulness neither cease nor change, as the next two verses attest: אתה ה' and זכר רחמיך ה' לא תכלה, nor do they depend upon the existence of the Sanctuary for their efficacy. נורא, תנו עז. (Ps. LXVIII, 35-36). The next two verses, too, if understood in the light of their exposition in the Talmud, follow the logical sequence of ideas we have delineated so far. The Jerusalem Talmud infers from the second verse that "the fear of G-d emanates from His Sanctuary" — אין נורא אלא בית המקדש (Ber. VII Halacha 4). Accordingly, when the Sanctuary was destroyed Jeremiah omitted the word נורא (feared) from his praise of G-d. For he said, "When the heathens swagger through His Sanctuary, can there be fear of G-d?" But the Men of the Great Assembly answered: "If there were no fear of Him, could one people exist among seventy (hostile) nations?" So they reinstated the original formula. On the basis of this explanation, the two verses become especially meaningful. The Temple is in ruins, but the miraculous survival of Israel in exile is proof of the enduring prevalence of the fear of G-d. — אל נקמות...הנשא. May He then continue to strengthen His people against all the trials of the Galuth; may He Make the extent of His powers known, by granting recompense for all we have suffered; may He punish the arrogant. The concluding verses ring out in a note of unshakable conviction and confidence that His salvation will ultimately be with us.

מזמור לתודה *Shout for joy unto the Lord, all ye lands. Serve the Lord with joy: come before him with exulting. Know ye that the Lord he is G-d, he hath made us, and we are his, his people and the sheep of his pasture. Enter into his gates with thanksgiving, and into his courts with praise: give thanks unto him, bless his name. For the Lord is good; his lovingkindness is everlasting; and his faithfulness from generation to generation.*

מזמור לתודה. Ps. C, like the preceding הודו, was chanted while a sacrifice was being offered (i.e. in this case the תודה). This might be the reason why the מזמור לתודה was placed immediately after the הודו.

The motive for reciting this Psalm of thanksgiving daily follows from the assumption that a person might be saved each and every day from some mortal danger without ever having been aware of it. אפילו בעל הנס אינו מכיר בניסו. The very one for whom the miracle was performed may have known nothing about it, declares the Talmud (Niddah 31a). The tractate Berachoth enumerates the occasions on which a person is obliged to offer a Todah, and to recite the blessing for deliverance, ברכת הגומל, in public. These occasions are mentioned in Ps. CVII, viz.; — after recovery from illness, completing a voyage by sea, a journey through the desert, or after release from captivity. However, for every deliverance from a known danger we are obliged to give thanks by reciting the Bracha (Orach Chaim 219, 9). It is for the unnoticed miracles in every day life על נסיך שבכל יום עמנו for which we are ever in debt to Providence, that we recite this Psalm.

Yet the מזמור לתודה assumes even greater importance in the light of a remark of the Midrash (Rabba to Lev. 9 and 27), viz., that in time to come all the other sacrifices will be abolished; only the prayers and sacrifices of thanksgiving will remain. An era of such purity of thought and deed, of such strict, virtuous conduct, will come to pass, that no prayers or sacrifices to atone for human failing will be needed. But the feeling of gratitude, for the mercies of Providence, will never die out as long as men live on earth.

For a detailed exegesis of this Psalm, see, in addition to the regular Bible commentaries, the עקדת יצחק, Shaar 52, and the Ikkarim of Albo (III, 33).

יהי כבוד. *Let the glory of the Lord endure for ever; let the Lord rejoice in his works. Let the name of the Lord be blessed from this time forth and for evermore. From the rising of the sun unto the going down thereof the Lord's name is to be praised. The Lord is high above all nations, and his glory above the heavens. Thy name, O Lord, endureth for ever; thy memorial, O Lord, throughout all generations. The Lord hath established his throne in the heavens; and his kingdom ruleth over all. Let the heavens rejoice, and let the earth be glad; and let them say among the nations, The Lord reigneth. The Lord reigneth; the Lord hath reigned; the Lord shall reign for ever and ever. The Lord is King for ever and ever; the nations are perished out of his land. The Lord hath frustrated the design of the nations; he hath foiled the thoughts of the peoples. Many are the thoughts in a man's heart; but the counsel of the Lord, that shall stand. The counsel of the Lord standeth fast for ever, the thoughts of his heart to all generations. For he spake, and it was; he commanded, and it stood fast. For the Lord has chosen Zion; he has desired it for his habitation. For the Lord hath chosen Jacob unto himself, Israel for his*

peculiar treasure. For the Lord will not cast off his people,
neither will he forsake his inheritance. And he, being merci-
ful, forgiveth iniquity, and destroyeth not. Yea, many a time
he turneth his anger away, and doth not stir up all his wrath.
Save, Lord, may the King answer us on the day when we call.

יהי כבוד, a symposium of verses taken from the Psalms,
forms the prelude to the main part of the פס' דז', the last six
chapters of the Book of Psalms. According to ancient sources,
the יהי כבוד and the succeeding אשרי prayer are connected by
an inner relationship.

As these sources have it, the number 21 is the key to
the understanding of both the יהי כבוד and the אשרי. The
Divine Name is mentioned 21 times in the יהי, (if we include
the one formed by taking the first letters of the words ישמחו
השמים ותגל הארץ); while there are 21 verses in the אשרי.
This number draws its mystic significance from the fact that
21 is the numerical value of the Divine name, אהיה, revealed
to Moses at the burning bush. Here, as in most instances, the
number mysticism, apparently quite irrational and formalistic,
alludes to profound implications and associations that lie hidden beneath the surface of the words. For as the designation
אהי' אשר אהי' proclaimed that the sublime and omnipotent
G-d is at the same time the helper and comforter whose lovingkindness is ever near to us (cf. Rashi to Ex. III 14), so
too are these aspects of the Divine extolled in the two pieces
יהי כבוד and אשרי respectively. — The Divine mastery over
nature and man is extolled in the יהי כבוד and His all-encom-
passing mercy in the succeeding אשרי. While the ב"ש gave
us the seven interpretations of the שם הויה, here the significance of the Divine Presence as אהי' אשר אהי' is set forth —
indeed a fitting overture to the Psalms of the פד', the songs
praising the activity of the Divine Presence in the cosmos.

The first verse is taken from Ps. CIV, the great nature hymn of the Psalter, termed the "the most grandiose
description of nature in world literature." (Alexander von
Humboldt). The words יהי כבוד etc., according to the Talmud (Chullin 60b), are uttered by "the Spirit of the World."
כבוד ה' (as will be explained in our commentary to טוב יצר.)
describes G-d's immanence in the world, and it is in this way
that man discovers G-d as the Creator of the Universe. May

His immanence continue for ever until the time of the universal Theocracy, when G-d will rejoice in His creatures,
ישמח ה' במעשיו (Lev. Rabba ch. 20). Throughout time (מעתה)
and space (ממזרח) may the Lord be praised, the Lord Who
is enthroned on high, far above the nations, yet Whose seal
is ה' מדת הרחמים (שמך ה'), boundless love. Though His throne
is established in heaven, His dominion extends over all ה'
בשמים וגו'. Thus apprehending the sovereign rule of G-d,
Heaven and Earth will join in joyous homage: ישמחו השמים
וגו'. The heavens shall rejoice and the earth be glad when the
nations shall proclaim, "G-d reigns!" Such expressions of
pure joy and perfect harmony in the universe will call forth
the שכינה which will return to dwell on earth. For the שכינה
rests only where pure joy prevails (Pesachim 117a) (an idea
also hinted at in the שם שלם, the full name of G-d יהו' formed by the first letters ישמחו השמים ותגל הארץ; as the
Kabbalist point out). At that time all mankind will heed the
message of Israel, viz. that the sovereignty of G-d is plainly
and utterly real, and that He always *was* and always *will be*
King. ה' מלך וכו'. This sentence is first found in the tractate
Soferim (14, 8) and is composed of portions of three verses
in the Psalms. The present, "G-d rules" (ה' מלך) is the premise, for here the speaker can rely upon his own, personal
observation. From this premise he makes the deduction that
G-d's rule is eternal both in the past and in the future (ה' מלך).

The second half of the יהי כבוד then goes on to describe the Master of History, before Whose omnipotence all
the scheming and plotting of man come to naught. He will
lead mankind in a steady advance towards the realization of
His plan. Zion the seat of His glory will become the center
of truth and enlightenment, His people the bearers of these
ideals. For, in spite of human weakness and failing, G-d will
never forsake Jacob, his chosen, since G-d is all merciful and
forgiving. המלך יעננו ביום קראנו "The Lord will answer us,
on the day we call on Him." This comforting promise brings
to a close the prayer that with its 21 Sacred Names, shows
the one aspect of the Divine essence, א'ה'י'ה' creation and sovereignty. The other aspect is, however, no less sublime.
This is his lovingkindness which is glorified in the 21 verses
of the succeeding אשרי. Thus the double significance of the
Name, אהי' אשר אהי', is brought out in the praise ascending
heavenward from the two poems, יהי and אשרי.

אשרי*Happy* are they that dwell in thy house; they will be ever praising thee. Selah. Happy is the people, that is in such a case. Happy is the people, whose G-d is the Lord.

תהלה לדוד. *I will extol thee, my G-d, O King; and I will bless thy name for ever and ever. Every day will I bless thee; and I will praise thy name for ever and ever. Great is the Lord, and exceedingly to be praised, and his greatness is unsearchable. One generation shall laud thy works to a-nother, and shall declare thy mighty acts. On the majestic glory of thy splendour, and on thy marvellous deeds, will I meditate. And men shall speak of the might of thy awful acts; and I will recount thy greatness. They shall pour forth the fame of thy great goodness, and shall exult in thy righteous-ness. The Lord is gracious and merciful; slow to anger and of great lovingkindness. The Lord is good to all; and his tender mercies are over all his works. All thy works shall give thanks unto thee, O Lord; and thy loving ones shall bless thee. They shall speak of the glory of thy kingdom, and talk of thy power; to make known to the sons of men his mighty acts, and the majestic glory of his kingdom. Thy kingdom is an everlasting kingdom, and thy dominion endureth through-out all generations. The Lord upholdeth all that fall, and rai-seth up all those that are bowed down. The eyes of all wait upon thee; and thou givest them their food in due season. Thou openest thine hand, and satisfiest every living thing with favour. The Lord is righteous in all his ways, and loving in all his works. The Lord is nigh unto all them that call upon him, to all that call upon him in truth. He will fulfill the de-sire of them that fear him; he also will hear their cry, and will save them. The Lord guardeth all them that love him; but all the wicked will he destroy. My mouth shall speak of the praise of the Lord; and let all flesh bless his holy name for ever and ever.*

ואנחנו. *But we will bless the Lord from this time forth and for evermore. Praise ye the Lord.*

אשרי. The Psalm properly begins at תהלה לדוד. The verse אשרי is added because it teaches that one should spend some time in silent contemplation in the house of worship before beginning to pray, as King David said, "Never have I begun my prayer to G-d before having composed and pre-

pared myself for it." (Yalkut to Samuel II, §146). Although
this reason is only applicable to the Minchah where אשרי is
recited at the very beginning of the service, the verse is also
included here (as well as in the אשרי preceding ובא לציון),
because of לא פלוג, to avoid differences in the various repetitions of the prayer.

תהלה לדוד opens the psalms which represent the פד"ז
in the narrower sense of the term. These psalms were included in the daily service because of Rabbi Jose, who said:
"May my lot be among those who complete the Hallel every
day." Hallel, here, does not refer to that group of psalms or-
dinarily called by that name, but instead to the whole book
of psalms (Sabbath 118b). Rabbi Jose may have been prevented by the lack of time and leisure from reciting the whole
book of Psalms every day. So he desired, at least, to "complete"
it, i. e. to read the last chapters, in order to recall, each day,
the final conclusion drawn in the last psalms of the book.
According to Rashi the "completion" consists of two chapters, CXLVIII and CL. According to the tractate Soferim,
17, 11, however, the six last chapters, including the תהלה לדוד
are meant. (So too Alfasi and Maimonides). The Talmud
(Berachoth 4b) gives another reason for including the תהלה
לדוד. "He who recites תהלה לדוד thrice daily will inherit the
world to come." For the exceptional evaluation of this psalm,
a twofold reason is given; — (a) its verses are arranged in
an alphabetical acrostic; and (b) it contains the phrase, פותח
את ידיך וגו'. The highest praise of the Creator arises from an
accord of all the letters of the alphabet, when the entire range
of sounds man is capable of uttering is used in a symphony
extolling G-d. This is the deeper meaning of the saying,
שמסדר שבח הקב"ה בכל האותיות according to the wonderful
explanation given by ר' בצלאל אשכנזי. But the climax of all
human praise is "פותח את ידיך" the proclamation of G-d's
undiscriminating, all-embracing sustenance of life in its struggle
for existence and survival. He who repeats this Psalm three
times every day, is ultimately sure to appreciate its deep significance, for the threefold repetition is certain to engrave its
truths indelibly in the very grain of his being.

ארוממך. The Jewish concept of Divine providence and
of G-d's merciful guidance of the world is diametrically opposed to that of the other peoples. "Be not like the rest," ex-

claims Rabbi Akiba. "When they prosper they honor their gods. When they suffer, they curse their gods. Do not treat G-d like an idol. You are a Jew. Therefore, when G-d bestows good fortune upon you, praise Him; and when He visits misfortune upon you, praise Him nevertheless!" (Mechilta 20, 20). It is this elevated mood allowing man to see G-d's mercy revealed in good fortune and in suffering as well, which time and again rouses Israel to worship and bless G-d. ארוממך וגו' — בכל יום אברכך וגו'. The theme is stated and repeated for emphasis. For גדלך זו מדת טובך "Thy greatness is Thy love," even though (ולגדולתו אין חקר), the methods and actions of His love often appear unfathomable to man. The others know to tell of גבורת ה' and עזוז נוראותיו, of His deeds of might and the irresistibility of His fearfulness. But, I, David, speaking as the personification of Israel, shall tell of Thy love: וגדלתך אספרנה. They speak of זכר רב טובך an intimation of love coming from afar זכר, as in זכר לדבר. They perceive only a faint glimmer of it. G-d, on the other hand, describes His love as כל טובי, the whole of His love which covers both reward and punishment. (Exodus Rabba 45). They acclaim רב טוב, His great love, by only praising His deeds of mercy וצדקתך ירננו. David, on the other hand, sang not only of His love but of His justice as well. (חסד ומשפט אשירה Ps. CI, 1). The rest of His creatures only render thanks unto Him; the pious alone bless Him for *all* His actions, וחסידיך יברכוכה. The elaboration of this blessing of the pious forms the content of the remainder of the psalm. כבוד and גבורתך correspond to the שם ומלכות which are the constituent parts of every blessing, (cf. above p. 15). The dominion of G-d lasts forever — מלכותך וגו' — and is manifest in His support of the bent and the falling (סומך).

At this point the letter "נ" which should have stood at the head of the next verse has been omitted from the acrostic. This has been done to avoid mention of נפילה, the downfall of man (Berachoth 4b). Only when referring to G-d's raising up of man סומך ה' לכל נופלים, is the letter "נ" included in this song of the Divine mercy. Man's falling and failing, his stumbling and wavering, are of his own making. But his rise, his progress, his success in the erratic course of life are due to the helping hand of G-d. עיני כל וכו', The eyes

of all are, therefore, directed towards Him, and He sustains
them all. פותח, He opens his hand wide and satisfies the needs
of all living creatures. If others, discouraged by pain and
suffering, lose faith, and feel constrained to deny Him blessing and reverence, we cry out loudly, untiringly: 'צדיק ה
בכל דרכיו G-d is just in *all* his ways; וחסיד בכל מעשיו and *all*
His deeds are replete with love and mercy. 'קרוב ה. G-d is
close to them that call on Him in earnest. Finally, 'שומר ה
He protects those that love Him, by destroying the wicked.
Israel, therefore, will not cease to proclaim His lovingkindness
until the coming of the Messianic era, when all mankind will
join together in blessing His Holy Name.

The significance of the prefatory verse, "אשרי העם
שככה לו" regarded in the light of the foregoing exposition of
the Psalm, now becomes apparent. אשרי העם שה' אלקיו. This
is Israel's blessing. To us השם, the G-d who loves and
gives, הוא אלקים, is also the G-d who judges and witholds
(מדת הדין). Both attributes of the Almighty find equal praise
in the תהלה לדוד. Our unshakable determination to sing his
praises forever, regardless of all the aberrations of the gentile world, is reiterated in the appended conclusion, ואנחנו
נברך יה מעתה ועד עולם הללויה. The prayer ends with the
triumphantly resounding call, the keynote which unites all the
succeeding פסוקי דזמרה into one rousing hymn of praise,
הללויה.

הללויה. *Praise ye the Lord. Praise the Lord, O my soul;
I will praise the Lord, while I live; I will sing praises unto my
G-d while I have my being. Put not your trust in princes, in
a son of man, in whom there is no help. When his breath
goeth forth, he returneth to his earth; in that very day his
designs perish. Happy is he that hath the G-d of Jacob for
his help, whose hope is in the Lord his G-d. Who made heaven and earth, the sea, and all that is therein; who keepeth
truth forever; who executeth judgement for the oppressed;
who giveth food to the hungry. The Lord looseth the prisoners; the Lord openeth the eyes of the blind; the Lord
raiseth up them that are bowed down; the Lord loveth the
righteous; the Lord guardeth the strangers; he upholdeth
the fatherless and widow; but the way of the wicked he
maketh crooked. The Lord shall reign for ever, thy G-d, O
Zion, unto all generations. Praise ye the Lord.*

הללויה. *Praise ye the Lord; for it is good to sing praises unto our G-d; for it is pleasant, and praise is seemly. The Lord doth build up Jerusalem; he gathereth together the outcasts of Israel. He healeth the broken in heart, and bindeth up their wounds. He counteth the number of the stars; he calleth them all by their names. Great is our Lord, and mighty in power; his understanding is infinite. The Lord upholdeth the meek, he abaseth the wicked to the ground. Sing unto the Lord with thanksgiving; sing praises upon the lyre unto our G-d. Who covereth the heaven with clouds, who prepareth rain for the earth, who maketh grass to sprout upon the mountains; who giveth to the beast its food, and to the young ravens which cry. He delighteth not in the strength of the horse, he taketh no pleasure in the vigour of a man. The Lord taketh pleasure in them that fear him, in them that hope for his lovingkindness. Extol the Lord, O Jerusalem; praise thy G-d, O Zion. For he hath strengthened the bars of thy gates; he hath blessed thy children within thee. He maketh peace in thy borders; he satisfieth thee with the fat of wheat. He sendeth out his commandment to the earth; his word runneth very swiftly. He giveth snow like wool; he scattereth hoar frost like ashes. He casteth forth his ice like morsels, who can stand before his cold? He sendeth out his word, and melteth them, he causeth his wind to blow, and the waters flow. He declareth his words unto Jacob, his statutes and his judgements unto Israel. He hath not dealt so with any nation, and as for his judgement, they do not know them. Praise ye the Lord.*

הללויה. *Praise ye the Lord. Praise ye the Lord from the heavens, praise him in the heights. Praise ye him, all his angels, praise ye him, all his host. Praise ye him, sun and moon, praise him, all ye stars of light. Praise him, ye heavens of heavens, and ye waters that are above the heavens. Let them praise the name of the Lord, for he commanded, and they were created. He hath established them for ever and ever. He gave a decree which none shall transgress. Praise the Lord from the earth, ye sea-monsters and all deeps, fire and hail, snow and smoke; stormy wind, fulfilling his word. Mountains and all hills; fruit trees and all cedars, wild beasts and all cattle; creeping things and winged birds. Kings of the earth and all peoples; princes and all judges of the earth. Both young men and maidens; old men and children. Let them praise the name of the Lord; for his name alone is exalted, his majesty is above the earth and heaven. And he hath lifted up a horn for his people, to the praise of all his loving ones. Even of the children of Israel, the people near unto him. Praise ye the Lord.*

הללויה *Praise ye the Lord. Sing unto the Lord a new song; his praise in the assembly of those that love him. Let Israel rejoice in his Maker; let the children of Zion be glad in their King. Let them praise his name with the dance, let them sing praises unto him with the timbrel and lyre. For the Lord taketh pleasure in his people, he adorneth the meek with salvation. Let those that love him triumph in glory, let them exult upon their beds. High praises of G-d are in their throat, and a two-edged sword in their hand; to execute vengeance upon the nations, and punishments upon the peoples. To bind their kings with chains, and their nobles with fetters of iron; to execute upon them the judgement written. This is an honour for all his loving ones. Praise ye the Lord.*

הללויה *Praise ye the Lord. Praise G-d in his sanctuary praise him in the firmament of his power. Praise him for his mighty acts: praise him according to his abundant greatness. Praise him with the blast of the horn: praise him with the harp and the lyre. Praise him with the timbrel and dance: praise him with stringed instruments and the pipe. Praise him with the clear-toned cymbals: praise him with the loud-sounding cymbals. Let everything that hath breath praise the Lord: praise ye the Lord.*

הללויה. The content and purpose of the succeeding five psalms can only be understood if they are taken for what they are, viz. פסוקי דזמרה, "Song-texts." The purely poetic and musical component of the psalms, felt by the emotions and the senses, is as important as the thoughts and ideas the words convey. To borrow a figure from music — a choir of harmonized voices begin to sing in soft low tones. As the song progresses, the voices rise in pitch and volume. Each movement adds new variations and modulations of the original theme, till finally all the voices together burst forth, fortissimo, in a jubilant, thundering climax. So are these Psalms. They form one hymn to G-d. The same chords are struck and reverberate in ever increasing force and intensity. Each new psalm adds its voice in praises to the concert, till finally the thundering jubilation of the whole chorus, sustained by a holy fervor rings out: ברוך ה' לעולם או"א. Just as the prophet Ezekiel, borne aloft by a stormwind, heard above the awful din, the mighty call ring out, ברוך כבוד ה' ממקומו, so the central chapters of the פסוקי דזמרה, make the call, ברוך ה' וגו', as it were, burst forth from the recesses of our own souls.

The glory of G-d, the Creator, extolled in the יהי כבוד וגו', and His boundless love praised in the אשרי, are dealt with in the פס' דז' as they apply to the individual, the nation and to all mankind.

The first of the five Psalms begins with man, the individual: הללי נפשי את ה' וגו'. From the contemplation of G-d's omnipotence and His ever-readiness to help, man acquires an unshakeable trust in Him. In the next Psalm, the group, "we" takes the place of the individual, "I," of the first Psalm. Now the השגחה כללית, solicitude for the community as contrasted with the השגחה פרטית, solicitude for the individual, is extolled. Returning time and again to the main themes — G-d's power as set forth in the יהי כבוד and His love as set forth in the אשרי, the Psalmist sings of the special protection and support G-d extends to all His people. Forever, therefore, shall Israel sing His glory: הללויה כי טוב זמרה אלקינו. In Psalm CXLVIII the enthusiastic adoration spreads over the whole cosmos. All that heaven and earth contain now join the chorus of praise, for the strength of all of them comes from G-d, and all creation obeys His command. The kings of earth and all the nations, the whole of mankind join the ranks of those who unreservedly praise the G-d of Israel, מלכי ארץ וכל לאמים . . .. This, however, is a vision of the future. Our eyes are drawn, therefore, to His kingdom yet to come. So the last Psalm but one becomes the "new song" of the future, שירו לה' שיר חדש. The day of His great judgment will free the earth of those who, in their blind obduracy, refuse to recognize His sovereignty, לעשות בהם משפט כתוב. The resplendent majesty of the Redeemer will not be darkened by any shadow of injustice and oppression. — הללו קל בקדשו, praise G-d in his Sanctuary; praise Him for His omnipotence; praise Him for the magnitude of His power. Here in the last Psalm the voices of all mankind join together in one mighty hymn of praise. Its 13 calls of Hallelu extol the Creator for the thirteenfold

manifestations of His lovingkindness, י"ג מדות. Both the instruments that inspire a trembling reverence בתקע שופר, and
the instruments that evoke the most blissful joy נבל וכנור,
together announce the triumphal appearance of G-d on earth.
Ever mightier grows the chorus of His servants — as the
increasing tonal power of the instruments mentioned shows
— until with overwhelming force, the presence of the Divine
will make itself felt throughout the whole world: כל הנשמה
תהלל י-ה.

     ברוך ה'. *Blessed be the Lord for evermore. Amen, and
Amen. Blessed be the Lord out of Zion, who dwelleth in
Jerusalem. Praise ye the Lord. Blessed be the Lord G-d, the
G-d of Israel, who alone doeth wondrous things; and blessed
be his glorious name forever; and let the whole earth be filled
with his glory. Amen, and Amen.*

     ברוך השם. The last verse of the last Psalm marks the
end of the פס' דז', in the narrower sense of the term. The
ever recurring theme of those hymns, the call to praise G-d,
Hallelu, now evokes the response ברוך ה' וגו'. The word ברוך
is expressive of the most perfect adoration, for it is the
acknowledgement of G-d as the ultimate, just source of all
blessings, מקור הברכה. (Cf. Intro. p. 14). The recognition of
G-d's creative omnipotence, as reflected in the word הלל, of the
פס' דז', leads to His blessing in the ensuing paragraphs ברוך
השם and ויברך. In fact the entire section of the פס' דז' is border-
ed by, and interlaced with the idea of Bracha. First comes the
thirteen-fold Bracha of ברוך שאמר, which apparently antici-
pates the 13-fold Hallelu of the last Psalm, and finally the
ויברך דוד. From the very outset, moreover, the Bracha is set
as the goal of the תהלה, for the תהלה לדוד begins with
ארוממך . . . ואברכך, and ends with the מעתה   ואנחנו נברך י-ה
ועד עולם הללויה.

     ברוך ה'. The next verses plot the course leading to the
universal recognition of G-d in the world. Starting out from
Zion, ברוך ה' מציון, the idea of G-d will be kept alive in
Israel ברוך ה' אלקי ישראל, even after the fall of Zion, when
His signs and miracles will be apparent to none but Himself,
עושה נפלאות לבדו, till finally His glory will fill the
whole world וימלא כבודו את כל הארץ.

     אמן ואמן. The most emphatic expression of the acknow-
ledgment of the truth of a statement. Derived from אמונה, the

word amen does not only endorse the absolute veracity of a statement, but it obliges the person uttering אמן to carry out the consequences inferred from the statement. (Cf. Isaiah LXV, 16). According to the Talmud (Shevuoth 29b), the אמן can have three meanings: the first, to take upon one-self the obligations entailed by a vow uttered by someone else; the second, to confirm the truth of a statement; and third, to pray for the fulfilment of a hope expressed in a statement, שיאמנו הדברים. (Cf. Magen Abraham 124, 10).

ויברך דוד. *And David blessed the Lord in the presence of all the congregation; and David said, Blessed art thou, O Lord, the G-d of Israel our father, from everlasting to everlasting. Thine, O Lord, is the greatness, and the power, and the glory; and the victory, and the majesty; for all that is in the heaven and in the earth is thine; thine, O Lord, is the kingdom, and supremacy as head over all. Riches and honour come of thee, and thou rulest over all; and in thine hand are might and power; and in thine hand it is to make great, and to give strength unto all. Now, therfore, our G-d, we give thanks unto thee, and praise thy glorious name.*

Thou art the Lord, even thou alone; thou hast made the heavens, the heaven of heavens, and all their host, the earth and all things that are thereon, the seas and all that are in them, and thou givest life to them all; and the host of heaven worship thee. Thou art the Lord the G-d, who didst choose Abram, and broughtest him forth out of Ur of the Chaldees, and gavest him the name of Abraham; and foundest his heart faithful before thee; And thou madest a covenant with him to give the land of the Canaanite, the Hittite, the Amorite, and the Perizzite, and the Jebusite, and the Girgashite, even to give it unto his seed, and hast performed thy words; for thou art righteous. And thou sawest the affliction of our fathers in Egypt, and heardest their cry by the Red Sea; and shewedst signs and wonders upon Pharaoh, and on all his servants, and on all the people of his land; for thou knewest that they dealt arrogantly against them; and didst make thee a name, as it is this day. And thou didst divide the sea before them, so that they went through the midst of the sea on the dry land; and their pursuers thou didst cast into the depths, as a stone into the mighty waters.

ויושע ה'. *Thus the Lord saved Israel that day out of the hand of the Egyptians; and Israel saw the Egyptians dead upon the sea shore. And Israel saw the great power which the Lord put forth against the Egyptians, and the people feared the Lord: and they believed in the Lord, and in Moses his servant.*

אז ישיר משה. *Then sang Moses and the children of Israel this song unto the Lord, and spoke, saying: I will sing unto the Lord, for he hath been highly exalted; the horse and rider hath he thrown into the sea. The Lord is my strength and song, and he is become my salvation; this is my G-d, and I will glorify him; my father's G-d, and I will exalt him. The Lord is a man of war; the Lord is his name. Pharaoh's chariots and his host hast he cast into the sea; and his chosen captains are sunk in the Red Sea. The floods cover them: they went down into the depths like a stone. Thy right hand, O Lord, that is glorious in power, thy right hand, O Lord, dasheth in pieces the enemy. And in the greatness of thy majesty thou overthrowest them that rise against thee: thou sendest forth thy wrath, it consumeth them as stubble. And with the blast of thy nostrils the waters were piled up, the streams stood upright as an heap; the floods were congealed in the heart of the sea. The enemy said, I will pursue, I will overtake, I will divide the spoil: my lust shall be satisfied upon them; I will draw my sword, my hand shall destroy them. Thou didst blow with thy wind, the sea covered them: they sank as lead in the mighty waters. Who is like unto thee, O Lord, amongst the mighty ones: who is like unto thee, glorious in holiness, revered in praises doing marvels? Thou stretchedst out thy right hand, the earth swallowed them. Thou in thy lovingkindness hast led the people which thou hast redeemed: thou hast guided them in thy strength to thy holy habitation. The peoples have heard it; they tremble: pangs have taken hold of the inhabitants of Philistia. Then were the dukes of Edom confounded; the mighty men of Moab, trembling taketh hold of them: all the inhabitants of Canaan are melted away. Terror and dread falleth upon them: by the greatness of thine arm they are still as a stone; till thy people pass over, O Lord, till the people pass over, which thou hast acquired. Thou wilt bring them in, and plant them in the mountain of thine inheritance, the place, O Lord, which thou hast made for thee to dwell in, the sanctuary, O Lord, which thy hands have established. The Lord shall reign for ever and ever. The Lord shall reign for ever and ever.*

כי לה'. *For the kingdom is the Lord's: and he is ruler over the nations. And saviours shall come up on Mount Zion to judge the mount of Esau; and the kingdom shall be the Lord's. And the Lord shall be King over all the earth: in that day shall the Lord be One, and his name One. And in thy Law it is written, saying, Hear, O Israel: the Lord our G-d, the Lord, is One.*

ויברך דוד. David's classic blessing (I Chr. XXIX, 10-13) which opens the ensuing paragraph follows the course set by the פס' דז', rising, however, to an even loftier height of devotional intensity, by accentuating the sublime grandeur and regal splendor of G-d's dominion which no force on earth can oppose. The theme is taken up by the laudation of the Levites: אתה הוא ה' לבדך (Nehemiah IX 6-11). A brief excursus takes us through Israel's past, citing examples of the wonder-working omnipotence of G-d, by recalling the promise given to Abraham and its fulfillment in the miracle of the division of the Red Sea.

The Song of Moses occupies a special place in the שחרית. Maimonides and other authorities, in fact, hold that it should be inserted after ישתבח. The Zohar too (II, 131b) considers it to be a prelude to the next section of the prayer rather than part of the פס' דז'. Indeed, according to the Talmud (Sabbath 118a) the praise of Divine miracles should be excluded from the פס' דז', for these psalms, do not, as the מהרש"א ad loc. explains, "recount His miracles; they are chapters of praise and homage." They describe the regular, rhythmical order of nature which to the thoughtful onlooker is no less a manifestation of G-d's omnipotence than sudden shocks and supernatural, cataclysmic events. The glorification of His miracles has its place in the succeeding ברכת היוצר, where the *direct* dependence of all the prime forces and elements on the grace of G-d is shown.

Nevertheless, the Song of Moses can justifiably be inserted before the ישתבח. The reason, given by ancient sources, is that "the fifteen expressions of homage contained in the ישתבח were taken from the Mechilta to the Song of Moses and from the verses of ויברך דוד." A profound idea lies hidden

beneath the surface of this apparently irrelevant statement:
The most perfect praise of G-d is not in the inspired panegyrics
of David, the שירי דוד, but grows out of the actual events of
history which our ancestors beheld with their own eyes. Only
since the day of the division of the Red Sea, when G-d for
the first time in history, revealed His mastery over nature
and mankind before the eyes of an astonished world — only
since then has "His throne been established for all time."

The blessing recited by ויברך דוד is essentially an elaboration of what the Torah itself considers the aim and purpose of
each and every Bracha. Enjoining us to say grace after meals,
the Torah next gives us the reason for so doing: "Thy heart be
then not lifted up, and thou forget the Lord thy G-d . . . and
thou say in thy heart, my power and the strength of my hand
have gotten me this wealth. But thou shalt remember the Lord
thy G-d; for it is He that giveth thee power to get wealth."
This omnipotence of G-d and His active guidance of
the world are brought out in this benediction, לך ה' הגדולה
והגבורה...והנצח. When the Kabbalist commentators recommend
that we give charity while pronouncing the words ובידך כח
וגבורה, following the example set by the saintly Rabbi Isaac
Luria (אר"י הק'), they expect us to realize the idea that G-d's
blessing will become activated only as a result of our own acts of
charity. As the Torah says it: כי בגלל הדבר הזה וגו' since for
the sake of this matter (charity) the Lord, thy G-d, shall bless
thee in all thy actions and in the work of thy hands (Deut.
XV, 10).

The rule that we stand while reciting this entire section,
has its origin in the words: קומו ברכו את ה'. "Arise and bless
the Lord" which immediately precede the אתה הוא ה' לבדך
in the book of Nehemiah. The reason for the omission of these
words in our מנהג, is that we are forbidden to quote fragments
of Scriptural verses (Taanis 27b), and the words referred to
here are part of verse 5 of chapter XIX of the book of Nehemiah.

אז ישיר משה. Cf. Torah Commentaries.

ה' ימלך לעולם ועד. The last verse of the song is repeated. Then various passages extolling G-d's sovereignty are
added. The selection and number of these verses is governed
by the desire to have the Song of Moses, as it is recited here,

consist of eighteen repetitions of the four-lettered Name of G-d, the שם הויה. Multiplying the eighteen by the four, we get the 72 letters of the "Great Name of G-d."

The Great Name so strongly emphasised here, is closely connected with the miracle of the division of the Red Sea. Abraham had already been promised that his descendants would be saved from Egypt with the "Name of the 72 letters" (Rabba to Gen. XV 14). The Name itself is in the Zohar (III, 150), derived from the three verses, Ex. XIV, 19-21, in which the miracles attending the division of the waters are recounted. While the four-lettered Name only alludes to the wonder-working might of G-d, as Nachmanides (Ramban) comments on Ex. VI, 3, its eighteen-fold repetition which yields the Great Name, brings out the fullest unfolding and the clearest revelation of this wonder-working omnipotence. This interpretation is also arrived at by the Kabbalist authors after examining the method by which the Name is deduced, and its composition. (Cf. קדושת לוי to Ex. XIV, 19). The account of the redemption from Egypt bore the sign of the Great Name, for there His power to work miracles as the Sovereign Ruler over nature and mankind revealed itself with the fullest clarity. No longer was it the "finger of G-d" which disclosed itself, but the unlimited, supreme power of His "Great Hand," וירא ישראל את היד הגדולה! Because of this special distinction, the song is to be recited standing and with the proper cantillation as if it were read from the Torah scroll.

Four verses glorifying the gradual spreading of the Kingdom of G-d on earth conclude the song. כי לה' המלוכה "For His is the kingdom. . .," and He will redeem His faithful, until ultimately G-d shall be acclaimed והיה ה' למלך על כל הארץ King of the World. (The sentence שמע ישראל is to be omitted, for according to the Vilna Gaon, it has been erroneously transferred from the Mussaf of Rosh Hashona where it follows upon the two preceding verses והיה וכו' ועלו וכו'.

ישתבח. *Praised be thy name for ever, O our King, the great and holy G-d and King, in heaven and on earth; for unto thee, O Lord our G-d, and G-d of our fathers, song and praise are becoming, hymn and psalm, strength and dominion, victory, greatness and might, renown and glory, holiness and sovereignty, blessings and thanksgivings from henceforth even for ever. Bles-*

sed art thou, O Lord, G-d and King, great in praises, G-d of thanksgivings, Lord of wonders, who makest choice of song and psalm, O King and G-d, the life of all worlds.

ישתבח. Concluding Bracha of the פסוקי דזמרה.

Since ישתבח refers back to ברוך שאמר, the initial Bracha, it does not begin with ברוך. The call, which issued forth from the ברוך, to praise G-d's glory forever, does not, however, as one might expect, "end" in this finale to the פס' דז'. On the contrary, the call goes forth with even greater vigor to all times and all generations to sing His praise "from now on until eternity." For only he "who can put the mighty acts of G-d into words, can utter *all* His praise" (Ps. CVI, 2). All that the human mind can invent in שיר ושבחה הלל וזמרה וגו' "song and praise, panegyric and chant, in tribute to might and dominion, victory, greatness and power, glory and splendor, holiness and sovereignty, in blessings and thanksgiving," is insufficient to grasp the essence of His rulership. As in David's fifteen "Songs of Ascent" the number 15 was used to reflect the highest degree attainable in the praise of G-d, so here the number 15 appears as the total summation of all humanly possible expressions of homage. It occurs again in the concluding Bracha, א-ל מלך גדול וגו', which, as the ancient commentators draw to our attention, consists of fifteen words.

To the Talmud and the later commentators, 15 was the symbol of creation. This is particularly evident from the Talmudic interpretation of the verse (Isaiah XXVI, 4) כי בי-ה ה' צור עולמים. The literal significance of the word י-ה. is used in the exposition of the sentence: "With י-ה has G-d created the world" (צור from יצר, created), i.e. with the two letters of the Divine Name: י and ה. With י, the perfect decimal, the perfect world of the future was created; while this incomplete and imperfect world was formed with the ה, which has the numerical value of 5. Hence the creation is symbolised by the number 15, reflecting the letters of the Divine Name. Therefore, when David sang his immortal hymns in praise of G-d, he chose, according to a Midrashic saying, the הללויה, as the most perfect expression of homage, consisting of praise הללו and the Creator's name י-ה in one word. For this reason too, the number appears at the end of this section of the Shacharis, the פס' דז', which, taken from the Psalms, carry into our daily lives the idea of G-d as the Creator and sustainer of nature. Fifteen is the sum-total of the laudations used, and fifteen is the number of words in the concluding Bracha. In its final three words, however, which are altogether the very last of the פס׳ דז׳, the essential message of the whole section is tersely re-affirmed. G-d is not צור עולמים, the first cause, creative and active only once in the distant past when the world was formed and fashioned, but He is חי העולמים, the constant living Source of all activity, the eternal perpetual Power dispensing life to all the worlds.

This idea, together with the declaration that G-d is elevated above all homage, is the theme of the concluding Bracha. Our praises, it is true, help bring out the final recog-nition of His greatness (cf. Midrash Ps. CIV, 1); nevertheless G-d is exalted above all grateful praise, א-ל ההודאות, for He is the Master of miracles, אדון הנפלאות, and as such His unlimited power extends beyond the compass of praise. (Cf. Midrash to Ps. CVI, 1). However, in spite of our limitations, we do not tire dedicating our hymns of praise to Him, הבוחר בשירי זמרה, who chose our songs of praise, for as yet He is the יושב תהלות ישראל, He dwells amidst the praises of Israel. As yet Israel is the sole bearer of His message to mankind. Whatever spirituality has penetrated into the hearts and homes of mankind has been carried there by the תהלות ישראל, the Psalms of Israel. Israel's concept of מלך א-ל חי העולמים, is still the sole harbinger of the coming Kingdom of G-d.

We see that the פס׳ דז׳ ring out in the Bracha which show us (by the measured choice of words) the wealth as well as the limits of the hymns of praise. Israel's deep yearning has led to the adding of praises and prayers to this section of the Shacharis far in excess of the original core of the 6 Psalms, CXLV to CL. In ever new songs and hymns our people has praised the greatness of G-d as revealed in the life of nature and mankind.

קריאת שמע

יתגדל. See translation after ובא לציון.

ברכו. *Bless ye the Lord who is to be blessed.*

ברוך. *Blessed is the Lord who is to be blessed for ever and ever.*

Blessed, praised, glorified, exalted and extolled be the name of the supreme king of kings, the Holy One, blessed be he, who is the first and the last, and beside him there is no G-d. Extol ye him that rideth upon the heavens by his name Jah, and rejoice before him. His name is exalted above all blessing and praise. Blessed be His name, whose glorious kingdom is for ever and ever. Let the name of the Lord be blessed from this time forth and for evermore.

ברוך. *Blessed art thou, O Lord our G-d, King of the universe who formest light and createst darkness, who makest peace and createst all things.*

יתגדל. The Kaddish here is to be considered as a conclusion of the preceding section and not as an introduction to the following part, beginning with the ברכו (Cf. ד"מ, par. 54). As in all cases when a certain inner connection exists between two adjoining sections of prayer the Half-Kaddish only is recited, omitting the three concluding sentences. In this form the Kaddish presents itself simply as a prayer for redemption. Composed by the Men of the Great Synod (Assembly) in the period following the destruction of the first Temple, during Israel's exile, the wording is culled from Ezekiel XXXVIII, 23. It portrays the eternal role of Israel among the nations, viz., קדוש השם, to strive for the restoration to its full glory of the Great Name of G-d, יתגדל ויתקדש etc. For the fulfilment of Israel's destiny as a nation, will be attained when G-d's Name is recognized by the whole universe. The gathering together of the dispersed ones of Israel is linked to this goal. (Cf. Ezekiel XXXVI 23-24, Rashi ad loc.).

The second paragraph יהא שמה רבא מברך, describes man's share in this process of restoration. It is to "bless, extol, praise, the Great Name" of G-d at all times, in all circumstances and environments. This is the essence of the Jewish task, to summon all the forces of the soul to *acts* of קדוש השם. The Sages accordingly appended the Kaddish to the end of every section of the service, for קדוש השם is the ultimate aim of every Jew's life. He must never allow it to fade from his consciousness. The Sages, therefore, ordained that the Kaddish is to be recited after the study of Mishnah or Talmud and after every public reading of scriptural verses as well. Thus the Kiddish came to occupy a central place in the Jewish Divine service. (For more information see our comments following ובא לציון, p. 184).

Kaddish, like every דבר שבקדושה (ברכו, קדושה וכו'), may only be recited when at least ten adult males are present. The idea is frequently encountered in Biblical and Rabbinical literature, that the Divine Presence dwells in the midst of the community, and that larger the congregation, the more resplendent the revelation of the שכינה will be. (Cf. Mishnah Berachoth VII, 3, Yebamoth 64a: אין השכינה שורה על פחות משני אלפים ושני רבבות מישראל.). Only the community can effectively guarantee the preservation and progress towards the highest ideals. The Torah was therefore entrusted to the "community of Jacob" (מורשה קהלת יעקב). To fulfil the Jewish ideal of life of קדוש השם, is far too great a task for the ephemeral individual, with his limited material, moral and spiritual capacities. אין צבור עני ואין צבור מת The community does not die; its power endures. It does not suffer from deficiencies. What is lacking in one individual, is made up by another. The individual, then, can only discharge his duties completely when he collaborates with the community. The Rabbis, therefore placed the strongest emphasis on תפלה בצבור, on prayer in the midst of the community. If we are prevented from going to the House of Worship, then, they urge, we should at least say our prayers at the same time as the community prays, and thus join them in spirit, if not in the flesh. The דבר שבקדושה, however, may be recited only in the assembly of the community, or in the presence of ten, the smallest number who may legitimately represent the community. Isolated and disunited individuals cannot achieve the proper sanctification of the Name of G-d with due solemnity and holy fervor. This can only be done by the rallying of all the spiritual powers found in the community.

ברכו. כל מילי דקדושה בעי הזמנה "All sacred acts require summoning." This dictum of the Zohar gives the reason for the recital of the ברכו, as well as the זמון, before the Grace after meals. (מג"א §192, 1.). In both instances the leader invites those present to join him in the benedictions. (For the same reason ברכו is recited by those called to the reading of the Torah, and this explains סברי preceding the Kiddush). Both formulas are essentially alike and are in fact compared to each other in the Mishnah (Berachoth VII, 3). First comes the initial invitation of the leader, ברכו את ה', to praise G-d. However, he must not exclude himself from the circle of the worshippers even if it be in appearance only. All must join in the benediction: גדלו לה' אתי etc. (Ps. XXXIV, 4). Hence, the leader adds the word המבורך, "Who is being blessed", to his call, and thus includes himself within the community. (Berachoth 49b, Tos: ד"ה לעולם, cf. further p. 173). To this invitation the worshippers respond with ברוך ה'.... They repeat the first sentence almost word for word, כענין שהוא מברך כך עונים אחריו. The leader, in turn repeats their words, to demonstrate, as it were, his complete accord with the congregation, and then proceeds with the service.

ברוך יוצר אור. The third main division of the Shacharis, which begins now, has to follow upon the preceding section without any interruption. Only to perform a מצוה, the fulfilment of which cannot be postponed, may one interrupt between ישתבח and קדיש.

Just as any break in the middle of the individual sections of the service would disrupt its sacred character, so too should no interruption disturb the following of one section upon another. In this way the prayer emerges as a complete, perfectly harmonious, flawless unity.

The content of this section and its place within the framework of the prayer as a whole have already been indicated in the introduction (p. 12). It forms the oldest part, the very core of the Shacharis. It consists of the שמע (with its three paragraphs) enclosed within three Berachoth; two preceding the שמע, and one linking it to the שמונה עשרה that follows.

The recital of the שמע, morning and evening, is an explicit Mitzvah of the Torah. In adding the accompanying Brachoth, the Rabbis of the Mishnah seem to have been guided by this consideration. They felt that the worshippers should not recite the basic truths of Judaism as proclaimed in the Shema, without giving vent to the thoughts and emotions which these truths evoke in those who were chosen to receive them. All the eager wholehearted assent to the grateful accept- ance and the faithful observance of those fundamentals of our faith reverberate from the words of these Brachoth.

The first paragraph refutes the theory of the agnostics who argued that "He who created light could not also have created darkness" (Shulchan Aruch §59, 1). The Bracha, יוצר אור, was composed in accordance with the Talmudic maxim (Berachoth 11b) that "the theme of the night should be mentioned at daytime." It is a paraphrase of Isaiah, XLV, 7 and approaches the first sentence of the Shema, which pro- mulgates the doctrine of the One and only G-d, from a novel angle. By declaring that the G-d of light and darkness is One and the Same, it repudiates the oldest aberration of human thought, the inference from the contrasts of the phenomena of nature that there was a plurality, or a duality of godheads, a power of the day, of life, of fortune, and a power of the night, death and evil. Basically it is the conflict between the dualistic and monotheistic weltanschauung round which all spiritual battles and philosophical arguments have ranged them- selves from olden times right until today. The spiritual de- velopment of mankind advancing painfully slowly, disgressing, and straying, is nevertheless moving along the road towards a monistic Theism which comes progressively closer to the Jewish concept of G-d. But in the midst of the most gigantic struggle of all times endeavoring to uncover the deepest secrets of the cosmos, the Jew stands his ground, unwavering, and daily reiterates his declaration of pure monotheism — that the G-d who created אור and חושך, light and its opposite, Who moulds this world so full of apparent contradictions and conflicts, is One and the Same. Therefore we remember G-d as the Creator of darkness in the Bracha of the day, and as the Creator of light in the Bracha of the night. (Rabbi S. R. Hirsch).

In the adaptation of this Bracha from the verse in Isaiah, a certain textual change has been made. The words ובורא רע, were replaced by ובורא את הכל. This was done, according to Berachoth 11b, in order to avoid mentioning the creation of evil in the daily prayer. The circumlocution ובורא את הכל, may have been chosen to allude to the final words of the verse: אני ה' עושה כל אלה, as though to indicate that evil is a force necessary for the existence of the world. It is not an autonomous power. It is created by G-d, and is used when it is needed for the ultimate benefit of the creation.

It has been pointed out in the introduction that the first Bracha of the ק"ש is by no means to be taken as a mere offering of gratitude for the dawn of a new day. This purpose was already fulfilled by the Bracha אשר נתן לשכוי בינה — יוצר אור is the blessing acknowledging G-d as the Creator of the universe. However, the Bracha centers in the creation of the great luminaries. It begins with the creation of the light, glorifies the splendor of the rays of the sun and concludes יוצר המאורות. This strong accentuation of the role played by the celestial sources of light in the creation, might be attributed to what the Psalmist phrases: "The heavens declare the Glory of G-d, and the firmament praises the work of His hands" (Ps. XIX cf. Is. XL, 26). The grandeur of G-d's creative might finds its most brilliant reflection in the celestial bodies. The panorama of the starry sky, the recurrent cycle of the lunar phases, but above all the steady course of the sun regulating all terrestrial activity, all these are, as the Psalmist goes on to say, אין אומר ואין דברים, a call without word or sound. It is the great Divine message descending from heaven to earth, to plant the consciousness of a Higher Power within the breast of man. It proclaims to the world: There is a G-d! — Moreover light was the first of the created things. On the first day G-d said: "Let there be light." Light was thus established as the prime source of all activity within nature. Through the action of light, matter becomes capable of motion. It is the "prime mover", the element which awakens all other forces to life.

Light does not only make the existent visible. It also causes the countless varieties of its forms to evolve. Light is taken here as the first cause of material existence and atomic structure. This view coincides wth that of physics which considers light as the basis of all physical phenomena. Among the many forms of energy known to man, light ranks as the foremost, as the one which stimulates all others. The close connection between light on the one hand, and heat and magnetism on the other, is well known. Whereas light is invariably accompanied by the generation of heat, heat does not always emit light. While light is capable of causing magnetic reactions, magnetic forces do not produce light. Moreover, light causes a great number of chemical reactions, and no living organism could live without the immediate or, at least, the indirect influence of light. Science teaches: "Light holds the seed of that infinitely variegated activity which, though hidden from direct observation, prevents the whole physical world from collapse. The state of darkness can never be reached without coming closer to destruction, to death. Whenever man has possessed a keen sensitivity and responsivness to the activity of nature he has associated light with life, and darkness with death." The idea, reiterated here so frequently, that the recreation of Nature each day is connected in some way with the celestial luminaries, seems to rest upon the concept of the power of light to set all other forces in motion.

While all other religious philosophies deny, or at least limit the absolute freedom of G-d to rule the material world, monotheism alone as understood by the Jew includes the teaching that the Will of G-d constantly activates all forces and elements in the universe with complete and absolute freedom. The world, therefore, can be regarded as a creation coming into existence anew each day, beginning at dawn with the appearance of the "great light". This daily renascence is produced by G-d בטובו, in His Goodness, for the orderly rhythm of the universe and the unchanging laws of nature provide the basis for the regulation of all human activity. No work could ever be planned in advance, no achievment ever attained without this regularity of the phenomena of nature. This is the greatest gift bestowed by G-d upon man. With the creation of light, the world began. With the first ray of morning light, G-d renews the universe each day. We, therfore, glorify the Almighty Creator and Sustainer of the world each day, with the ברכת המאורות, the blessing on the "great lights".

המאיר. *Who in mercy givest light to the earth to them that dwell thereon, and in thy goodness renewest the creation every day continually. How manifold are thy works, O Lord! In wisdom hast thou made them all: the earth is full of thy possessions. O King, who alone wast exalted from aforetime, praised, glorified and extolled from days of old; O everlasting G-d, in thine abundant mercies, have mercy upon us, Lord of our strength, Rock of our stronghold, Shield of our salvation, thou Stronghold of ours! The blessed G-d, great in knowledge, prepared and formed the rays of the sun; it was a boon he produced as a glory to his name; he set the luminaries round about his strength. The chiefs of his hosts are holy beings that exalt the Almighty, and continually declare the glory of G-d and his holiness. Be thou blessed, O Lord our G-d, for the excellency of thy handiwork, and for the bright luminaries which thou hast made; they shall glorify thee forever.*

תתברך. *Be thou blessed, O our Rock, our King and Redeemer, Creator of holy beings, praised be thy name forever, O our King; Creator of ministering spirits, all of whom stand in the heights of the universe, and proclaim with awe in unison aloud the words of the living G-d and everlasting King. All of them are beloved, pure and mighty; and all of them in dread and awe do the will of their Master; and all of them open their mouths in holiness and purity, with song and psalm, while they bless and praise, glorify and reverence, sanctify and ascribe sovereignty to—*

The name of the Divine King, the great, mighty and dreaded One, holy is he; and they all take upon themselves the yoke of the kingdom of heaven one from the other, and give sanction to one another to hallow their Creator: in tranquil joy of spirit, with pure speech and holy melody they all respond in unison, and exclaim with awe:

Holy, holy, holy is the Lord of hosts; the whole earth is full of his glory.

*And the Ophanim and the holy Chayoth with a noise
of great rushing, upraising themselves towards the Seraphim,
thus over against them offer praise and say:*

Blessed be the glory of the Lord from his place.

המאיר לארץ. G-d grants light to the earth and its
inhabitants — ברחמים — with mercy. The gradual transition
from night to day, at dawn, protects man from being blinded
by the sudden impact of the sunlight. The twilight warns him
of the impending darkness, which he would otherwise face
unprepared, helpless. — מה רבו מעשיך ה' (Ps. CIV, 24). The
insertion of this verse here proves that this paragraph of
our prayers is not merely to be taken as a praise of the celestial bodies, but of the whole of creation. The context (Ps.
CIV) is a hymn of praise of the wonders of nature—and this
verse, in particular, gives articulation to our admiration for
the abounding variety of G-d's works, each one of them
product and proof of His infinite wisdom. — המלך וכו' (as
in Ps. XCIII, 2). G-d has always been the one and only, the
Supreme King, אדון עולם אשר מלך וכו'. Yet it is only since
the world came into existence, מימות עולם, that He has been
praised and acclaimed as King לעת נעשה בחפצו כל וכו'. We
find a similar idea in the saying (Aboth VI, II) כל מה שברא
הקב"ה בעולמו לא ברא אלא לכבודו, cf. also Midrash to Psalms
XCIV.

אלקי עולם. This sudden cry for mercy in the
midst of a paean of praise requires some explanation. אבודרהם
has this to say: According to the Jerusalem Talmud (Taanis
IV, 3) the light we perceive, is not the light as it was created
in its original purity and power. It comes to us in a diminished
form — "יהי מארת", מארת חסר כתיב — to correspond to
our own state of imperfection. Child and infant mortality,
which could only have been caused by the transgressions of
their parents, was held to be a manifestation of this imperfection. Accordingly, the אנשי משמר would fast on the fourth
day (Wednesday), the day of the creation of the "great
lights," על התינוקות שלא יעלה עליהם אסכרה. This explains
also the inclusion of this cry for mercy in the Bracha יוצר אור.
א-ל ברוך. The words here are arranged alphabetically. This
points to a special significance in their content. The Midrash (to
the Song of Songs I, 4) remarks: — בך, "נגילה ונשמחה בך"

בכ"ב אותיות שכתבת לנו בתורה. At the moments when our devotional joy reaches its climax, we praise G-d with all the 22 letters with which the Torah was written. (בך has the numerical value 22). The present piece merits this distinction in its style because as is evident from its concluding words: פנות צבאיו, it forms the prelude to the recital of the קדושה of the Angels. — לא-ל ברוך refers to the paragraph לא-ל ברוך נעימות יתנו which comes later. — גדול דעה as in Berachoth 33a — הכין ופעל. Ps. LXXIV, 16.— גדולה דעה שניתנה בין ב' אותיות. טוב יצר. "The Good One created כבוד for His Name," Maimonides, in the 64th chapter of his Guide, distinguishes three meanings in the term כבוד. Besides the subjective human concept "glory," it can also be explained as referring to the "Divinely created *light*" אור הנברא, or else, finally, as the *immanence* of G-d within nature. (כבוד related to כבד, weighty). It is in this last sense, that Moses' petition הראני נא את כבודך is to be understood. אור הנברא is that primordial light, which, as the direct emanation of the Deity, represents the initial stage of the creation, the first step in the transition from the metaphysical to the material world. Its supernatural splendor is too great for the human eye, bounded by the limits of time, to bear. It is therefore hidden away in the "storehouse of life" אור עולם באוצר חיים to be kept there till man reaches a higher level of spiritual existence, and to be given to him as the crowning reward for his ethical perfection. Flashes of this "hidden light" have penetrated into our world at special, exalted moments, as, for instance, when G-d revealed His שכינה at Mount Sinai. וישכון כבוד ה' על הר סיני.

Moreover, the entire world is a reflection or rather a dull afterglow of this hidden light, when, illuminated by the radiance of the sun, moon and stars, "it declares the "Glory of G-d." Malbim to Ex. XXXIII, 18 (cf. also Abarbanel, Commentary on the Guide to the Perplexed I. 8) adds a fourth explanation of כבוד השם to the three given by Maimonides, viz., the idea of the *"evolving creation"*. To him the whole cosmos as it evolved from formless, metaphysical being to a finite material world (alluded to in the words והיה בעבור כבודי) is also כבוד ה'. However this interpretation seems merely a logical development of Maimonides' line of thought, for taken in this sense, כבוד השם is the entire material world which, in all its beauty, represents the unfolding of the Divine

immanence, His "raiment of glory". To this revelation of
the Divine immanence, the passage: "The Good One created
כבוד for His Name", refers.

However, the attribute כבוד acquires a new significance,
when it is employed parallel to קדושה. Kedusha designates
the detached and purely spiritual transcendence of G-d, whereas כבוד, as has been explained, refers to His immanence within the world of material phenomena, His communication with
the universe. In the phrase תמיד מספרים כבוד א-ל וקדושתו, the
two contrasting attributes, viz. קדושה, His transcendence beyond the world and כבוד, His immanence within it, are acclaimed. The climax of the entire Bracha, the Kedusha of the
Angels, ק' ק' ק' ה' צבאות, is anticipated here. (Cf. our commentary ad loc.). — מאורות נתן. The light is held to be the
cloak and the reflection of the Divine Omnipotence (cf. עוטה
אור כשלמה Ps. CIV, 2 and Midrash ad loc.) — . . . תתברך ה'
Man concludes his hymn of praise with this sentence. In the following paragraph the Angels begin theirs. The human laudation refers to the entire created world. — על שבח מעשה ידיך
yet again, special emphasis is laid on the great luminaries ועל
מאורי אור וגו'. — שבח וגו'. Cf. commentary to ב"ש p. 64.
סלה means "forever", like נצח, ועד, according to the explanation given by Rabbi Eliezer ben Jacob in Eruvin 54. The
Targum and Rashi interpret the word thus wherever it occurs
in the Psalms. It has the same meaning in the five places
where it is found in the prayers. Ibn Ezra rejects this view. He
quotes the Latin translation of Jerome which takes סלה as a
musical symbol signifying a pause. Then he gives his own opinion. He holds סלה to be a particle which expresses affirmation
and corroboration: כן הוא ואמת הדבר. According to Kimchi, who
derives the word from סלו המסילה, it is used to indicate where
the voice is to be raised. (Cf. his commentary to Psalms III,
3. cf. also the view of Gesenius.). —— תתברך צורנו. "We
have exalted the G-d who grants light to the world each day,
and guides the sun and stars according to His Will. Since,
however, there are people who still worship the sun and the
stars, our prayers now describe the whole Host of Heaven
as offering praise to G-d and sanctifying Him as the Lord
and Creator of the universe. We expose the belief of those
people as an idle delusion, and show that the sun and the
stars as well, obey the Creator's Will." (כל בו). The Ke-

dusha that follows being descriptive in character, the worshipper may remain seated while repeating it, nor does it require the quorum of ten for its recital. It serves, at this point, to complete the logical argument of this Bracha, by repudiating any notion that the first causes of the actions of nature are independent prime forces, subject to their own laws. The אחד of the Shema, taken in its cosmologicol meaning is anticipated here.

From the above quoted remarks, it is evident that the host of Angels mentioned here, is merely a personification of the Host of forces of the universe. All Jewish philosophers agree that the word מלאך (messenger) refers to the vocation of the Angels, that is, to be the heralds and the executors of the Divine Will. (The word משרתים, "ministers", employed here carries this implication with even greater clarity). Purely spiritual beings by nature, the Angels occasionally acquire human form. Like all other beings they are created by G-d and depend entirely on Him. The belief in the existence of Angels follows from the assumption of a supernatural act of creation. It is this premise which makes the necessity for angel-like beings logically understandable. They form the link between the incorporeal, purely spiritual Divine Being and the world of material phenomena. Pantheism which lets G-d dissolve in nature may do without such an assumption. Yet it is just this tension between the transcendental and the material, force and matter, essence and attribute, which has moved man most profoundly since time immemorial, and stirred him to probe and to question. Polytheism accepted the idea of intermediate beings, but later developed the naive belief in independent gods. A relic of this pagan belief found its way into Christianity as the dogma of the Trinity, which was to provide the mediating link between the Creator and the world.

Judaism on the other hand rejects any assumption of a mediator between G-d and man. It strives to repudiate most emphatically the erroneous belief in the existence of free and independent god-like beings or "forces" who share in determining man's fate, by the recital of the Kedusha which the Angels offer daily to G-d. This declaration proclaims loudly and unequivocally that there is only One G-d to whom the whole host of heaven must humbly submit וכלם מקבלים עליהם עול מלכות שמים. However even to the Angels (the messengers between the two worlds) the unity of G-d, this mystery of mysteries of the coalescence of His transcendental existence with His presence that fills the earth, remains an eternal enigma. Man's inquiring mind has endeavored from time immemorial to penetrate beyond the veil that hides the answer, כסוד שיח שרפי קדש. However, it is just this unity, incomprehensible and therefore so wondrous, which is the theme of the Angel's שירה. The thundering climax of their hymn, in which all their voices are united, is the mighty declaration: ק' ק' ק' ק' ה' צבאות מלא כל הארץ כבודו, "G-d is exalted in holiness above heaven and earth and above time." — yet "the whole earth is filled with His immanence."

The word קדושה means separation — hence freedom, detachment from the sensory, the material. Translated into human terms, the word signifies moral and ethical perfection, finally holiness. When it refers to G-d it has the parallel meaning viz., transcendence. This detachment from the material is always the criterion of holiness. There is no difference in essence between human and Divine holiness only one of degree. The threefold repetition of the קדוש (in the Kedusha) expresses the absolute detachment of holiness of G-d. The number 3 as the root of all relativity forms the basis of the material world. By the threefold קדוש, G-d is acclaimed as exalted above the three dimensions of the expanse according to the Targum: He rules above space (קדיש, קדיש על ארעא, בשמי מרומא) and time (קדיש לעלם וכו') in splendid isolation, yet מלא כל הארץ, "The earth is full of His Immanence." The proclamation of His absolute exaltedness above all phenomena of this world is placed next to the declaration of His Omnipresence. It has been pointed out before, that the concept כבוד ה' takes in the entire world of physical phenomena, and hence, by contrast to the term קדושה, signifies the immanence of G-d, G-d's activity within the material universe. By showing the striking contrast between these two notions קדושה and כבוד השם, the lesson is driven home that the supra-mundane Deity who dwells in the infinite Heavens, is as manifest in the smallest particle of matter as in the unattainable reaches of pure spirit, and that all is animated by His breath. Yet this immanence does not impair the independence of His existence. The Deity has not confined or limited itself within the material world. The world is not G-d; it is only one concrete manifestation of G-d, over which He rules in sovereign omnipotence. The term ה' צבאות used here also seems to convey this idea, for the Talmud (Ber. 31b) regards this attribute as designating G-d as the Creator of the Universe. The ויכלו השמים והארץ וכל צבאם (Gen. II, 1), furnishes the basis for this interpretation (cf. also Chullin 87a). The universe, according to this view, is not a rigid, determined and immutable mass, but an array of a stupendous number of forces, subject at all times to G-d's command. The chorus of the Angels daily proclaims the simultaneous existence of His sacred detachment from this world and His glory that fills the creation. "Thrice holy and exalted is the Divine creator of nature, free above the earth that is filled with His Glory."

The Kedusha, however, does not give the answer to the basic question. The deep mystery enshrouding the relationship of the Creator and the world, spirit to matter, soul to body, energy to mass, is not solved by the glorification of the miraculous unity of G-d.

Yet the question cannot be suppressed. Every new glorification of the unity of G-d only provokes anew the eternal question: where is the ultimate ground of all material existence? What is it? In which way did the concrete world designated as כבוד, the glory of G-d evolve? From where did it originate? Time and again the Angels, awe-struck in their bewilderment, ask one another: משרתיו שואלים זה לזה איה מקום כבודו.

The answer comes from the אופנים and חיות הקדש, the highest group of Angels (cf. Maimonides יסודי התורה §2, 7) which form part of the Divine throne itself. (cf. Chullin 92a and Rashi ad loc.). The Zohar, as well as Maimonides distinguishes ten groups of Angels which correspond to the various stages of the transition from the spiritual to the physical world. Among them are the Seraphim. They are the animated spirits which, according to Isaiah Chap. VI — chant the Kedusha cited above. It is however the Angels closest to pure spirit, the אופנים and חיות הקדש who are most likely to be able to solve the riddle of the origin of all existence.

What is the answer they give? ברוך כבוד ה' ממקומו. "Blessed be the glory of G-d from His Abiding Place." The Glory of G-d, which, as we have pointed out, alludes to the totality of creation — derives its blessing, its sustenance, its growth and development ממקומו. This last term means, according to Targum Jonathan, "מאתר בית שכינתה," "from His Abiding Place." Even the אופנים and חיות are unable to give a direct answer to the question: איה מקום כבודו. Where can we look for the very beginning of the creation? מכלל דמקומו ליכא דידע ליה. "No one knows where His abode is." (Chag. 13b). Yet by responding with ברוך to the קדוש of the שרפים, the אופנים and חיות lead us to a more profound knowledge of G-d's creation. His transcendental holiness was proclaimed by the former as קדוש. The latter answer by giving ברוך as the ultimate source of the material manifestation of His Glory: לעמתם ברוך יאמרו. A fundamental principle of all existence in its variegated forms is revealed here: In the world of nature, יש מאין, matter was created out of the void, and all material blessing (ברוך) comes from the incorporeal, transcendental being of G-d, (קדוש). With man too, every ברכה bestowed upon him is but the consequence of קדושה, of his moral perfection. מי יעלה בהר ה' ומי יקום במקום קדשו ... ישא ברכה מאת ה' (Ps XXIV, 3; CXXXIV, 2). Here the supreme host of Angels proclaim a fundamental law of nature and the basic principle of ethics. The question of the ultimate origin of all existence may well remain unanswered forever. The homage of the אופנים, however, discloses to us the great universal principle which is of foremost importance for the moral outlook of man.

The Kedusha here ends with the ברוך כבוד. The verse ימלך usually recited as the third verse of praise in the Kedusha is omitted. This verse is the tribute paid by man to G-d as King and the G-d of Zion ימלוך ה'...אלו-היך ציון; it has no place in the Kedusha of the Angels.

Now that the general explanation of the Kedusha has been concluded, we shall proceed to give a running commentary on the text.

תתברך צורנו מלכנו וגואלנו. Three attributes of G-d are mentioned in this passage: גואל, מלך, צור. They present in fine, the ideas underlying the three blessings between which the Shema is embedded. צור is to be understood as Creator,

an interpretation frequently applied to this term. אל תקרי
צור אלא צייר (cf. also above p. 86). However the attribute
מלך too occurs frequently in this section. (למלך א-ל חי וקים,
ומקדישים וממליכים, את שם הא-ל המלך.) This is because
the Kedusha should lead to קבלת עול מלכות שמים. We find this
expressed in the ימלוך, the human share of the Kedusha, and
in the frequent mention of G-d's Kingship in this paragraph.
גואלנו, finally refers to the Bracha before the גאל ישראל.
— בורא קדושים, refers to the Angels who are unaffected
by passion, greed or other emotions and live in perfect serenity
and harmony. — ואשר משרתיו refers, according to Abudraham,
to the two Archangels possessing eternal life, Gabriel and
Michael (Gen. Rabba ch. 78). — יוצר משרתים, on the other hand
includes the vast host of other Angels who are created anew
each day and vanish at its close. Michael and Gabriel represent
the elemental forces of fire (wrath, justice) and of water
(love, fertility) (cf. Berachoth 4b and the commentators ad
loc.). They are immortal. — ואשר referring back to מלכנו
ומשמיעים ביראה דברי. Isaiah XIV, 18. כל מלכי גוים כלם cf.
Every word of command going out from G-d creates
an Angel (Chag. 14b). Each one of them is G-d's word translated into a force animating the universe; each proclaims His
Regal Might. — כלם אהובים. The Jewish view, as opposed
to the polytheistic perversity which regarded the universe as
peopled by a host of quarreling, competing deities, is set forth
here. Surrounded by His love, His chosen Angels possess
power. They all do His Will in fear and awe. They sing His
praise. — רצון קונם. This version is the correct one, according
to most authorities, among them the Gaon of Vilna. —
בקדשה ובטהרה בשירה וגו'. Ethical perfection and aesthetic
harmony are the ideal basis for the panegyric of the Angels
to rise with ever greater jubilation and ardor.

Six expressions of praise ומברכים ומשבחים וכו', corresponding to the six attributes of the Divine את שם הא-ל
המלך הגדול וכו' are used to glorify Him. There is a hidden
allusion here to the six wings of the Angels seen by Ezekiel
in his vision. ואשמע את קול כנפיהם (I, 24, Chag. 13b) "with
their six wings, i.e. with all the forces of their beings, they
unite in His praise," extolling the three basic attributes revealed by Moses (Deut. X, 17), גדול גבור ונורא קדוש הוא,
"Who is unattainable in His Holiness." — וכלם מקבלים...ונותנים

רשות זה לזה. By the interaction of opposing and interpendent forces within the universe the harmony of nature is achieved. Each element and each type of energy has its complement; every action causes a reaction. All this activity results in the perfect harmony and rhythm of nature. As these forces of nature limit, restrain or counteract the forces that oppose them, the former forces are in turn subject to the influence of the latter. In this way they all "receive the yoke of the kingdom of Heaven from one another, and give permission to one another to sanctify their Creator." All inequalities in the distribution of power and wealth vanish in the common ground of Divine worship, for it gives rise to justice and love, tolerance, mutual guidance and understanding. True enthusiasm for an idea suffuses the devotees of that idea with joy and zeal. It does not degenerate into fanaticism. Instead is intensifies the desire to break away from the confusing complexity of ideas and proceed towards the ultimate goal: to sanctify G-d, our Creator.

בנחת רוח. Tranquility of spirit, clear articulation, and sacred melody are the elements which make up the peculiar soul-stirring quality of religious recitation. According to most authorities קדושה qualifies נעימה (viz. especially באר היטב אורח חיים §59, 3). There is a spiritual, moral grandeur ennobled by purity and holiness which is called הדרת קדש. The music of Angels expresses this grandeur, each word uttered by the heavenly choir is permeated with holiness and purity. את פיהם וכו' ברעש גדול. — וכלם פותחים. While the chant of the שרפים rises softly, serenely to G-d, the אופנים proclaim their homage in a tempestuous roar. The former (as we have mentioned before) promote activity on the earth — the laws of which are steady and regular. Accordingly, they sing their song in measured harmony. It is otherwise with the song of the אופנים. They surround the immediate vicinity of the Divine throne מכסא הכבוד עצמו. They are the naked, elemental forces of nature which form the very foundations of the universe. As the tumultuous uproar of nature, the thunder, lightning and quaking of the earth, heralded the coming of the Almighty Master of Nature at Sinai, so, in the same way the message of the prime forces of heaven were revealed to the prophet amidst a mighty uproar, an upheaval of all elemental forces proclaiming and adoring G-d as the Creator of the Universe. ואשמע אחרי קול רעש גדול ברוך כבוד ה' ממקומו.

ברוך ל-א‑ל. *To the blessed G-d they offer pleasant melodies; to the King, the living and ever-enduring G-d, they utter hymns and make their praises heard; for he alone performeth mighty deeds, and maketh new things; he is the Lord of battles; he soweth righteousness, causeth salvation to spring forth, createth remedies, and is revered in praises. He is the Lord of wonders, who in his goodness reneweth the creation every day continually; as it is said, (O give thanks) to him that maketh great lights, for his lovingkindness endureth for ever. O cause a new light to shine upon Zion, and may we all be worthy soon to enjoy its brightness. Blessed art thou, O Lord, Creator of the luminaries.*

ברוך ל-א‑ל. The concluding section of the Bracha reverts to the theme of the beginning. This scheme is general to all prayers. (Pesachim 105a). The initial idea of G-d as constantly present, constantly fashioning nature, led to the praise of G-d, as the Creator of Nature, in the words ברוך כבוד. The first thread is taken up again in ברוך ל-א‑ל, and is interwoven with the second concept of G-d as Omnipresent source of all activity כי הוא לבדו. — למלך א‑ל חי. Again the prayer stresses: He and only He performs Almighty deeds. גבורות—specifically refers to the Creation of the world, as the Talmud proves (Taanis 2a in reference to Ps LXV, 8). It is the Creator of the world עושה גבורות, Who also עושה חדשות, renews and sustains the universe each day. — בעל מלחמות. The conflicting trends in the life of nature and mankind are not to be traced back to two opposing universal principles; G-d is the "Lord of wars", Who also "plants mercy," "makes salvation grow forth" etc. He is the איש מלחמה, ה' שמו. He is the "Creator of war" but His Name is ה' (מדת הרחמים), the G-d of love. In the political arenas of the nations, the Father of Mankind makes the longing for peace, and amity emerge from the horror of the blood-soaked battlefields; and in the life of the individual too, enduring friendships often result from the airing, and settlement of personal conflicts. Thus the G-d of wars appears to us as

the זורע צדקות, "Planter of Mercy," Who, מצמיח ישועות,
makes "salvation grow forth." Man becomes aware of a blessing only once it becomes manifest; he is ignorant of it while
G-d is preparing it in the recesses of the future. — בורא
רפואות, "He creates healing." The healing of the hopelessly
sick is a creative act comparable to the birth of a new being.
For this reason this attribute is included among the גבורות
ה'. — נורא תהלות. A midrashic comment on the verse מי
ימלל (Ps CVI. 2) "Who can utter *all* the praise of G-d?",
reads as follows: "When a mortal king enters a new country,
he is acclaimed rich, merciful and strong, even though he be
weak and cruel. Not so G-d. As much as we may praise
Him, we can always find a higher praise applicable to Him.
That is the meaning of the verse: נורא תהלות עושה פלא —
G-d performer of miracles, is exalted above all praise. Bearing out this explanation, the enumeration of the praises of
G-d ends with נורא תהלות as if to show the futility of the
attempt to sing "all His praise."

We have to determine what it was that prompted the
choice of just these attributes of G-d, their number and their
kind. To this problem an ancient commentary provides an
interesting answer. It reminds us of the fact that the Kedusha
of the Angels is recited here to contradict the view of those
who maintain that the sun, moon and stars move according
to their own laws and are independent of the Will of The
Creator. In opposition to this view, the Psalmist cries out:
ינאץ אויב שמך לנצח, "Shall the enemy blaspheme Thy Name
forever?" (LXXIV, 10). Now the letters of the two words שמך
לנצח are those with which the names of the seven planets of the
Ptolemaic system begin (Sabbath 156a, 120b. Rashi to Berachoth 59b). These seven planets symbolise the powers mentioned
in this passage. The idea is brought out that the planets are not
the sources of those powers but שמך לנצח "Thy Name forever." The first planet, the sun, ruling on Sun-day is alluded
to by פועל גבורות ("כצאת השמש בגבורתו"). The moon, star
of Mon-day, is referred to by עושה חדשות, its outstanding
characteristic being its monthly cycle of renewal. בעל מלחמות
points to מאדים, the blood-red star of the third day, Mars
the god of war of the Romans, called Tiu (Tuesday) by the
ancient Germans. מצמיח ישועות hints at כוכב, the morning

star that brings salvation (Mercury — Wednesday, French Mercredi.) Jupiter, called in Hebrew צדק, is referred to by זורע צדקות. בורא רפואות is the designation used for the star of Friday, Venus, (known in Hebrew as נוגה) which brings "peace, joy, bliss and health." The Sabbath star, שבתי (Saturn, Saturday) is finally alluded to in נורא תהלות because ruling on the day of rest, it pays homage to the Creator alone.

אור חדש. According to §59 טור אורח חיים, this sentence is a later addition. It is inserted here "because the Bracha, יוצר אור, refers to the primordial light of the creation. Humanity was not worthy to enjoy it. It was, therefore, hidden away to be granted to the צדיקים at some future date. We pray, therefore, that we may soon be privileged to share in the eternal light." Thus in a very significant way, this closing sentence reveals an important insight: The daily alternation of light and darkness, the theme of this Bracha, is never to be taken for granted as an immutable and final act. Like every other contrast and every other conflict in nature, this הבדלה בין אור לחושך too, will be reconciled in the Messianic future by the moral endeavor of mankind united in a higher harmony. The coming of this era of light is inseparably linked with Zion, the place from where the light of the moral and ethical perfection of mankind emanates to illuminate the world.

אהבה רבה. *With abounding love hast thou loved us, O Lord our G-d, with great and exceeding pity hast thou pitied us. O our Father, our King, for our fathers' sake, who trusted in thee, and whom thou didst teach the statutes of life, be also gracious unto us and teach us. O our Father, merciful Father, ever compassionate, have mercy upon us; O put it into our hearts to understand and to discern, to mark, learn and teach, to heed, to do and to fulfil in love all the words of instruction in thy Law. Enlighten our eyes in thy Law, and let our hearts cleave to thy commandments, and unite our hearts to love and fear thy name, so that we be never put to shame. Because we have trusted in thy holy, great and revered name, we shall rejoice and be glad in thy salvation. O bring us in peace from the four corners of the earth, and make us go upright to our land; for thou art a G-d who worketh salvation. Thou hast chosen us from all peoples and tongues, and hast brought us near unto thy great name forever in faithfulness, that we might in love give thanks unto thee and proclaim thy unity. Blessed art thou, O Lord, who hast chosen thy people Israel in love.*

אהבה רבה. Two halachic considerations govern the second Bracha of the ק״ש, and point the way to a deeper understanding of this section. The first states that this Bracha (as distinct from the יוצר אור) — does not begin with ברוך because it follows immediately upon the preceding one and is closely connected with it in content. The second consideration is, that the אהבה רבה has the character of a ברכת התורה, a Bracha over the Torah. In fact in certain circumstances, the Bracha may serve as a substitute for the בר' התורה (Orach Chaim §46). These two rules, then, establish the significance of the אהבה רבה as a transition from the blessing of creation, to the בר' התורה, the blessing of the Torah, of the revelation to Israel.

Creation and Revelation are the two cornerstones of Judaism. They support one another. The belief in the creation of the world by a free Divine act is the logical basis for the doctrine of the free-will of man. Without the acceptance of this doctrine, the revelation of G-d's will to man would be meaningless. For if we were to deny or limit the free, sovereign power of the Creator over His Creation, then man would be a product of a predetermined, fettered nature, and would hardly be master of his own will and volition. He would be powerless to obey the revealed law. However, the Bible teaches us that everything, the form and nature of all that exists, emerged from the free, omnipotent Will of the Creator. G-d ruling in free sovereignty over His world, breathed a spark of this freedom into man endowing him with the mastery over his own small world, his body and his faculties. Thus man is an image of the free G-d, possessing freedom in a world ruled by G-d's omnipotence. In this manner the belief in man's free will follows from the belief in a Divine creation, while man's free-will in turn is the logical prerequisite for the idea of creation.

However a second train of thought treating of creation and revelation connects the two Brachoth. True, the existence of a Creator is clearly and irrefutably manifest to the thoughtful observer, in the marvels of an harmonious nature

and especially in the grand panorama of the firmament, השמים
מספרים כבוד א-ל. However, nature remains silent on the question
of man's position within the cosmos, how he is supposed to
act in this world pervaded by G-d's immanence. Heaven and
earth and all their laws do not provide the guide for man's
conduct. Nor have philosophers and lawgivers after many
thousands of years of searching, been able to formulate a
code of ethics which would have found universal recognition,
were it even for a short period of time only. The history of
philosophy is a history of human trial and error. Only G-d's
revealed law, תורת השם, gives man the guidance which is
suited to his innate urges and desires, and which leads him to
develop in accordance with the Divine plan. תמימה, in its
perfection, the Torah "satisfies the Soul" (משיבת נפש). The
Psalm just mentioned begins as a hymn of nature השמים
מספרים, and then proceeds with the praise of the Torah תורת
השם תמימה. ברכות ק"ש following this line, open the book
of nature in their first part and the book of revelation, the
Torah, in the second, as the twin guide of faith and morals.

אהבה רבה. G-d's love of Israel is the first and the
final subject of this Bracha. The sentence, שמע ישראל, which
proclaims the permanent election of Israel, is enclosed between
the expressions of G-d's love of Israel הבוחר באהבה, and Israel's
love of Him, ואהבת. In their love for each other, G-d and
Israel meet. It is impossible to conceive a more categorical
repudiation of the assertion that Judaism is a dry, legalistic
burden to its adherents, a cumbrous yoke which dooms its
carriers to suffer throughout the centuries. Israel has never
regarded her destiny within the family of nations as being
other than a special privilege and gesture of "great love"
proffered to her by G-d. No matter how horribly Israel suffered at the hands of her oppressors, she always reassured
herself and affirmed once more: אהבה רבה, "With great
love hast Thou loved us." This blissful conviction, that she
was the beloved of the Highest One, instilled new strength
in Israel each day to fight with the courage of a lion for the
שמע ישראל, to suffer for it, to live and, if need be, to die for
it.

The difference between the morning and evening Brachoth are fully explained by what has been said in the intro-

duction about the respective characteristics of the two services (p. 6, cf. צל"ח to Berachoth 11b, ברכות 12a, תוספות
ד"ה להגיד). The Maariv looks toward the future. Accordingly
its Bracha begins with אהבת עולם — and concludes with the
words ואהבתך אל תסיר ממנו לעולמים. The Shacharis, on the
other hand, refers to the love we have been vouchsafed in
the past. It emphasises the אהבתנו (past tense) and singles
out the fact of Israel's election from among the other nations,
as the most outstanding manifestation of the Divine love: הבוחר
בעמו ישראל באהבה. — חמלה is associated with אהבה as in
Isaiah LXIII, 9, באהבתו ובחמלתו הוא גאלם. The fact that
we have been freed from the labyrinth of rival and conflicting
philosophies, and have been shown the road to truth and harmony, is a demonstration of G-d's love for us. כי מאהבת ה'
אתכם וכו' (Deut. VII, 8).—והאר, ודבק. Besides praying for Divine assistance that we may learn with understanding, and practice in faithfulness, we ask that we be given acess to a deeper
knowledge, and for the complete gratification that results from
submission in love to the demands of the Mitzvoth. Only those
who know the scholar's passionate desire for truth, and the
saint's ardent longing for holiness, can sense the fervor of
the plea burning in these words. — ויחד. The very last of
all the petitions, all of which are concerned with the ethical
perfection of ourselves, is this plea for our hearts to unite
in the fear and love of G-d. This reconciliation of two apparently mutually exclusive emotions, love and fear, is the final
achievement of a life devoted to training the self to ethical perfection. It projects a ray of the perfect unity of G-d Himself
into our hearts. The unity of ה' (מדת הרחמים) and אלקינו
(מדת הדין) in ה' אחד produces a harmony and unity in the
human soul by making all its emotions and affections converge
upon one center, G-d. For fear and love are the two emotions
of the human heart which correspond to the two attributes of the
Divine, justice and mercy. (Ramban to Exodus XX, 8), and
are called forth by them. Whoever achieves this harmony in
his heart, has G-d in his heart. His heart is not affected by
revolt, apathy, dejection. Instead, complete accord, unconditional
submission to the Divine and infinite serene faith permeate his
soul. That is what it means to be "perfect with G-d": to possess
tranquility of conscience, true peace of mind and soul. This
fusion of even the most contradictory affections into one per-

fect unity is the secret of the truly pious. Only in the relation of man to G-d is it conceivable, as Rabbi Simeon points out so significantly: אין לך אהבה במקום יראה ויראה במקום אהבה אלא במדת הקב"ה בלבד. (Sifre Deut. VI, 5). It causes the same person who trembles in abject fear before G-d to feel, at the same time, the most ardent desire to be near Him.

G-d found you worthy of His love. In your nature He found the spiritual and ethical qualities which the nearness of G-d to man evokes. To use human terms, we say He found Himself drawn to you. At the same time He had to honor the pledge which He gave to the patriarchs בעבור אבותינו שבטחו בך. The following sentences contain all those wishes which every truly conscious Jew carries in his heart for himself and his children. The fulfilment of these wishes is the supreme aim of his life. — דברי תלמוד תורתך are the words of the traditional interpretation of the Divine Law, called Talmud — באהבה. Love of knowledge and conscientiousness in practising the Law should be our guide in "learning and doing" (Nedarim 62a). — ולא נבוש, "That we may never be put to shame," a direct outcome of the ethical perfection sought for above. The further Israel drifts away from the realization of its ideals of justice and mercy, the louder and more violently is the Jewish honor assailed and vilified. But the closer the Jewish people comes to the ideal, the more assurance is there that the oppressors and slanderers will remain silent. — כי בשם. It has been prophesied that not until the time of the Messiah will monotheism become the common heritage of all mankind. ביום ההוא יהי' ה' אחד. The proclamation of G-d's unity in the שמע is therefore preceded by the plea for a speedy redemption. (Cf. a similar sequence in the earlier recital of the שמע p. 37.) Not in our own power, nor in the might of secular rulers do we put our trust, but in Thy great and feared Name, כי בשם קדשך. This trust makes us rejoice in Thy help even though we remain exiled and dispersed. — והביאנו לשלום. Only in our homeland shall we find the peace denied to us among strangers. — קוממיות following Leviticus XXVI, 13. ואולך אתכם קוממיות (Cf. Numbers Rabba Ch. 13, "Upright and fearless"). — כי א-ל. Cf. Ps. LXXIV, 12. — וקרבתנו. The concluding words of the Bracha, as usual take up the theme of the beginning. G-d's love for us brings us near to Him.—באמת. The election of Israel was not an act of arbitrary favoritism, but of justice. Only after all other nations had failed morally, had refused to shoulder the yoke of duty and devotion to G-d, of obedience to His commands, did Israel become the special object of G-d's love. — ליחדך, points to the שמע which follows immediately. It contains the Jewish doctrine of the unity of G-d. — The Bracha concludes not with the unity of G-d but with the love of G-d. As Abudraham remarks, the affirmation of the unity of G-d is valueless if it does not spring from the love of the integrated heart. The skeptics are weighed down by indifference and apathy. Only those who are roused to enthusiasm, who are suffused by love, possess indomitable courage and never give in. They carry and preserve the great idea of pure monotheism. The love of Israel for G-d is reciprocated by His love for Israel, הבוחר בעמו ישראל באהבה. Recipients of this love, possessors of this ideal, sharers in common historical experiences and ideals, the Jews were given the heavenly message שמע ישראל. A call to humanity for peace, it is at the same time, a battle cry for Israel. It is the ultimate of cultural evolution. It is the raison d'etre of the Jew. It is the ancient, yet forever new, Divine mission שמע ישראל.

שמע ישראל. *Hear, O Israel, the Lord our G-d, the Lord is One.*

Blessed be His name, whose glorious kingdom is for ever and ever.

And thou shalt love the Lord thy G-d with all thine heart, and with all thy soul, and with all thy might. And these words, which I command thee this day, shall be upon thine heart; and thou shalt teach them diligently unto thy children, and shalt talk of them when thou sittest in thine house, and when thou walkest by the way, and when thou liest down, and when thou risest up. And thou shalt bind them for a sign upon thine hand, and they shall be for frontlets between thine eyes. And thou shalt write them upon the door-posts of thy house, and upon thy gates.

And it shall come to pass, if ye shall hearken diligently unto my commandments which I command you this day, to love the Lord your G-d, and to serve him with all your heart and with all your soul, that I will give the rain of your land in its season, the former rain and the latter rain, that thou may-

est gather in thy grain and thy wine and thy oil. And I
shall give grass in thy field for thy cattle, and thou shalt eat and
be satisfied. Take heed to yourselves, lest your heart be deceived,
and ye turn aside, and serve other gods, and worship them;
and the anger of the Lord be kindled against you, and he shut
up the heaven, that there be no rain, and that the land yield
not her fruit; and ye perish quickly from off the good land
which the Lord giveth you. Therefore shall ye lay up these
my words in your heart and in your soul; and ye shall bind
them for a sign upon your hand, and they shall be for frontlets between your eyes. And ye shall teach them your children,
talking of them when thou sittest in thine house, and when
thou walkest by the way, and when thou liest down, and when
thou risest up. And thou shalt write them upon the door-posts
of thine house, and upon thy gates; that your days may be
multiplied, and the days of your children, upon the land which
the Lord swore unto your fathers to give them, as the days
of the heavens above the earth.

And the Lord spoke unto Moses, saying, Speak unto
the children of Israel, and bid them that they make them a
fringe upon the corners of their garments throughout their
generations, and that they put upon the fringe of each corner
a cord of blue; and it shall be unto you for a fringe, that
ye may look upon it, and remember all the commandments
of the Lord, and do them; and that ye go not about after your
own heart and your own eyes, after which ye use to go astray;
that ye may remember and do all my commandments, and
be holy unto your G-d. I am the Lord your G-d, who brought
you out of the land of Egypt, to be your G-d; I am the Lord
your G-d.

שמע. The 3 paragraphs of the Shema form the oldest
part, the center of the morning and evening prayers. The
Talmud begins with the discussion of the precepts concerning
the daily recital of the Shema. Although the 3 paragraphs are
regarded as making up one unit, the actual command of the
Torah can be fulfilled by the recital of the first sentence. ("Thou
shalt say these words when thou liest down and when thou
risest up"). Proper attention must therefore be paid to the
meanings of the words while reciting the paragraph.

The foundation of Jewish ethics, their basis in dogma
and their program in practice, is the theme of the Shema.

The Bracha dealing with the creation יוצר אור was followed
by its logical sequel, the Bracha dealing with the revelation
at Sinai, אהבה. This leads directly to the essentials of this
revelation, the Shema. In the solemn proclamation of the
true moral ideal the daily prayer thus reaches its climax. The
three paragraphs of the Shema set down a triad of ethical
precepts: the first, according to the Talmudic interpretation
— treats of קבלת עול מלכות שמים, the acceptance of the Divine rule; the second, קבלת עול מצות, submission to the Divine law, and the third, the road to personal sanctification
והייתם קדושים. This last state is attained by resisting material
temptation, ולא תתורו אחרי לבבכם ואחרי עיניכם. The three
questions basic to moral and ethical legislation are answered
here: the origin of the law, its demands and its purpose. They
are presented here in brief but precise outline from the Jewish
point of view. The first sentence, unexhaustible in the abundance of its meanings and implications, has a cosmological, an
ethical and a historical significance. All the opposing trends
in the profusion of the phenomena of nature, history and in
the soul of man, which more than anything else produced the
error of polytheism, are seen by Judaism to be the activity
of the one G-d, ה' אחד. To us He appears as ה', the absolute Prime Spirit. He ruled even before the world began, as
the creative, wonder-working love, מדת הרחמים. As אלוקים,
the Omnipotent, He communicates with the universe by means
of the laws of nature, and with His people by means of the
laws of the Torah. He is the ideal personification of law and
justice, מדת הדין. This revealed wisdom perpetually replenishes
human thought, as the teaching of the unity of love and justice,
spirit and matter, freedom and necessity, of the Infinite and
the multitude of finite forces. Moreover, it is the very foundation of the unity of our lives and our own selves, and thus
the basis of Jewish ethics. For only if mercy and justice, joy
and pain, life and death flow from one source, only if our
health and wealth are granted and withheld by the order
of the One G-d, only then are we His, with every fibre of
our being, with all our heart, all our soul and all our wealth.
Therefore, the immediate consequence of the ה' אחד is ואהבת
— not a theoretical concept echoing in a vacuum, but the direct
challenge to lead a moral existence, that we should love and
serve G-d in all the diverse phases of our life and being.

Complete, unreserved submission to the One indivisible G-d, makes man into a harmonious and integrated personality. יחוד תתאי, the unity below is a reflection of the יחוד עלאי, the unity above.

ברוך שם. The world is still far from accepting G-d as the Father of all mankind. Only a tiny segment of the human race responds to the proclamation of pure monotheism by reciting ברוך שם, the expression of joyous, permanent, unqualified assent. Hence this verse is said in a whisper at all times, except on the holy day of יום כפור. Then we proudly proclaim it aloud as though anticipating the day when אלקינו, *Our* G-d will be ה' אחד, the G-d of *all* mankind.

Until that time, Israel utterly alone, carries this idea through the ages, for her sake as well as for the sake of the whole human race. Living for this idea and because of it, Israel perennially bears witness to its absolute veracity. The two last letters of the words שמע and אחד form עד witness. They forever remind Israel of her function, among the nations, to be the witness to the One G-d. The Jew closes his eyes to exclude all the distracting influences of the outside world when he says the Shema. He concentrates his mind completely on his intention to live for the ideal of אחד, and if, need be, to die for it. He reaches, as it were, beyond the confines of his own being (צריך להשביע את יצרו — Sifre) and vows himself to emulate Rabbi Akiba who suffered torture and died a martyr's death for the sanctification of G-d's Name. As his life expired, his dying lips pronounced the אחד.

The knowledge of G-d (שמע ישראל: Know, Israel) flows from the love of G-d ואהבת. This love in turn, can only grow as a result of earnest research into the depths of the revealed wisdom והיו וכו' from an *education* in the responsibilities religion entails ושננתם לבניך, and the constant awareness of the concrete *reminders* of the Divine, the תפילין and the מזוזות. This, in brief, is the thread of ideas running through the first paragraph. The second, והיה, emphasises practical religious observance לעבדו as the means to attain "oneness" with G-d. The general outlines of the first paragraph are thus filled in by the specific demands of the second. He who has the "acceptance of the Divine Kingdom" firmly embedded in his soul will be prepared to hallow his life by the practice of Judaism.

Last comes the third paragraph, ויאמר. It has been
chosen (according to Berachoth 12b) as the concluding paragraph of the Shema because it contains five basic ideas of
Judaism: the Mitzvah of ציצית, the redemption from Egypt,
the "yoke" of the מצות, the suppression of heresy, and the
avoidance of sinful thoughts ולא תתורו וכו'. It is the ideal
of holiness which is proclaimed here, and of which man is re-
minded by the ציצית (וראיתם אותו וכו'). Holiness is the real
motivating force, guiding our steps towards the ultimate
goal, and only by a persistent striving for holiness, does life
ascend to a higher level of existence. Through it alone, can
man, the finite being, become the image of G-d the *Infinite*.
There need be no other reason for the Jew to pursue this
ideal of becoming holy, than אני ה' אלקיכם, than the very
existence and the Will of G-d.

אמת. The word is to be added immediately after the
end of the last paragraph of the Shema without any pause
or interruption, as in Jeremiah X, 10, "וה' אלקים אמת". It
is an expression of our deepest conviction, the unqualified
belief of the worshipper in the ideas mentioned in the Shema.
"True", is the echo which the recital of the Shema evokes
instantaneously in the human soul.

According to the Zohar פ' וירא, the three words ה' אלקיכם
אמת, should be repeated by the worshipper after the conclusion
of the Shema in order to reach a total of 248 words (245
words of the Shema plus these three). This is the number of the
organs of the human body (Orach Chayim §61, 3). The Midrash interprets this regulation in a most striking manner.
The underlying idea is, that the observance of the Divine ethical
laws guarantee not only the health of the mind and soul, but
of the body as well.

The living human being is an indivisible entity—
as the state of the body has its profound effects upon the
activity of mind and soul, thus, the operations of the soul in
turn influence the body. This indeed is the wonderful greatness of Judaism — that the hallowing of the soul, the express
aim of the law, also guarantees the health of the body as a consequence. He who hallows his life, thereby protects and prolongs
it. The 248 expressions of Jewish morals, the Mitzvos, as it
were, raise a protective wall around the 248 organs of the

body, our physical being (Enumerated in Mishna Oholoth I, 8). There is no better healing power than the good life, no more effective hygiene than morality, no more capable physician than G-d Himself. Religion is the true psycho-somatic medicine. The 248 words of the Shema allude in a concealed but pointed manner to this basic· principle of Judaism.

אמת.*True and firm, established and enduring, right and faithful, beloved and precious, desirable and pleasant, revered and mighty, well-ordered and acceptable, good and beautiful is this thy word unto us for ever and ever. It is true, the G-d of the universe is our King, the Rock of Jacob, the Shield of our salvation; throughout all generations he endureth and his name endureth; his throne is established, and his kingdom and his faithfulness endure for ever. His words also live and endure; they are faithful and desirable for ever and to all eternity, as for our fathers so also for us, our children, our generations, and for all the generations of the seed of Israel his servants. For the first and the last ages thy word is good and endureth for ever and ever; it is true and trustworthy, a statute which shall not pass away. True it is that thou art indeed the Lord our G-d, and the G-d of our fathers, our King, our fathers' King, our Redeemer, the Redeemer of our fathers, our Maker, the Rock of our salvation; our Deliverer and Rescuer from everlasting, such is thy name; there is no G-d beside thee.*

אמת ויציב. We had occasion, before, to refer to the far reaching significance which the verse להגיד בבוקר חסדך ואמונתך בלילות, possesses for the understanding of the morning and evening prayers (cf. p. 7, also Berachoth 11b). It is said, in reference to this verse, that he who does not recite אמת ויציב in the morning and אמת ואמונה, in the evening, has not properly fulfilled his duty, i.e. to mention G-d's lovingkindness (which He has shown to us in the *past*) and His faithfulness (which we hope to experience in the *future*), every day. The Gaon of Vilna sees this interpretation borne out by the two words "ויציב" and "ואמונה" following the word אמת in the morning and evening prayers respectively, for in Daniel (II 45), ויציב חלמא points to an established fact of the *past* (the dream), and ומהימן פשרה points to the fulfilment of the dream in the future. Thus in our prayers too, the two terms signify that G-d's truthfulness is attested to by our history, and forms the basis for our belief, in the future. — ויציב ונכון וכו, 15 affirmations follow. They express the deep conviction of the worshipper of the veracity of the ideas expressed in the Shema. (The significance of the 15, is explained in our comments on ישתבח, p. 86).

The following sentences lead to the main section of this ברכה which begins with עזרת אבותינו. The ציצית, which the worshipper holds in his hand during the Shema, and the next paragraph, are released after the words ונחמדים לעד, for with these words the reference to the Shema ends, and a new subject begins. (Mogen Abraham §24, 1). The entire section is an elaboration of the ה' אחד, the idea that G-d is the perfect unity, the most exalted, unattainable, infinite אלקים, and the most personal, close and intimate ה'. Judaism considers just this the greatness of G-d, as Rabbi Yochanan taught: "Wherever you find His exaltedness, you also find His nearness to you" (Megillah 31, 2). This basic harmony is echoed in innumerable variations in the words of the Bible: G-d is the Highest and the Nearest.

The Jew has taught man to feel G-d's nearness, and to turn in prayer to Him. The Jew has found this direct approach: "My G-d and G-d of my fathers." The authors of the prayers wanted to bring out this idea in ever new and different forms. This explains the broadness of concept in this Bracha, the repetition and the elaboration of similar trends of ideas. It conforms to the "leitmotif" להגיד בבוקר חסדך, not only to mention His lovingkindness but להגיד, to tell, to *talk* about it (as in הגדה). — דבריו חיים. The words of His law are *"alive";* they revitalise and ennoble the minds and souls of all who are imbued with them. (מגן אברהם §24, 1).

עזרת. *Thou hast been the help of our fathers from of old, a Shield and Saviour to their children after them in every generation; in the heights of the universe is thy habitation, and thy judgments and thy righteousness reach to the furthest ends of the earth. Happy is the man who hearkeneth unto thy commandments, and layeth up thy Law and thy word in his heart. True is that thou art indeed the Lord of thy people, and a mighty King to plead their cause. True is that thou art indeed the first and thou art the last, and beside thee we have no King, Redeemer and Saviour. From Egypt thou didst redeem us,*

O Lord our G-d, and from the house of bondmen thou didst deliver us; all their first-born thou didst slay, but thy first-born thou didst redeem; thou didst divide the Red Sea, and drown the proud; but thou madest the beloved to pass through, while the waters covered their adversaries, not one of whom was left. Wherefore the beloved praised and extolled G-d, and offered hymns, songs, praises, blessings and thanksgivings to the King and G-d, who liveth and endureth; who is high and exalted, great and revered; who bringeth low the haughty, and raiseth up the lowly, leadeth forth the prisoners, delivereth the meek, helpeth the poor, and answereth his people when they cry unto him; even praises to the Most High G-d, blessed is he, and ever to be blessed. Moses and the children of Israel sang a song unto thee with great joy, saying, all of them:

Who is like unto thee, O Lord, among the mighty ones? Who is like unto thee, glorious in holiness, revered in praises, doing marvels?

With a new song the redeemed people offered praise unto thy name at the sea shore; they all gave thanks in unison and proclaimed thy sovereignty, and said,

The Lord shall reign for ever and ever.

O Rock of Israel, arise to the help of Israel, and deliver according to thy promise, Judah and Israel. Our Redeemer, the Lord of hosts is His name, the Holy one of Israel. Blessed art thou, O Lord, who hast redeemed Israel.

עזרת אבותינו. The paramount importance of the redemption from Egypt and the division of the Red Sea in the history of the Jewish nation, as well as their indispensibility for a true understanding of the Jewish creed, has been explained in our comments on the Song of Moses. We refer the reader to our notes there.

One of our historical experiences became the prime source of the Jewish faith. Similarly, the experience derived from our individual lives on earth gives us the evidence of the existence of G-d. The frequent repetition of the word אמת in this paragraph emphasises this idea. Whereas in the Bracha preceding the Shema, אהבה רבה, G-d's great *love* for the chosen people was repeatedly asserted, so in אמת ויציב, the paragraph succeeding

the Shema, "Truth" is the key-word, the theme of Israel's affirmation before G-d. For אמת מארץ תצמח וצדק משמים נשקף,
truth grows from the earth, while lovingkindness looks down
from heaven. (Ps. LXXXV, 12). Love is a gift from heaven.
Israel received it at her election. Truth, however, "must grow
from the earth." The certainty of the Divine must grow out
of the reality of life, from historical experience. (Six times
the word אמת is repeated in this paragraph, for corresponding to
the six days of creation and the six directions of space, the
Six is considered the symbol of concrete reality). Then חסד
ואמת נפגשה, truth and lovingkindness meet — The lovingkindness which chose Israel to be G-d's nation; and truth which
founded the Kingdom of G-d on earth.

ברוך - גאל ישראל. The Bracha concludes with Israel's redemption. The flow of ideas of the Brachoth of the Shema
reaches its climax here. An incomparable treasure of moral
strength lies in the idea of redemption, the belief in the Messianic future. It gives us the assurance that the ideal can be
realized. It gives us the faith in moral progress, and in the ultimate unity of all mankind. It gives meaning to human history.
Future is the future that is salvation. Time leads ever nearer to
this end. Just as Judaism will reach its fulfilment in the Messianic future, so the cycle of the three blessings reaches its
conclusion with the mention of redemption. These blessings
teach us to regard Judaism as built upon three pillars: Creation
יוצר, Revelation הבוחר, Redemption גאל.

The Talmud stresses the importance of joining the ש"ע
to the idea of redemption לסמוך גאולה לתפלה, (Berachoth 4b).
We have essayed in our introduction (p. 13) to interpret the
meaning of this striking enjoinder. Our petitions and prayers
(in the ש"ע) should grow out of historical experience גאולה. The
Kabbalist commentators, however, explain the extraordinary
emphasis laid on סמיכת גאולה לתפלה in a different way. To
them גאולה comprises the sum-total of all our individual and
national aspirations. Only he who looks to G-d and blesses
Him for the fulfilment of all his hopes and longings, he "who
links his hope for redemption to fervent prayer," he, indeed,
has a share in the future, is heir to the world to come.

שמנה עשרה

The שמנה עשרה or תפלה forms the fourth and main
section of the morning service. All that precedes it is merely
preliminary to, and culminates in it. The Talmud describes the
relationship of the Shema to the ש"ע in a Midrashic interpretation of the verse in the Psalms: כן אברכך בחיי זו ק"ש
(Berachoth 16b). "I praise thee so long as I live," refers to
קריאת שמע — "and raise my hands in prayer," בשמך אשא כפי
זו תפלה, refers to the ש"ע. The blessing and praise of the Divine Name in the שמע and its accompanying Brachoth are followed by the section containing our prayers and requests. This
section is called the Tefillah, the Prayer.

The Tefillah may be divided into three sections: "The
first three benedictions form the introduction. The worshipper
reciting these ברכות may be compared to a servant offering
homage to his master. In the middle ברכות, he asks his master
for sustenance, while in the final, three ברכות he takes his
leave in gratitude, as if his petition had already been fulfilled"
(Berachoth 34a).

According to Talmudic tradition, the ש"ע was instituted
by the 120 men of the Great Assembly, among whom were
the last of the Prophets. This statement seems to contradict the
assertion that שמעון הפקולי, Simon the flax-worker, arranged
the 18 benedictions under the aegis of Rabban Gamliel II.
Several hundred years separate these two periods in history.
The Talmud (Megillah 17b) reconciles the two conflicting
statements by asserting (an assertion which has been variously
discussed and interpreted) that the Tefillah had been forgotten during the interim and had to be reinstituted. For more
information on the historical problems see our comments on the
ברכה ולמלשינים.

Without going further into detailed historical investiga-
tion, we may point out that although the exact order and wording of the middle Brachoth were established later on, the number

of the benedictions, 18, must have been fixed in very early times. Many ancient Midrashim derive the number 18 from Scriptural passages, even though they have nothing to say about the specific content of the ברכות. This proves, also, that a special significance attaches to the number itself.

Moreover, it becomes evident from the sources that the guiding principle was not the number of the requests inserted in the Tefillah. Instead it was to repeat the Divine name 18 times in the benedictions. In most of the sources (Berachoth 28b, Levit. Rabbah I, etc.) the number of the benedictions is derived from the number of times (18) the Divine Name is mentioned in Ps. XXIX (הבו לה' בני אלים), in the three paragraphs of the Shema, or in the Song of Moses. The significance of the eighteenfold repetition of the Tetragrammaton is that, thereby, the "Great Name" of 72 letters is uttered. This was pointed out in the comments on the ברכות השחר (p. 31) and the Song of Moses (p. 85). It refers to G-d in the fullest unfolding of His Omnipotence as manifest in the miracle of the Redemption from Egypt. The "Great Name" casts its radiance over all sections of the Shacharis. However, only in the ש"ע does the Name determine the very structure of the prayer itself, as if to express the idea that G-d's real greatness is manifest in His wonder-working intervention, for which we pray in the ש"ע.

Immediately after the invocatory blessing of G-d, "Who redeemed Israel from the slavery of Egypt," the Tefillah begins, צריך לסמוך גאולה לתפלה. It calls upon the eighteen times repeated Holy Name "which once divided the waters." In this way it acknowledges the fundamental truth that the daily sustenance and satisfaction of all creatures is no less miracle than the supernatural intervention at the Red Sea. As the Talmud expresses it: קשה פרנסתו של אדם כקריעת ים סוף.

However by concluding each one of the eighteen petitions with the formula ברוך אתה ה', the ש"ע becomes much more than a mere supplicatory prayer. It is lifted far above the lowly plane of purely opportunistic and selfish petition, to the high level of true קידוש השם, a sanctification of the blessed, omnipotent and merciful G-d.

The clearest and simplest outline of the logical structure of the ש"ע is given in the Talmudic dictum quoted above, according to which the first three Brachoth represent the introductory formula of homage; the last three, the concluding thanks offering; while the intermediate section contains the requests themselves. The first three are, above all, distinguished by their invocation of the main attributes of G-d — גדול, גבור נורא. The prayer, which thus far was primarily concerned with the relationship of G-d to the world, now penetrates to the Holy of Holies and pays homage to the Supreme Being Himself by mentioning these prime attributes which were revealed by G-d to Moses (Megillah 25a).

These three first Brachoth describe G-d as the source of all that exists, the Master of Nature. They provide an answer to the three ultimate questions: Who governs the universe? What are His powers? What influences Him? And the answers are: — "You are the G-d of our fathers, אבות; You are the merciful Provider and Protector; You are not influenced by earthly considerations." The first Bracha is consequently called, אבות. In the second we declare G-d to be omnipotent, גבורות. Finally in the קדושה, He is praised as the Holy One Who guides the world in holiness, detached from all earthly influences and Who is, therefore feared by all. קדוש אתה ונורא שמך.

The last three Brachoth of the Tefillah treat of the relationship of the receiver to the giver. They run parallel to the first three, and answer the questions: "Who are *we*? What are *our* powers? What influences *us*?" The answers are "We are G-d's servants עבודה. We are powerless, dependent upon Him, and therefore, filled with gratitude הודאה. In everything we are subject to Divine rule, and only the heavenly harmony of peace, within and without, maintains our existence amidst the conflict of discordant forces שלום.

However, in order to gain a real understanding of the order of succession of the 12 (or 13) intermediate Brachoth, some preliminary remarks must be made. They will reveal a most striking and penetrating insight into the structure of the ש"ע as a whole.

We pointed out that, according to Berachoth 26b, the daily תפלות are considered a substitute for the morning and evening sacrifices תפלות כנגד תמידים תקנום. The meaning of this saying has already been explained in connection

with the התמיד 'פ. Specifically, it is the זריקת הדם,
the offering of the blood upon the altar for which
the Tefillah acts as a substitute. (מג"א א"ח א' יעב"ץ,
ר' יונה רפ"ד דברכות). The Torah itself (Lev. XVII, 11)
designates the blood as נפש, the substance and essence of the
human personality. The offering of the blood on the altar
effects atonement: כי נפש הבשר בדם היא ואני נתתיו...לכפר וכו'....
The offerer of the sacrifice secures atonement through
the act of the sprinkling of the blood on the walls of the altar,
אין כפרה אלא בדם (Zev. 26b); כיון שהגיע דם על המזבח נתכפרו בעלים
(יומא 5a). The Tefillah parallels the performance of this
rite. We follow in our subsequent explanations those of the
Kabbalist commentators (cf. סידור של"ה) who find in the
12 (or 13) intermediate Brachoth an exact replica of the
blood-offering on he altar, while the three preparatory and
three concluding Brachoth obviously serve as the introduction
and conclusion respectively.

The precept for the Tamid (עולת צאן) reads as follows:
וזרקו בני אהרן הכהנים את דמו על המזבח סביב (Lev. I, 11).
According to the traditional interpretation, this means שתי
מתנות שהן ארבע (Zevachim 53b, Mishnah Tamid IV, 1).
The priest approached the northeast corner of the altar and
poured blood on it. The blood thus ran over both the east
and the north sides, נותן מזרחה צפונה. He walked
around the altar till he reached the southwest corner.
Then he repeated the act, ונותן מערבה דרומה, thus completing
the rite, על המזבח סביב. Now it seems an accepted fact, confirmed in Biblical and traditional literature, that each one of
the four sides of the altar and indeed of the four points of
the compass, possesses a definite and specific ritualistic significance. Each always represents the same or a related
idea. The *East,* for instance, as is evident from many
passages of Jewish literature, symbolizes the Spirit (cf. Num.
Rabbah Ch. 2 מזרח שממנו אור יוצאה לעולם). This is shown
by the position of the Menorah placed at the East wall of
the sanctuary. The *North,* the side where the Table with the
Shewbread was placed in the sanctuary represents *material
prosperity* (Job XXXVII, 22 מצפון זהב יאתה). Towards
the *West* we always look for the Shechinah (שכינה לעולם
במערב cf. Zevachim 118b), while the *South,* where the sun

rises to its zenith, is considered the source of the beneficial forces of fertility (Num. Rabbah Ch. 2 דרום טללי ברכה יוצאין ממנו לעולם). According to this view, then, the northeast corner of the altar is the meeting place of the spiritual and material powers of the individual, while the southwest corner symbolizes the same forces as they affect the community (Shechina and fertility). The sprinkling of the blood on the 4 corners of the altar then expresses the readiness of the worshipper to surrender the powers of His Body and Spirit, both as an individual and as a member of the nation to the Divine. The twelve intermediate Brachoth of the ש"ע — which, we said, correspond to the offering of the blood — contain, as we shall presently show, four groups of three blessings each which correspond to the ב' מתנות שהן ארבע, and refer to the spiritual and physical forces of the individual and the nation.

However this connection between the four basic categories of forces and the four points of the compass is not a mere symbolism. It is, rather a profound insight according to which the basic harmonies of the cosmos, rest on a firmly established order held in check by the interaction of the forces of nature. As the interaction of the streams of power flowing from all four directions produces an equilibrium in nature, so in the affairs of men, the proper cooperation of all forces for the good of society has its basis in a meaningful and harmonious Divinely established order.

The ideal exemplification of this order was the encampment of the twelve tribes round the Sanctuary in the desert. This in turn has its ultimate prototype in the Divine Throne itself, supported by the four Cherubim כשם שברא הקב"ה ד' רוחות העולם כך סיבב לכסא ד' חיות וכנגדן סידר הדגלים למשה (Num. Rabba Ch. 2). This order has, therefore, timeless significance, and the scale of values revealed and reflected in it was adopted by our sages when they set out to arrange the petition man makes, in his תפלה, for the goods and benefits he needs. As we now proceed to describe the arrangement in detail, we shall follow the course from East to West (as did the Priest on the altar) and encircle the Sanctuary. It is the same direction the firmament follows, traversing its daily course from East to West, paying homage in the immutability of its measured rhythm, to its Creator. (וצבא השמים לך משתחוים. Nehemiah IX, 6. cf. Baba Bathra 25a).

Thus we pace, beginning from the East, round the holy camp of the tribes of G-d. On the East, the side associated with the spirit, stood the tribe of Judah, and with it Issachar and Zebulun, אלו שלשה נעשו גדולים בתורה (Yalkut). These three tribes excelled in the knowledge of the Torah. Accordingly the first of the twelve intermediate Brachoth of the ש"ע seeks the gifts of *reason* and *understanding* אתה חונן. The pattern for the first group of three benedictions was set by the verse ושב ורפא לו (Is. VI, 10). True understanding (אתה חונן) leads to a return to G-d (השיבנו) which in turn results in moral rehabilitation (רפואה דסליחה). However the elements of each group of Brachoth are interdependent. There is no real atonement without rehabilitation; and without repentance no true understanding, for sin allows no unprejudiced thinking. Thus the first group is a unit composed of moral and spiritual aims מרבה לסלוח — הרוצה בתשובה — חונן הדעת.

The second group comprise the physical, material goods, just as the tribes encamped on the Northside were distinguished by their *material prosperity*. Asher received the blessing מאשר שמנה לחמו from Jacob; Naftali was designated by Moses as שבע רצון ומלא ברכת ה'; while Dan, who is called מאסף לכל המחנות, is the leader of the group. Hence the second unit of Brachoth contains all those petitions which ask for the preservation of our material welfare.

In the first Bracha of this section we seek protection from poverty עניות, and in our struggles ריב and, generally speaking, the liberation of the individual גאולה. In the second Bracha we ask for physical health רפואה and in the third for our material sustenance פרנסה. These three Brachoth too presuppose each other, and form an homogeneous entity. In the absence of material wealth, poverty and struggle endanger health and, consequently, personal freedom of action. While the first group of Brachoth referred to the Spirit the second is concerned with the needs of the body.

At this juncture, the seventh and central blessing of the thirteen Brachoth follows. It stands by itself. It forms the transition from the needs of the individual to those that can be fulfilled only through the community. This Bracha aptly refers to the קבוץ גליות, to the reunion of all individuals, the gathering of the exiles into the community. Its character is similar to the function of the tribe of Dan, the מאסף לכל המחנות, who was to gather the stragglers of all other camps. Placed in middle of all the Brachoth, it is their focal point. Like the sanctuary in the desert, it is surrounded by four groups, דגלים, each containing three tribes. It represents the transition from the spiritual and material gifts bestowed on the individual, to the incorporation and development of these benefits in the life of the nation as a whole.

The third group comprises the spiritual preconditions for the reunion of the nation of Israel under the rule of G-d. According to the prediction of the prophets, the spiritual and moral foundations will have to be laid before the rehabilitation of our people can take place. Isaiah, in the first chapter of his prophecies, declares the initial stage in the rise of a new Israel to be the reinstatement of an equitable, impartial and authoritative system of justice. "And I shall reinstate your judges as before, and your counsellors as in the beginning. Afterwards you will be called: City of Righteousness, the faithful fortress. Zion shall be redeemed with justice and its returning ones with deeds of mercy." Immediately after this prediction, the prophet denounces the sinners who persistently hinder the progress of mankind. The second stage in the redemption will be their destruction. "And the destruction of the sinners and transgressors altogether; and those that desert the Lord will perish." But after all evil is finally vanquished, the men of good intentions, those who have fought the wars of the Lord, shall use their talents with complete freedom, aided by the blessing from above, for the establishment of the foundations of the Messianic kingdom on earth.

These three stages of redemption (as foretold by the prophet) represented in the third group of Brachoth in the Tefillah: The reinstitution of a system of justice השיבה, punishment of the G-dless ולמלשינים, and the vindication of the righteous על הצדיקים. This group has the character of the camp of Ephraim located on the West, which united with Ephraim, the tribes of Menasseh and Benjamin. It is the side

where the Shechinah stood, i.e. in the territory of Benjamin
(cf. Deut. XXXIII, 12). The return of the Shechinah and
its reappearance also heralds the "awakening of G-d's power."
i.e. the punishment of the wicked: — יושב הכרובים הופיעה
(Ps. LXXX, 2). לפני אפרים ובנימין ומנשה עוררה את גבורתך
These three petitions for the establishment of the spiritual background for the גאולה are followed by the last three which
mention the material blessings necessary for the welfare of
the Jewish nation.

They too follow the order set by the prophetic prediction according to which at the end of days, "Israel's sons
shall return and seek the L-rd, their G-d, and David, their
King (Hosea III, 5). The return to G-d then, will precede
the installation of the Messiah of the House of David (Meg.
18a). The two Brachoth, בונה ירושלים and את צמח דוד, bear
this out. The erection of the City of G-d, where He will
establish His glory, will come first. Then the royal heir, the
משיח בן דוד, will be enthroned. On the South side of the
camp (which we have finally reached) the tribes of Simon
and Gad are united under the leadership of Reuben. The Midrash regards Reuben as the prototype of the בעל תשובה
"Who turns repentant to G-d" (Num. Rabba ch. 2). תשובה
hastens the redemption, as it is said: "And the Redeemer will
come unto Zion and to those among Jacob who turn away from
transgression" (Isaiah LIX, 20). The last Bracha, שומע תפלה,
represents, according to the Talmud (Megillah 18a), the
very summit of the spiritual ascent; for in the coming realm
of eternal nearness to G-d, all our individual and national
prayers will receive generous fulfilment (Isaiah LVI, 7).

The cycle of the Thirteen intermediate Brachoth is
now completed. Man, free as an individual, but at the same
time a member of his nation, lays all his spiritual and
material requests before G-d, seeking fulfilment and spiritual
elevation from Him. This idea was expressed symbolically
in the עבודה of the daily Tamid sacrifice, when the life blood
was offered on the altar. It is faithfully reflected in the Tefillah, the עבודה שבלב, the service of the heart. Though we
have no altar, we walk in spirit round its corners daily to
receive purification. ארחץ בנקיון כפי ואסובבה את מזבחך ה',

(cf. Berachoth 15a where this verse is interpreted as referring to ‫ע"ש‬).

The structure of the ‫שמונה עשרה‬ is therefore revealed, as follows:

INTRODUCTION.

1. Thou art G-d.
2. Thou art omnipotent.
3. Thou art independent.

WE SEEK FOR:

I. *Spiritual blessings*: (*East*)

4. Understanding.
5. Repentance.
6. Atonement.

II. *Material benefits*: (*North*)

7. Freedom of the individual.
8. Health.
9. Prosperity.
10. Gathering of all individual forces.

III. *Spiritual aid for the nation*: (*West*)

11. Justice.
12. Retribution for the G-dless.
13. Reward for the Righteous.

IV. *Material aid for the nation*: (*South*)

14. Re-building of Jerusalem.
15. Coming of the Messiah.
16. Acceptance of our prayers.

CONCLUSION

17. We are Thy servants.

18. We have no power, but to thank Thee.

19. We are lost without the harmony of Thy peace.

אדני. *O Lord, open thou my lips, and my mouth shall declare thy praise.*

We now proceed to explain the ש"ע in detail. — אדני. Rabbi Chanina ben Dosa whose prayers were known to be particularly effective, was once asked how he knew whether his prayer had been accepted. He replied: "Whenever the prayer comes easily to my lips I know that it has been accepted. When it does not, then I know that it has been rejected." R. Jochanan found this observation borne out by the verse בורא ניב שפתים שלום . . . ("the words flowing freely from the lips are a message of peace from on High"). It was he who suggested appropriately that אדני שפתי be recited here, as a petition for G-d's aid for an undisturbed prayer. Moreover, the Divine Name used in this verse (from Ps. LI) is the שם אדנות, the most personal invocation of G-d, which Abraham first called upon; אדני אלקים במה אדע כי אירשנה. He was the first to recognize not only that G-d is the exalted Creator, but that He is also the Being, upon whom everyone is personally dependent. To everyone He is, therefore, אדני, "My G-d." Only this very intimate and individual relationship lends meaning and warmth to prayer. Similarly, Moses too, began his personal petition: אדני אלקים אתה החלת להראות ות' (Deut. III. 24).

ברוך. *Blessed art thou, O Lord our G-d and G-d of our fathers, G-d of Abraham, G-d of Isaac, and G-d of Jacob, the great, mighty and revered G-d, the most high G-d, who bestowest lovingkindness, and possessest all things; who rememberest the pious deeds of the patriarchs, and in love wilt bring a redeemer to their children's children for thy name's sake.*

(Remember us unto life, O King, who delightest in life, and inscribe us in the book of life, for thine own sake, O living G-d.)

*O King, Helper, Saviour and Shield. Blessed art thou
O Lord, the Shield of Abraham.*

ברוך. At beginning and end of this Bracha we are to
bow; we bend our knees at ברוך, bow down while saying אתה,
then stand erect when we utter the שם: "The Jew, even when
depressed and downcast always has a blessing on his lips. But
it is the knowledge of the nearness of ה' the מדת הרחמים
which time and again gives time and strength to straighten up
and stand erect with uplifted heads."

As has been pointed out before, the first Bracha answers
the question: Who is the Being to whom we address our prayer?
The answer is, the one given to Moses, when he first encountered G-d at th Burning Bush. Our knowledge of G-d
rests, in the first place, on the ancient tradition of His revelation to the Patriarchs. It is not based on a philosophical
or mystical proof. Nor is it a dogma. It is based on the simple,
historically confirmed fact, that each one of the Patriarchs
sought G-d and found Him. ויאמר עוד אלקים אל
משה כה תאמר וגו' (Ex. 3, 13). He became their
"personal" G-d. Abraham became the "Friend of G-d"
אברהם אוהבי, Yitzchak His "only One" יצחק יחידו,
Jacob His "Firstborn." We inherited this concept of the "Personal G-d" from our fathers. To Him we turn in prayer,
אלקינו ואלקי אבותינו. To Him for Whom our fathers lived
and died, Who is not a Being remote from world and mankind, nor an abstract concept, to Him we call, when we prepare to pray for the satisfaction of our demands. This is
why the words אלקינו ואלקי אבותינו here, take the place of the
words אלקינו מלך העולם prescribed for all other Brachoth.

גומל חסדים טובים . . . באהבה. When for the first time
in the history of Mankind G-d demonstrated His power, He
appeared as the Liberator of oppressed Israel. As such we encountered Him first and therefore we are confident that He
is, and always will be our Redeemer. Just as He has shown
Himself as מלך עוזר ומושיע ומגן, the helping, saving and pro-
tecting King ever since the days of Abraham so He will also
show Himself to be our Redeemer, ומביא גואל לבני בניהם.
For He remembers the love of the Patriarchs וזוכר חסדי אבות
and He will bring redemption to their sons even if they are un-

worthy of their fathers, למען שמו באהבה, for the sake of His Eternal Lovingkindness.

הא-ל הגדול, הגבור והנורא. These are the "Prime attributes" of G-d, the only ones invoked in the Tefillah. A Reader was reciting the ש"ע in the presence of R. Chanina. To these three attributes "Great, Mighty and Revered G-d" he added others such as "Powerful, Proud, Fearful, Strong, Surely Existent and Honored G-d." R. Chanina waited until the Reader had finished. Then he said to him: "Have you now exhausted all the praises of thy Master? Why did you recite all these? We would not have been allowed to utter even the three, had they not been revealed by our teacher Moses in the Torah and introduced by the Men of the Great Synod in the Tefilla, yet you keep adding others. This may be compared to praising an earthly king, for being the owner of a few silver denars when, in fact, he possesses countless thousands of golden denars. — It is not praise it is disparagement." (Ber. 33b).

אתה גבור. *Thou, O Lord, art mighty for ever, thou quickenest the dead, thou art mighty to save.*

(משיב. *Thou causest the wind to blow and the rain to fall*).

Thou sustainest the living with lovingkindness, quickenest the dead with great mercy, supportest the falling, healest the sick loosest the bound, and keepest thy faith to them that sleep in the dust. Who is like unto thee, Lord of mighty acts, and who resembleth thee, O King, who killest and quickenest, and causest salvation to spring forth?

(Who is like unto thee, Father of mercy, who in mercy rememberest thy creatures unto life?).

Yea, faithful art thou to quicken the dead. Blessed art thou, O Lord, who quickenest the dead.

אתה גבור. From the praise of גדולה, G-d's Great Mercy in the first Bracha, the Tefilla proceeds to the praise of גבורה, His boundless power. In this second Bracha we therefore find an account of the omnipotent acts of the Divine, the greatest being the conquest of death. G-d's power is most signally manifest where human power fails. Hence we enumerate here all those phenomena, the key to which G-d retains in His own hand: "the resurrection of the dead, the rain fall and the sustenance of all living beings." (Taanis 2a; Tur §114). Next all those events are mentioned which reveal G-d's creative might. When He reverses the course of the seemingly inexorable laws of Nature, turning imminent disaster into salvation: He supports the morally "fallen," סומך נופלים (cf. Yoma 69b) — heals the sick, רופא חולים, even though their suffering may seem hopeless — and מתיר אסורים, He frees the innocent captives, even as He once freed Israel from Egypt's gigantic might. Five times the miracle of the resurrection of the dead is mentioned in this Bracha, for it is man with his five senses and with the five regions of his soul who will come to life again.

Between the revival of the dead and the support of the living בחסד, the granting of wind and rain is mentioned during the summer season. The Talmud (Ber. 33a) suggests this place for משיב הרוח because the beneficial gift of rain which re-awakens the lifeless earth to new and fruitful activity is comparable to the revival of the dead. At the same time the rain provides sustenance for the plant, beast and man.

אתה גבור...מי כמוך...ומי דומה לך. More than anything else the adduced instances of G-d's Mastery over Nature show His incomparable and unfathomable גבורה.

ברוך מחיה המתים. The Rabbis remark: אמונים נוצר מחיה אלו שאומרים אמן באמונה ה'. When the reader recites מחיה המתים, בונה ירושלים or גואל ישראל, we respond with the "Amen" although we have never witnessed a revival of the dead, the redemption of Israel or the re-building of Jerusalem. G-d rewards such faithfulness with faithfulness.

נקדש. (Reader). *We will sanctify thy name in the world even as they sanctify it in the highest heavens, as it is written by the hand of thy prophet: And they called one unto the other and said,—(Cong.) Holy, holy, holy is the Lord of hosts: the whole earth is full of his glory.— (Reader). Those over against them*

אתה קדוש. *Thou art holy, and thy name is holy, and holy beings praise thee daily. (Selah.) Blessed art thou, O Lord, the holy G-d. (the holy King.)*

say, Blessed.—(Cong.) *Blessed be the
glory of the Lord from his place.*—
(Reader.) *And in thy Holy Words it
is written, saying,*—(Cong.) *The Lord
shall reign for ever, thy G-d, O Zion,
unto all generations. Praise ye the
Lord.* — (Reader.) *Unto all generations we will declare thy greatness, and
to all eternity, we will proclaim thy
holiness, and thy praise, O our G-d,
shall not depart from our mouth for
ever, for thou art a great and holy G-d
and King. Blessed art thou, O Lord,
the holy G-d.*

אתה קדוש. The third Bracha refers to the third of
the attributes of G-d: נורא. However His קדושה is emphasized
because the holiness of G-d, that is, His exaltedness above
material needs and moral deficiency, is considered more than
anything else as the source of the fear of G-d: ״נורא אלקים
ממקדשך.״ (Ps. 68, 36). A direct allusion to this connection
between Fear and Holiness was retained in the text of the
Kedusha for the High Holidays, קדוש אתה ונורא שמך, which
originally was the form for every day.

The Kedusha is recited in the most solemn manner
as a responsive chant between the reader and congregation.
It may be spoken only when a quorum of at least ten adults,
as representatives of the community is present. It forms the
climax of public worship. It extols the unfathomable Unity
of the Divine Being, as we explained in detail in the קדושת
יוצר (p. 99). Israel possesses no Kedusha of her own as
distinguished from the Kedusha of the Angels. We endeavor
rather to fashion our Kedusha in perfect accord with that of
the upper Beings: נקדש את שמך בעולם כשם וגו׳. "Let us
sanctify Thy Name in the world, even as they sanctify it in
the highest heavens." The testimony to the Unity and Sanctity of G-d proclaimed by man, shall in no way differ from
that revealed by the active Forces of the Universe. There is no
discrepancy between human perception and the higher revelation which speaks to us from the Prime Forces and Prime
Elements of Nature. Microcosm and Macrocosm are in har-

monious accord, and proclaim to us the Unity of the Creator
in identical terms. Even in his outward behavior the Jew
endeavors to resemble the Hosts of Heaven when he recites the Kedusha. We stand still, with our feet closed like
the Angels who surround the Divine throne (Ez. 1, 7), and
we rise on the tips of our feet as though striving to unite
the "Lower Host of G-d" with the "Upper Host" (Shir
Rabba 2), to break the bonds of earthly restraint and to speed
to the service of the Creator like the Angels who are ever
ready with winged alacrity to appear before His throne.
(Is. VI, 2) — The Kedusha ends with the ardent wish,
which at the same time is our unwavering belief, that: "Thy
G-d, Zion" may reign forever and be universally recognized,
ימלך ה' אלקיך ציון. Until that time we shall not cease to
"Proclaim and sanctify" His Greatness and Holiness, לדור
ודור. —

אתה חונן. *Thou favourest man with knowledge, and
teachest mortals understanding. O favour us with knowledge,
understanding and discernment from thee. Blessed art thou,
O Lord, gracious Giver of knowledge.*

אתה חונן. The first gift for which the Jew prays is
spiritual enlightenment. "Great is Enlightenment for it was
set at the beginning of the daily requests" (Ber. 33a). The
desire for mental alertness and perspicacity, which have been
the secret of Jewish strength through centuries of suffering
and exile, were implanted deep within the consciousness of
the Jewish soul as the very first request which the Jew places
before his Creator. Even on workdays, our first plea is not
for Divine support in the struggle for our daily bread. This
preferential position impresses the lesson upon us that even
our daily work must not be permitted to overshadow the care
for our spiritual needs. Instead the reverse is true: the intense
longing for spiritual energy always takes first place; for to
the Jew to be a human being always means to strive inde-
fatigably towards spiritual perfection. (cf. ח"א §115).

דעה, is the clear appraisal of the nature of things and
of situations; בינה, the insight into their connections and in-
terrelations. השכל, finally, is the ability to employ the insights
gained. Hence follows logically the order: דעה בינה והשכל

(Albo Ikk. I, 16). The Kabbalists, however, explain דעה as
רוח הקדש, Divine intuition, the highest degree of knowledge
attainable to man (cp. Rashi Ex. 31, 3) and accordingly place
דעה at the end (חכמה בינה ודעת). — דעה, clear perception
is largely an innate talent, whereas בינה is gained only by man's
active co-operation therefore . . . אתה חונן.

השיבנו. *Cause us to return, O our Father, unto thy
Law; draw us near, O our King, unto thy service, and bring
us back in perfect repentance unto thy presence. Blessed art
thou, O Lord, who delightest in repentance.*

השיבנו. The recognition of the truth allows us to find
the road back to G-d; without it even the most earnest endeavor to act in accordance with the dictates of morality
and ethics must fail. However, תשובה, no less than the recognition of the truth, requires Divine assistance, as explained
in detail with the prayer ויהי רצון שתרגילנו בתורתך וגו' (p. 35).
If a man is filled with the earnest desire to return, then
G-d helps him on his way. (Yoma 38b). We, therefore, pray
that G-d help us to complete what we began, that our תשובה
may be a full and perfect one והחזירנו בתשובה שלמה. —
אבינו מלכנו. The choice of these appellations is explained by
a Midrash to Deut. 33, 4 where the text refers to Torah
as מורשה קהלת יעקב, the heritage of the community of Jacob:
"This may be compared to a King's son who in his youth was
abducted to a far-away land; whenever he wishes to return
he may do so without shame, for it is to his own inheritance
that he returns. Similarly one who has studied the Torah,
even though he may have abandoned it and had been estranged from it for many years, he may return to it at any
time; for the Torah is מורשה, the heritage of the community
of Jacob." Therefore we pray: "Lead us back, our Father
to Thy Torah," for G-d will always receive us again whenever
we come to Him.

This Bracha contains 15 words — the same number
as the verse יעזב רשע דרכו וגו' (Is. 55, 7). According to the
Kabbalists a profound association connects the number of
words of each one of the Berachoth of the ש"ע to the idea
which they express. The טור proves those connections throughout the entire ש"ע. However, generally speaking, we have
disregarded them. We follow the view of the בית יוסף who

confesses: "I too, investigated the number of words. Later on, however, I recognized, that this has no deeper significance, for there is no generally accepted uniform text of the ש"ע in the whole world. Some add this, others omit that. Therefore the number of words is quite irrevelant."

סלח לנו. *Forgive us, O our Father, for we have sinned; pardon us, O our King, for we have transgressed; for thou dost pardon and forgive. Blessed art thou, O Lord, who art gracious, and dost abundantly forgive.*

סלח לנו. Recognition of the truth — Return to G-d — Moral Purification; this is the moral development of the ethical personality, progressing toward the height of perfection, the first concern of the Jew. Only after תשובה has been achieved, can we hope for atonement for our sins. — סליחה is the personal subjective expiation. Here the trangression is consigned to oblivion; מחילה is the objective indemnification absolving the culprit from punishment. From "our father" we invoke atonement for those sins that we have committed as חטאים, without intent or plan. Such sins a father's heart can condone. But when we have sinned wilfully, פשענו, we have severed the bond between the Father and His children. We have become estranged and remote from Him and consider ourselves as servants. Here we pray for forgiveness to "Our King."

ראה. *Look upon our affliction and plead our cause, and redeem us speedily for thy name's sake; for thou art a mighty Redeemer. Blessed art thou, O Lord, the Redeemer of Israel.*

ראה בענינו. The triad of pleas for our spiritual welfare is followed by that setting out our petitions for material welfare. This group begins with the prayer for personal freedom. Outward freedom is thus regarded as the direct consequence of the spiritual freedom attained through atonement (Rashi, Meg. 17b and Bes Yoseph par. 115 emphasize that this Bracha refers to freedom from the worries and sorrows of daily life, not to national redemption) — ראה בענינו from Ps. 25, 18: ראה עניי ועמלי. The correct version is. therefore the one without the "נא" interposed. During the repetition of the ש"ע on Fast days, the reader, inserts the תפלת תענית after this Bracha. By way of analogy to סמיכת גאולה לתפלה, the prayer for

help in distress is thus adjoined to the invocation of His
Redeeming Power as גואל ישראל. The individual worshipper
however, reads the ענכו in the middle of שומע תפלה; for
the addition of special Berachoth is permissible only in the
communal prayer.

רפאנו. *Heal us, O Lord, and we shall be healed; save
us and we shall be saved; for thou art our praise. Grant a
perfect healing of all our wounds; for thou, O mighty King
art a faithful and merciful Physician.*

*Blessed art thou, O Lord, who healest the sick of thy
people Israel.*

רפאנו. After Jer. 17, 14. However, the singular form
of the scriptural verse is turned into the plural form in the
Tefilla, because all requests have to be made for the community; never for the individual alone. רפואה is the recovery
of the disrupted or weakened organism; ישועה (related to
יש) is essentially the gift of a new, fresh and vigorous being.
Much as human skill and knowledge achieve in helping and
healing, ultimately we owe praise to Him, תהלתנו אתה who
gives us the means to heal and on whom the success depends.
G-d alone combines in ideal perfection the two qualifications
which make a great physician: consummate skill in diagnosing
the disease and in providing proper and effective remedy
on the one hand, and love of the human being on the other
to restore fully the sufferer's physical and psychical strength:
He is רופא נאמן ורחמן.

ברך. *Bless this year unto us, O Lord our G-d, together
with every kind of the produce thereof, for our welfare; give
a blessing upon the face of the earth. (Give dew and rain
for a blessing upon the face of the earth). O satisfy us with
thy goodness, and bless our year like other good years. Blessed
art thou, O Lord, who blessest the years.*

ברך עלינו. Bless "on us" this year "לטובה." The year may
be a blessed one, yet not bring blessing to *us,* may not be blessed
"on us." Fields and orchards may abound with fruits yet
no benefit may accrue to man from it: "The vine may offer
its fruit, yet wine be expensive" as our Sages expressed it.
There might be an abundance of agricultural products yet human
unreason and mismanagement may cause scarcity, famine and

starvation. Hence we pray for the blessing of field and meadow, but also for blessing of the conduct of human affairs in order that the years may shower its blessing "on us" and "מטובך — "לטובה. Some read מטובה instead of מטובך, referring to the land as in טוב הארץ תאכלו (Is. 1, 19). In this case the Bracha would express our plea for the prosperity of the Holy Land, as the inclusion of טל ומטר would also suggest, טל ומטר is said during those months which are the rain season in Eretz Israel. This simple, little prayer "And give dew and rain as a blessing on The Land" spoken throughout the winter, shows the deep inner connection between Israel and the Land, more emphatically and more clearly than all the enthusiastic speeches and avowals of allegiance combined. Whereas משיב הרוח merely expresses the praise of G-d as the Source of Rain, טל ומטר is a prayer for its beneficial dispensation and is therefore included only when the rainy season in ארץ ישראל actually begins (i.e. 59 days after the תקופת תשרי).

תקע. *Sound the great horn for our freedom; lift up the ensign to gather our exiles, and gather us from the four corners of the earth. Blessed art thou, O Lord, who gatherest the banished ones of thy people Israel.*

תקע. With this Bracha, the tenth one, we have reached the center of the Tefilla. The Bracha preceding it spoke of the needs of the individual whereas those following it treat of the needs of the nation (cp. p. 126). This Bracha, praying for a gathering of the dispersed and divided parts of Jewry, forms the proper transition between them. Like a powerful lens it gathers the divergent and dispersed individual rays to send them forth in united strength and enhanced brilliancy.

The text of this Bracha follows Is. 27, 13 and 11, 12, closely. Shofar and Ensign נס are, according to Kimchi, (Is. 18, 3) symbols only to illustrate the re-gathering of Israel: "When a dispersed nation is to be gathered an ensign will be raised on a mountain and the trumpet sounded as signals for all to assemble. In a similar manner Israel, at the time of the Redemption, will be gathered from everywhere." The sounding of the Shofar and the raising of the ensign, according to this merely serve to symbolize the universal gathering of the scattered people. The Midrash, however, recognizes in the "Great Shofar" the great, right horn of the ram which was sacrificed at the עקדה. His smaller, left horn was sounded at the gathering at Mount Sinai (Yalkut Is. 27, 13); while the great, right horn will be sounded by G-d in the future, on the day of Redemption. At the root of this interpretation seems to lie the idea that the call of the heavenly Shofar-sound at Sinai was heard and understood only by Israel, a small fraction of humanity. In the mighty call of the "great, right Shofar" of Redemption however, all mankind will recognize the voice of the Almighty.

The Bracha also refers to the return of the ten lost tribes of Israel, who will also hear the call of the great Shofar. (Sanh. 110b). The term נדחי ישראל applies specifically to them (Midr. Ps. 147, 2) and has, therefore, been placed into the concluding Bracha, מקבץ נדחי עמו ישראל.

השיבה. *Restore our judges as at the first, and our counsellors as at the beginning; remove from us grief and suffering; reign thou over us, O Lord, thou alone, in loving-kindness and tender mercy, and justify us in judgment. Blessed art thou, O Lord, the King who lovest righteousness and judgment.* (During the Ten Days of Penitence conclude: *the King of judgment*).

השיבה, opens the group of pleas for spiritual help for the nation. It refers to the restitution of the old and proven system of Jewish Justice as the fundamental prerequisite for the return of the שכינה into Israel's midst and for her future redemption. Only where Justice prevails within the circle of men can G-d dwell. The first command of the Seven Mitzvoth of the Noachidic legislation given to all mankind was, threfore, the institution of an orderly system of Justice. (Sanh. 56b).

Many thousands of years of the history of Law have proven to us only too clearly that a truly just social order will hardly ever be achieved by human effort alone. Scholars and Philosophers have been laboring incessantly to create a system of legislation which would guarantee a just and equitable balance between the conflicting claims of all members of society, and thus would achieve peace and security on earth. Their failure reveals the human insufficiency in the face of this problem. It can be solved only by Divine act, and within a social system founded by Him. In this Bracha we pray for the establishment of such an ideal system of Justice, and allude to the text of the prophetic presage (Is. 1, 26) referred to above (p. 138). The abolition of injustice and oppression of tyranny and intolerance, will achieve, as an immediate result, the abolition of יגון ואנחה, of sorrow and sighing. Only within such a society living in serenity and peace will G-d reign in sovereign supremacy ומלך עלינו אתה ה' לבדך. The key to the miraculous ability of the Jewish system of Law to create a society free of the tensions and class-conflicts besetting all other known social systems, lies in the harmonious blending of the two principles of משפט, Justice, and צדק, Love or Mercy. We have commented on this characteristic of the Jewish social order before (p. 29), in connection with the Morning Blessings. (For a brief but comprehensive outline of the Jewish Social Order cf. SOCIAL ORDER by R. Jos. Elias (Jewish Pocket Books); for a more detailed account, LA JUSTICE SOCIALE EN ISRAEL by the author).

During the Ten Days of תשובה (between Rosh Hashono and Yom Kippur) we conclude this Bracha with the המלך המשפט instead of מלך אוהב וגו'. (Ber. 12b). In this formula G-d is praised as "the King who administers Justice" or, according to other expositors "The King (who is) Justice." During the days when man is summoned to self-judgment and repentance, G-d's Judge-ship is the predominant aspect of His rule.

ולמלשינים. *And for slanderers let there be no hope, and let all wickedness perish as in a moment; let all thine enemies be speedily cut off, and the dominion of arrogance do thou uproot and crush, cast down and humble speedily in our days. Blessed art thou, O Lord, who breakest the enemies and humblest the arrogant.*

ולמלשינים. "In the days of R. Gamliel the unbelievers multiplied in Israel. They oppressed her and strove to lead her astray to heresy. When the Rabbi recognized that here the greatest of all human needs for aid [from on High] had developed, he and his בית דין arose and created an additional Bracha petitioning G-d that He may destroy the atheists, and he incorporated it in the Tefilla so that all may become familiar with it. Thus the number of Berachoth in the ש"ע was increased to nineteen." In these terse remarks based on the Talmud (Ber. 28b), Maimonides explains the history and purpose of this much discussed Bracha (הלכ' תפלה פ"ב ה"א). Hardly any other portion of the Siddur has been misunderstood as often and as thoroughly as this one.

Right from the outset a problem arose which R. Gamliel placed before the Sages in this form: כלום יש אדם שיודע לתקן ברכת המנים "Is there a man who would be able to formulate the Bracha concerning the Minim (according to Rashi: Those who deny the Divine Origin of the Torah)?" It is clearly evident from the wording of the question that there was no doubt about the justification of such a Bracha. There was no question that one was at least as justified in praying for the removal of the threat of spiritual contamination of the body of the Jewish people, as for help from danger of physical destruction. Moreover, as long as the enemies of G-d are at work "neither His throne nor His Name is complete," and therefore, "He is at war with them from generation to generation."

However, the unavoidable necessity of introducing a Bracha against heretics did not become apparent until the period of R. Gamliel who lived during the first century of the common era. The schism which the founder of Christianity had introduced in Judaism had to be counteracted. When that movement began, its dogmas and teachings were not so clearly defined and formulated. The common man could not recognize the unbridgeable gap between Jewish Monotheism and Christianity. To assure the survival of the pure Monotheism of Judaism and of the Torah, a sharp line of demarcation had to be drawn between Judaism and the new teachings.

This is the outspoken purpose of this Bracha. It is not only evident from the period of its origin, but is confirmed by clear indications in the הלכות גדולות, the מחזור ויטרי and רש"י commentary in uncensored editions of the Talmud (cf. דקדוקי ספרים, Ber. 28b). The justification and need for such a Bracha were obvious; the problem was to provide the proper formula as is apparent from the question which R. Gamliel put to the Sages.

The difficulties — aside from the natural reluctance to compose a prayer for the destruction of fellow human beings — seem to have been caused by the following questions: Who is to be combatted, the individual heretics or the entire sect as such? Were only those to be denounced who had deserted Judaism and embraced the new Faith or were those adversaries who still remained within Judaism, e.g. the Sadducees, Minim etc. to be included? Should the prayer be directed against the *persons* of the adversaries of G-d, or against the spirit of heresy? The answers to these questions can be inferred from the caption of the Bracha which was given to it by שמואל הקטן upon the request of R. Gamliel.

It is not for us human beings to condemn a group in its entirety. True, a sharper distinction could have been drawn by denouncing the groups or sects themselves. Instead, the formula refers to the individual persons who have forsaken Judaism. We do not say ומלכות זדון (the reign of wickedness), but והזדים (the wicked). (ח"א par. 24, 17). The Jewish atheists as well as those who had deserted Judaism, were included, כולל זדים עם המינים (Meg. 17b), a fact which clearly shows that the Bracha was not *exclusively* directed against the Jew-Christians or Nazarenes, as later on claimed by the Fathers of the Church. It refers to all elements estranged from the Jewish teachings since their activities seriously endangered the continuity of Judaism. First, the עוזבי ה' are mentioned, who have deserted G-d and turned to the new Belief. To the Jewish leaders of that epoch, this new Belief, developed from Judaism yet preaching quite divergent views, must have appeared as a dangerous schismatic movement, to be countered with all available means. (Only much later a different attitude towards Christianity was adopted, about which we shall say more later on). The dissidents were called משומדים and in all the oldest known editions of the Siddur the Bracha begins with the words למשומדים אל תהי תקוה (the term משומדים means "estranged" cf. Ex. 12, 43, Targum and Ramban). Later the term was changed to ולמלשינים, the slanderers, after the most violent accusations on the part of the Christians, (מפחד אויב for fear of the enemy, as מחצית השקל remarks). The rest of the text of the Bracha was subjected to so many emendations and alterations, that it is almost impossible to determine the original version.

It may be considered certain, however, that the זדים, cited
by the Talmud, have to be mentioned. They are the intentional
and habitual sinners who remain within the boundaries of
Judaism. Against them the strongest and harshest terms of con-
demnation are used. Furthermore כל עושי רשעה, all those
who do evil, are mentioned directly after the משומדים. This
seems to underline the fact that the petition for the disappearance
of evil is not confined to those who have turned their backs
on Judaism. All those who oppose and undermine His Reign
are included. (According to the Gaon of Vilna כל הרשעה
should be said instead of כל עושה רשעה, because we pray
for the disappearance of evil rather than for the destruction
of the evil-doers).

In all the violent attacks which the adherents of the "Religion of Love" have directed against this Bracha (and in
general against the "Jealous G-d" of the Old Testament as
compared to the God of Love of the Gospels), the most important point has been overlooked. The failure to understand
the holy wrath expressed in this Bracha against the evil-doers,
is very often caused by the lack of moral sensitivity, by a deficiency of feeling for the sinfulness of all existing injustice.
He whose emotional equilibrium remains undisturbed when
violence is done to justice and right, can easily afford to
glory in his moral "advance" beyond the stage of belief in
the "Jealous G-d."

If we do not consider an amoral act as a sin against G-d,
as a flagrant disregard of our Creator and King, then we
have not understood the just G-d of wrath, of the wrath
against sin. The belief in G-d is incompatible with indifference
to injustice committed on earth. To love G-d, to fear G-d means
to hate and despise evil. "Thou who love G-d, hate the evil."
"Truly, those who hate Thee, O G-d, I hate, and those who
revolt against Thee, I shall fight." For to be able to revere,
one must be able to despise too; to be capable of striving
for Justice, one must be capable of anger also. Where there
is no moral indignation against all blasphemers and contemners
of law and morality (as the concept of the wrathful G-d of
Justice teaches), there can be no fight for Justice, no co-
operation in the moral progress of humanity. The strict,
Divine Justice obligates us, each in his place, to fight against

injustice, to work towards the ideal goal of history; for His design of the world is founded on Justice. — It is no mere coincidence that the Bracha against the מינים has been placed to follow immediately upon the ברכת המשפט, the Bracha of Justice. The battle against injustice is a direct outcome of the quest for Justice. The connecting "ו" at the beginning of ולמלשינים points to this inner association.

This Bracha was introduced at a time when the Jewish Culture was threatened with dissolution. Its relevance for our times is disputed in many quarters. The Reformers have omitted it from some editions of their Prayer Book. Christianity, it is true, is no longer considered as much of a danger to Judaism as it was at the time of its inception. On the contrary our greatest halachic authorities — Maimonides, for instance, and more recently R. Yechezkel Landau (the נודע ביהודה) and R. Yakov Emden, have looked upon Christianity as one of the factors in awakening and spreading the idea of G-d, in attaining the universal knowledge of G-d on earth. "Yet despite all this," יעב"ץ remarks in his siddur, "the Bracha is still necessary since the words of evil still remain. They must not grow again and ripen into fruits of poison and hemlock." Our age with its strong atheistic and anti-religious movements and its terrifying outbreaks of religious *hatred* strikingly illustrates the justification of his arguments.

על הצדיקים. *Towards the righteous and the pious, towards the elders of thy people the house of Israel, towards the remnant of their scribes, towards the proselytes of righteousness, and towards us also may thy tender mercies be stirred. O Lord our G-d; grant a good reward unto all who faithfully trust in thy name; set our portion with them for ever, so that we may not be put to shame; for we have trusted in thee. Blessed art thou, O Lord, the stay and trust of the righteous.*

על הצדיקים. This Bracha has been placed after the Bracha against the מינים, because "the horn of the pious will rise only after the מינים have been destroyed" (Meg. ibid). Until that time the pious, in quiet devotion, prepare the ground for the Reign of G-d, in "the desert of the nations." They bear with patience and fortitude their sufferings as the servants of G-d, their eyes always directed towards the future.

To them, pioneers of this future, this Bracha is dedicated, — its prayer that G-d may be their hope and support at all times.

There are four categories of pious mentioned in our version of this Bracha: Those whose motive is צדק, the sense of justice; those who act out of חסד, Love; a third group "the Elders of Thy people," i.e. the counsellors and leaders, and finally "the remnant of their scholars," the teachers and instructors. Then the גרי צדק, those who have converted to Judaism because of conviction (not of fear or other motives) are included. Our Torah already places them together with the pious and the elders (Levit. XIX, 32) and the Talmud (Meg. ibid) assigns the same rank to them as to the others mentioned above.

ותן שכר טוב refers to the reward in the future world for, "know that the reward of the pious is in the world to come." (Ab. II, 21).

ולירושלים. *And to Jerusalem, thy city, return in mercy, and dwell therein as thou hast spoken; rebuild it soon in our days as an everlasting building, and speedily set up therein the throne of David. Blessed art thou, O Lord, who rebuildest Jerusalem.*

ולירושלים עירך וגו'. May G-d Himself return to Jerusalem; for wherever Israel went in exile His שכינה accompanied them and it returns, as it were, with them. It was R. Shimon bar Yochai who discovered this thought hinted at in the words ושב ה' אלקיך את שבותך etc. (Deut. 30, 3, Meg. 29a). The word ורחמך in that verse, explains the insertion of ברחמים in our Bracha. For although Zion's redemption will be brought about by justice (ציון במשפט תפדה), the rebuilding of the Temple and the return of the שכינה only can come about as an efflux of the Divine Mercy. (עטרת זקנים par. 188 and מטה משה par. 325). — The Jerusalem of the future will last for all eternity. The Jerusalem of old was built by human effort and was therefore destructible, the new Jerusalem will be created by G-d Himself, עוד אבנך ונבנית, and will therefore endure forever. Hence the Bracha ends: בונה ירושלים alluding to Ps. 147, 2. — The words וכסא דוד etc. are inserted in order to comply with the precept of the Jerusalem Talmud (Ber. II, 4) כולל של דוד בבונה ירושלים, the plea for the rebuilding of Jerusalem must be combined with the one prayer for the establishment of the Messianic Kingdom. This arrangement was to show clearly the indivisibility of these two issues. Later, a special Bracha for the coming of the Messiah was introduced צמח דוד. Hence the reference to it in ולירושלים is omitted in many old Siddur texts. However, the "ו" at the beginning of our Bracha points to a time when both formed one Bracha. It began with רחם (similar to the corresponding Bracha in the Grace after meals), and ended אלהי דוד ובונה ירושלים.

את צמח. *Speedily cause the offspring of David, thy servant, to flourish, and let his horn be exalted by thy salvation, because we wait for thy salvation all the day. Blessed art thou, O Lord, who causest the horn of salvation to flourish.*

את צמח דוד. There are many widely diverging opinions regarding the date of the composition of this Bracha and the reason for its introduction. The Babylonian Talmud holds that it should be a separate Bracha (Meg. 17b), whereas according to the Jerusalem Talmud it is to be united with the preceding one (cf. above), so that the original number of 18 Berachoth be maintained after the addition of ולמלשינים. However, later on את צמח was generally recognized as a separate Bracha. A Midrash leads us to conjecture that the motives for the introduction of both ולמלשינים and את צמח might have been the same. It is not at all unlikely that the danger to Judaism from the new teachings of the rising wave of Christianity prompted the addition of את צמח, just as it had caused the introduction of ולמלשינים. For by teaching the belief that the Messiah, in the person of its founder, had already arrived, Christianity immediately set itself in direct opposition to a fundamental teaching of Judaism. The entire question of the right of Judaism to exist was dependent upon the recognition of the founder as the Messiah. It was, therefore, decided to accentuate the petition for the Messiah until then included within ולירושלים, by creating a special Bracha for it. The hope of coming of the Messiah should thus be kept awake in the heart of the Jew at all times.

The true Messiah will not be of unknown origin but "a branch of the house of David." (Is. XI, 1), and his

descent is considered so significant that צמח, "branch" has
even become one of the names of the Messiah (Jer. Ber.
II, 4). Like a צמח, a plant which has a small and insignificant
beginning, then grows imperceptibly towards maturity, Redemption too will come gradually, not abruptly and suddenly,
but slowly, leading Israel out of despair and distress towards
freedom. — וקרנו תרום בישועתיך. The "horn" is a symbol
of strength and vigor, it is used to describe the success of
the just as well as the wicked Ps. LXXV, 11 and XCII, 10.
— ישועה points to the great historical event of the re-building
of Jerusalem: וראו כל אפסי ארץ את ישועת אלקינו. Is. LII,
10, Ps. XCVIII, 3 (Abudr.). Every day, we look for the
coming of the Redeemer. On the Day of Judgment every
soul will have to answer the question: צפית לישועה? Did you
look forward to the Redemption? (Sab. 31a).

שמע. *Hear our voice, O Lord our G-d; spare us and
have mercy upon us, and accept our prayer in mercy and favour;
for thou art a G-d who hearkenest unto prayers and supplications; from thy presence, O our King, turn us not empty
away;* (On fast days the Cong. say here the following:
—*Answer us, O Lord, answer us on this day of the fast of
our humiliation, for we are in great trouble. Turn not to
our wickedness; conceal not thy face from us, and hide not
thyself from our supplication. Be near, we entreat thee, unto
our cry; let thy lovingkindness be a comfort to us; even
before we call unto thee answer us, according as it is said,
And it shall come to pass that, before they call, I will answer;
while they are yet speaking, I will hear; for thou O Lord,
are he who answereth in time of trouble, who delivereth and
rescueth in all times of trouble and distress;*) *for thou hearkenest in mercy to the prayer of thy people Israel. Blessed art
thou, O Lord, who hearkenest unto prayer.*

שמע קולנו. The Talmud has already raised the question
why this Bracha which we would have expected at a much
earlier stage of the Tefilla — was placed at the end of all
the supplicatory Berachoth. (Jer. Ber. II, 4). The answer
is given by referring to a verse in Isaiah (56, 7) והביאותים
אל הר קדשי. According to this, the joyous elation evoked by
acceptance of our prayer is as yet a matter of the distant future.

שומע תפלה is a Bracha the realization of which is an ultimate goal — like גואל ישראל and בונה ירושלים. For "since the day when the Sanctuary was destroyed, the Gates of Prayer have been closed, and only the Gates of Tears remained open." (Ber. 32b). Only when Israel has found the road back to her G-d, may she hope for fulfillment of her prayers. Therefore this Bracha was placed at the end of all supplications. — ברחמים וברצון. As long as human beings remain morally weak and insufficient they have to plead for "mercy and benevolence" for their prayers to be accepted. — "Hearken to our voice." Since the prayer is to be spoken silently this can only refer to the "voice of the heart" (Cp. כתב וקבלה Deut. 30, 10).

ה' אלקינו. Moses too, in his personal prayer ואתחנן uses this Double Name to invoke the Mercy of G-d in Judgment" (Rashi Deut. 3, 24). — ומלפניך cf. Ps. LXXIV, 21: אל ישוב דך נכלם "Let not the downcast turn away in shame."

At this juncture of the Bracha personal requests and special supplications may be interjected. Thus on Fast days the individual worshipper inserts the עננו Prayer here in his Tefilla, (cf. our commentary p. 137). However the permission to express personal wishes at this point should be used only in cases of urgent need. It should not lead to a permanent enlargement of the Tefilla. (Oruch Hashulchan par. 119, 2). Here too the rule obtains: "Better a little with devotion than a great deal without devotion" (ח"א 1, 4). The following כי אתה is a variation of an idea previously expressed. It serves to have all additional special requests joined to the main stream of the prayer, in accordance with the principle מעין חתימה סמוך לחתימה. (Pes. 104a). — ברחמים. Thirteen attributes, the י"ג מדות הרחמים describe the relationship of G-d to His world and to His children. 13 norms gives us an understanding of His revealed word (cf. Comm. to ר' ישמעאל p. 54); and in 13 Berachoth we pray for perfection — to find the road to G-d. (From אתה חונן to שומע תפלה.). May their prayer then be accepted ברחמים, into the eternal spring of Divine love, מדת הרחמים, the sole source of fulfillment and reward (Ab. II, 13). The Amen with which the congregation responds when the reader recites this Bracha which closes the ring of the 13 Middle Berachoth, therefore, acquires special significance and ranks together with קדיש and קדושה in importance. (ח"א 109, 1).

רצה. *Accept, O Lord our G-d, thy people Israel and their prayer; restore the service to the oracle of thy house; receive in love and favour both the fire-offerings of Israel and their prayer; and may the service of thy people Israel be ever acceptable unto thee.*

On New Moon and during the Intermediate Days of Passover and Tabernacles the following is added:

Our G-d and G-d of our fathers! May our remembrance rise, come and be accepted before thee, with the remembrance of our fathers, of Messiah the son of David thy servant, of Jerusalem thy holy city, and of all thy people the house of Israel, bringing deliverance and well-being, grace, lovingkindness and mercy, life and peace on this day of — The New Moon — The Feast of Unleavened Bread — The Feast of Tabernacles. Remember us, O Lord our G-d, thereon for our well-being; be mindful of us for blessing, and save us unto life; by thy promise of salvation and mercy, spare us and be gracious unto us; have mercy upon us and save us; for our eyes are bent upon thee, because thou art a gracious and merciful G-d and King.

And let our eyes behold thy return in mercy to Zion. Blessed art thou, O Lord, who restorest thy Divine presence unto Zion.

רצה. Here the last group of Berachoth begins. It is in its entirety an expression of gratitude for the love and mercy received from above. (Maimon. Hil. Tef. I, 5). Petitions for acceptance of our prayers and for lasting peace are interwoven with it. They are presented on behalf of the nation as a whole. The character of this group of Berachoth is not disturbed by the inclusion of these requests, for "the greatest homage paid to G-d is when the entire nation turns to Him for help." (cf. שבלי הלקט 28).

רצה. This Bracha called עבודה was already part of the service during the days of the Temple. According to the Mishna (Tamid V, 1) the priests recited it as they completed the sacrifices, correspondingly we say it at the end of the Tefilla, which, as has been pointed out before, replaces the sacrificial service. The wording of the Bracha, of course, has been changed. After the destruction of the Sanctuary, the hope for the reinstitution of the Temple Service was substituted for the plea of its maintenance previously contained in this Bracha. Tradition endeavors most emphatically to keep awake the faith in the sanctity of Zion, "the site of our Sanctuary." To the fervent hope for its speedy resurrection, this Bracha is dedicated. — רצה בעמך ישראל. Before we ask G-d to accept our prayer in grace, we ask for acceptance of "Thy people Yisroel." For we may hope that our prayer be heard, only if we have striven, with our whole being and willing, to prove worthy to be heard. — והשב...ואשי ישראל. On the question whether the words ואשי ישראל are to be joined to the preceding sentence or whether they are the beginning of the following ואשי ישראל תקבל באהבה, cf. א"ח par. 120 and commentaries. According to the Vilna Gaon they are to be read in connection with the preceding verse, praying for the re-institution of the sacrificial service. — לדביר (connected with דבר, word) "The place of the Sacred word." — ותפלתם באהבה, Prayer is the "Service of the Heart," עבודה שבלב. It is deduced from the Biblical passage   לאהבה את ה' אלקיכם ולעבדו בכל לבבכם (Deut. XI, 13). After we have prayed for the revival in Zion of the Temple-Service, we ask that it be לרצון תמיד, forever, that we may not, through our own unworthiness, be deprived of it once more, as we have been in the past. — ותחזינה (acc. to Micha 4, 11 - Is. 52, 8) — ברחמים cf. comm. to ולירושלים עירך.

On Rosh Chodesh and on Chol Hamo'ed, יעלה ויבא is interjected here "as a supplication for Israel and Jerusalem, for the reinstitution of the Temple service and of the sacrifices of the day." (Rashi Sab. 24a). However the prayer itself contains no reference to those matters. Continuing the trend of ideas of the בר' עבודה it expresses the wish that our זכר ascend to G-d on Rosh Chodesh and Holy Day, and receive blessing and grace. The Torah ordains that "On your days of rejoicing and your holy days and on your month's beginnings, you shall blow the trumpets over your offerings that they may be to you *memorial* before your G-d." (Num. 10, 10). We say this prayer as a substitute for the trumpet sound, in the Tefilla, the substitute for the offerings, והיו לכם

לזכרון לפני אלקיכם. — Eight expressions connoting ascent and acceptance of the prayer are mentioned in it. They symbolize, as the Vilna Gaon points out, the eight celestial spheres, behind which He has hidden His countenance since the time of Israel's fall. On Rosh Chodesh and Holy Day, Israel feels nearer to G-d. We, threfore, pray that our Tefilla penetrate beyond those intervening spheres, until it reaches His Presence and evoke His Grace and Mercy. — זכר, to remember, פקד, to remember and act in accordance with the facts remembered. — זכרון אבותינו, the Past — זכרון משיח, the Future — זכרון ירושלים, the present state of decline and destruction in which the ruins of Jerusalem wait for the day when its destiny as the Holy City of Israel will be fulfilled.

מודים. *We give thanks unto thee, for thou art the Lord our G-d and the G-d of our fathers for ever and ever; thou art the Rock of our lives, the Shield of our salvation through every generation. We will give thanks unto thee and declare thy praise for our lives which are committed unto thy hand, and for our souls which are in thy charge, and for thy miracles, which are daily with us, and for thy wonders and thy benefits, which are wrought at all times, evening, morning and noon. O thou who art all-good, whose mercies fail not; thou, merciful Being, whose lovingkindness never cease, we have ever hoped in thee.*

מודים דרבנן. We give thanks unto thee, for thou art the Lord our G-d and the G-d of our fathers, the G-d of all flesh, our Creator and the Creator of all things in the beginning. Blessings and thanksgivings be to thy great and holy name, because thou hast kept us in life and hast preserved us: so mayest thou continue to keep us in life and to preserve us. O gather our exiles to the holy courts to observe thy statutes, to do thy will, and to serve thee with a perfect heart; seeing that we give thanks unto thee. Blessed be the G-d to whom thanksgivings are due.

מודים. According to Maimonides this Bracha too was recited by the priests in the Temple (Mishna Comm. Tamid V, 1). It forms one unit with the preceding עבודה, עבודה והודאה חדא מלתא היא, since, "the rendering of thanks too, is part of the service of the Almighty" (Rashi Meg. 18a). Any expression of gratitude which is not preceded by the

acceptance of the obligation to observe the Divine Law is
blasphemy. The duty to thank Him at this stage of the Tefilla
is therefore aptly inferred from the verse: זובח תודה יכבדנני.
However the meaning of הודאה is a threefold one. In Samuel
II, 16, 4 it occurs as the Targum's translation of השתחוה,
meaning to bow down. Hence we are enjoined to bow down
at the beginning and end of this Bracha. But הודאה is also
an expression of confession and faith, as Rashi defines it
(Sukkah 45b). The word is used in this sense in the opening
phrase where we acknowledge that He is our G-d as He was
the G-d of our fathers, and that He is צור, our Creator, the
Fashioner of our fates, our Support and our Protector. Finally
מודים means "thank" (as in the scriptural passage: ועתה ה' מודים
אנחנו לך ומהללים לשם תפארתך, Chron. 1, 29, 13). — Our
gratitude is all embracing. We thank for our lives, which are
always in His hands and for our souls which are under His
care as long as we live (Sifre, Num. 27, 16). Further for
the נסים, the visible and invisible miracles, and for the
נפלאות, those miracles that occur without our being aware
of them as the טובות, the thousands of benefits woven into
the texture of our daily lives.

The causes of these miracles, the principles of His
Rulership are now invoked. הטוב כי לא כלו רחמיך, He is
kind, for His mercy never ends. Mercy flows from the eternal
spring of Love. This pure Love, חסד, is the ultimate source
of Kindness for which therefore we thank G-d: הודו לה' כי
טוב כי לעולם חסדו. In its sign the world was created, עולם
חסד יבנה (Ps. 89, 3) and through all eternity He remains
רב חסד, replete with Love.

רחמים signifies the mitigation of the demands of Justice
by the addition of compassion and pity. It is therefore, not
quite free of "wrath" and accompanied by יסורים. In חסד,
however, Justice has been overcome, it is "beyond the boundaries
of Justice." Hence חסד is at work at all times, not only when
the world is visited by distress and punishment. It is the ever
renewed gift of love which holds the world together. Thus
חסד is the spring which feeds מדת הרחמים, and רחמים, Mercy,
is in the final analysis but a function of חסד, the all embracing
Love. This explains the sentence הטוב...והמרחם כי לא תמו
חסדיך, which textually is based on Lam. 3, 22 (cf. Rashi

ibid.; cf. further צל"ח Ber. 16b; Bachya Ex. 34, 6; Malbim Ps. 40, 12). — מעולם. "We *have* forever hoped for you," instead of the usual לעולם, we *shall* forever hope for you. In this way we provide the transition to the על הנסים which on Purim and Channukah is added here and which refers to the past.

On Chanukah and Purim the following is added:

We thank thee also for the miracles, for the redemption, for the mighty deeds and saving acts, wrought by thee, as well as for the wars thou didst wage for our fathers in days of old, at this season.

On Chanukah.

In the days of the Hasmonean, Mattathias son of Johanan, the High Priest, and his sons, when the iniquitous power of Greece rose up against thy people Israel to make them forgetful of thy Law, and to force them to transgress the statutes of thy will, then didst thou in thine abundant mercy rise up for them in the time of their trouble; thou didst plead their cause, thou didst judge their suit, thou didst avenge their wrong; thou deliveredst the strong into the hands of the weak, the many into the hands of the few, the impure into the hands of the pure, the wicked into the hands of the righteous, and the arrogant into the hands of them that occupied themselves with thy Law; for thyself thou didst make a great and holy name in thy world, and for thy people Israel thou didst work a great deliverance and redemption as at this day. And thereupon thy children came into the oracle of thy house, cleansed thy temple, purified thy sanctuary, kindled lights in thy holy courts, and appointed these eight days of Chanukah in order to give thanks and praises unto thy great name.

On Purim.

In the days of Mordechai and Esther, in Shushan the capital, when the wicked Haman rose up against them, and sought to destroy, to slay and make to perish all the Jews, both young and old. little children and women, on one day, on the thirteenth day of the twelfth month, which is the month Adar, and to take the spoil of them for a prey, — then didst thou in thine abundant mercy bring his counsel

*to nought, didst frustrate his design, and return his recompense
upon his own head; and they hanged him and his sons upon
the gallows.*

The על הנסים being an expression of our gratitude
and not a supplication — is spoken here, in the ברכת הודאה.
(Sabbath 24a Tos.).

ועל כלם. *For all these things thy name, O our King, shall
be continually blessed and exalted for ever and ever.*

(During the Ten Days of Penitence say:— *O inscribe
all the children of thy covenant for a happy life.*)

ועל כלם. This sentence concludes the enumeration of
the benefits for which we owe a debt of gratitude to our
G-d, (corresponding to the sentence beginning with ועל הכל
in the Grace after Meals).

וכל החיים. *And everything that liveth shall give thanks
unto thee for ever, and shall praise thy name in truth, O G-d,
our salvation and our help. Selah. Blessed art thou, O Lord,
whose name is All-good, and unto whom it is becoming to
give thanks.*

וכל החיים. The contents of this passage remind us
of the prayer which Hezekia, King of Judah recited after
his recovery from mortal illness: "For the grave cannot
praise Thee, nor Death extol Thee; they that go down into
the pit cannot hope for Thy truth." (Is. 38, 18). The belief
in the existence of G-d does not, as pagan religions teach,
arise in man as an attempt to escape from his inevitability
of death. Instead it is learned from the experience of G-d's
proven faithfulness, the record of which is handed down from
one generation to another. The sentence spoken at this place
during the Ten Days of תשובה fits appropriately: "Inscribe for a good life all the children of Thy covenant."

הטוב שמך. The concluding Bracha should have read,
according to Jer. Yoma VII, 1, and Rashi Yoma 68b,: הטוב
לך להודות, in allusion to הודות לה' (Ps. 92, 2) "For Israel has
nothing with which to pay her debt to G-d, but the gratitude
for all the benefits she received; and he who expresses his
gratitude shall receive His benfits once more; therefore, הודו

לה' כי טוב, praise G-d for He is kind" (Midr. Ps. 118, 1). The two ideas aired in this Midrash find expression in the Bracha הטוב שמך.

מודים דרבנן. "When the reader repeats the ש"ע, he bows down at the beginning of the Bracha of Gratitude. The congregation thereupon bows down as well and recites a short prayer of thanksgiving beginning with מודים. For it does not befit a servant to have his confession of thanks to his master recited through a messenger. Each one should render his thanks in person. It is different with the other Brachoth, which contain requests, for one may well put forward a request through a שליח" (Abudraham). The passage is composed of various versions adopted by different Rabbis. It is therefore called the מודים דרבנן. (Sota 40a).

At the repetition of the Amidah by the Reader, the following is introduced, but is omitted in the house of mourning:

אלקינו. *Our G-d and G-d of our fathers, bless us with the three-fold blessing by the Law written by the hand of Moses thy servant, which was spoken by Aaron and his sons, the priests, thy holy people, as it is said, The Lord bless thee, and keep thee; the Lord make his face to shine upon thee, and be gracious unto thee; the Lord turn his face unto thee, and give thee peace.*

ברכת כהנים. We read in Levit. 9, 22 that Aaron, having completed the sacrificial service, raised his hands and blessed the assembled people. His descendants too, the priests used to recite the prescribed blessing (Num. 6, 23-26) after having performed the sacrifices in the Temple. Hence we also have the Priests' Blessing at the end of the ש"ע, which, as pointed out before, corresponds to the sacrificial service (cf. p. 123).

The ברכת כהנים is recited only in the repetition of the ש"ע, as the blessing itself may be pronounced only when the required quorum of 10 is present. (Meg. IV, 4). Today the Minhag has been adopted almost universally that the כהנים utter the blessing on Holy-days only. Then the festival spirit of the day creates that atmosphere of serenity and harmony which is the precondition for all blessings. (א"ח Par. 128, 44).

The blessing itself and its meaning have been explained in connection with the ברכת התורה (p. 49). The ברכת כהנים forms the closing link in the chain of the 18 blessings. It is not an isolated, independent act. Only as a result of the preceding עבודה, the service, can the blessings pronounced in it, and culminating in the blessing of peace, be obtained. Peace is, as the Rabbis express it, "the vessel containing and preserving all blessings." It is not the first but the last of our requests; and no peace can exist without the preceding עבודה and הודאה; for our peace is perfect only if it grows out of common gratitude and common submission to the service of His Law.

שים שלום. *Grant peace, welfare, blessing, grace, lovingkindness and mercy unto us and unto all Israel, thy people. Bless us, O our Father, even all of us together, with the light of thy countenance; for by the light of thy countenance thou hast given us, O Lord our G-d, the Law of life, lovingkindness and righteousness, blessing, mercy, life and peace; and may it be good in thy sight to bless thy people Israel at all times and in every hour with thy peace.*

Blessed art thou, O Lord, who blessest thy people Israel with peace.

During the Ten Days of Penitence say:—

In the book of life, blessing, peace and good sustenance may we be remembered and inscribed before thee, we and all thy people the house of Israel, for a happy life and for peace. Blessed art thou, O Lord, who makest peace.

שים שלום. G-d promised, in conclusion of the ברכת כהנים: ואני אברכם, And I shall bless them. According to the explanation of R. Akiba (Chulin 49a) this means, that G-d Himself grants the blessings, which are uttered by the priests. And since שלום, peace, is foremost among the blessings which G-d bestows, השם עז לעמו יתן וגו', we first pray שים שלום טובה וכו', "give peace," and then add five requests for realization of the blessings, so that there are altogether six requests advanced here, as many as the individual expressions of blessing contained in the ברכת כהנים, יברכך וכו'. We then pray: "Bless us, our father, all of us (encompassing כהנים and

ישראלים.) with the light of Thy countenance." This expression
is invariably used to signify the blissful, invigorating and
joyous aspect of His Rule, the essence of Divine favor.
Thus in this Bracha we finally condense all our prayers in the
wish: Bless us with the light of Thy Countenance, for in its
shine Thou hast given us the most coveted goods of life:
The most precious, spiritual possession in תורת חיים, the
Law of Life, and the sublime gift of the heart in אהבת חסד.
the Love of Kindness, which always has distinguished Israel
among the nations (Yeb. 79a).

Seven blessings are mentioned here (up to ושלום)
which G-d has granted us in the "Light of His Countenance,"
the same as the number of the colours of the rainbow. For
the Light of His countenance is faintly reflected in the rainbow,
the symbol of His Covenant with Man. And "as the appearance of the bow that is in the clouds on the day of rain,
so was the appearance of the brightness round about, so was
the appearance of the likeness of the glory of G-d." (Ez.
1, 28). In the same manner as the rainbow shows the seven-
colored reflection of light, thus the radiant "Light of His
countenance" too appears as the emanation of a sevenfold
blessing.

שלום רב. Instead of the שים שלום, with its direct reference to the Priests' Blessing, a different piece שלום רב is
said on all those occasions when the Priestly Blessing is
omitted, e.g. in מנחה and מעריב (at which times the כהנים
might lack the absolute sobriety required for the utterance
of the יברכך).

The שלום רב is thus chiefly an evening-prayer. Its sole
request is for "abundant peace" from the unknown dangers
of the impending darkness, a request also repeated in other
parts of the evening prayers המפיל, השכיבנו. The concluding
words and the final blessing, המברך etc., are the same for
שים שלום as for שלום רב. During the 10 days of Teshuva
however, this Bracha is changed to עושה השלום with the
article "ה," so as to reach a numerical value of 381 corresponding to that of the Angel Safriel who is in charge of the
Book of Life. The word עושה too has the same numerical
value. Both are referring back to the interpolated, בספר חיים,
added on these days.

It is significant that the request for peace is the last of the eighteen. Peace, this seems to imply, is, according to Jewish concept, not the basis but the ultimate aim of our endeavors. For to the Jew, peace means the harmonisation of all contracts, the solution of all earthly conflicts, the final aim, and the supreme task, as Albo explains in the last chapter of his Ikkarim. שלום is perfection par excellence, e.g. absolute lack of conflict, in the relation of man to man in his own soul, and in his relation to G-d. Peace thus becomes an ideal, forever to be striven for as long as we live; it is — according to a dictum of R. Jona ben Levi — to the world, what yeast is for the dough, the perennial "mover of human fate," (which the Greek concept, in contradistinction, finds in War). According to the Jewish view, peace is to be considered the father of all happening, the element of fermentation and development. Therefore, it is the creator of all that is great and good, furthering the progress of mankind, ennobling the individual, leading the community towards harmony, and humanity towards perfection. Life is one long struggle for lasting and absolute peace. The prayer for G-d's blessing in this struggle is the last and most comprehensive of all the pleas we direct towards Heaven.

אלקי נצור. *O my G-d! guard my tongue from evil and my lips from speaking guile; and to such as curse me let my soul be dumb, yea, let my soul be unto all as the dust. Open my heart to thy Law, and let my soul pursue thy commandments. If any design evil against me, speedily make their counsel of none effect, and frustrate their designs. Do it for the sake of thy name, do it for the sake of thy right hand, do it for the sake of thy holiness, do it for the sake of thy Law. In order that thy beloved ones may be delivered, O save with thy right hand, and answer me. Let the words of my mouth and the meditation of my heart be acceptable before thee, O Lord, my Rock and my Redeemer. He who maketh peace for us and for all Israel, and say ye, Amen.*

יהי רצון. *May it be thy will, O Lord our G-d and G-d of our fathers, that the Temple be speedily rebuilt in our days, and grant our portion in thy Law. And there we will serve thee with awe, as in the days of old, and as in ancient years. Then shall the offering of Judah and Jerusalem be pleasant unto the Lord, as in the days of old, and as in ancient years.*

אלקי נצור. The ש"ע ends with the Bracha המברך וכו'.
The paragraph אלקי נצור has been adjoined to it to conform with
the precept of the Rabbis: "Do not let your Tefilla become a
mere act of routine, but [a petition for] mercy and a supplication to G-d." (Ab. II, 18). Everyone is therefore bidden to let
his prayer flow out of the spontaneous urge of his heart, and
not to let it to degenerate into the mechanical recital of a text.
"Since the Tefilla created by the Men of the Great Synod
has been made a regular duty and is recited by us as such,
the "mercy and supplication" do not always become apparent.
Therefore the Rabbis used to add personal prayers to it in order
to comply with that rule" (צל"ח Ber. 16b). The Talmud
(ibid.) quotes several such personal prayers, and the one
that Mar the son of Rabina used to recite at the end of the
ש"ע has been chosen universally as the conclusion for the
Tefilla. In it we ask for the humility and self-control which
will keep us silent even in the face of slander and calumny —
and humble "as dust" in the intercourse with our fellow men.
On the other hand, we ask for alertness in the study of the
Torah, פתח לבי..., and diligence in the pursuit of the Mitzvoth
עשה למען — . ובמצותיך תרדוף נפשי. In the last resort, it is
not national honor or personal happiness which we seek in
our prayers, but the honor of "His Name, of His Sanctity
and of His Torah," which are being desecrated among the
nations even now, as it is emphatically stated in the 36th chapter
of יחזקאל. At the very end of the Tefilla comprising all our
demands and requests, we pray so that the Divine Name
appear again in the full brightness of its glory, עשה למען
ימינך. The right (hand) of G-d symbolizes His redeeming
power. It shows itself "highly exalted" to Israel in victory
(Ps. 118, 16), and He withdraws it before the enemy when
Israel is defeated (Lam. 2, 3). — למען יחלצון וכו'. Said David:
למען יחלצון ידידיך, "Lord of the Universe redeem them for
the sake of thy beloved ones, ידידיך, Abraham, Isaac and
Jacob. If they are not worthy to benefit from the merits
of those, save them for sake of Thy Right Hand, and hearken
unto me. Whereupon G-d said: "So shall I do," as it is said:
"He saves them with His Right Hand and with His holy arm."
(Ps. 98, 1. Midr. Ps. 137, 5). Thus with the verse from the
Psalms, למען וכו', the preceding sentences are complemented,
expressing the wish that G-d, for the sake of His own honor

and might, symbolized in His "Right Hand," may redeem
the nation whose fate is, as it were, linked to His own. —
יהיו לרצון. This verse (Ps. 19, 14) which David set at the end
of the first 18 Psalms, is, according to R. Yochanan, the
conclusion of the ע"ש. (cf. Ber. 9b). "May what we have said,
אמרי פי, and what we have allowed to remain in the depths of
the heart unsaid, והגיון לבי, be לפניך לרצון before G-d." — At
this juncture each one should, following a custom mentioned
in the של"ה, recite a Biblical verse the first and the last letters
of which are the same as the first and last letters of his
Hebrew name, "so that the Torah may save him from bad
fortune."

עושה שלום. "When a man prays, he stands as it were,
on holy ground. Therefore when he has concluded his prayer,
he steps back three paces, to leave the holy ground and to return to the profane. When he has returned, the worshipper
gives the שלום greeting in order to announce his return to the
worldly matters." (Beis Yosef par. 123). The sentence עושה
שלום paraphrasing Job 25, 2 — points to the harmony of the
upper regions, where each and every celestial body follows its
appointed orbit without interfering with another's course. May
such perfect harmony also be granted to earthly life. While
pronouncing the words עושה שלום we bow to our left (which
corresponds to the right side of the שכינה, thought facing
us). At הוא יעשה שלום עלינו we bow to the right (corresponding to the left of the שכינה) and at ועל כל ישראל we finally bow
forward towards the שכינה itself, (Yoma 53b). Peace is created
on High by the harmonisation of two opposing forces. One is
symbolized by the Archangel Gabriel, the representative of
fire and destructive vengeance. He stands at the left side
of the heavenly throne. Michael, standing at the right hand
side of the throne symbolizes the spirit of assuaging mercy.
By our deferential bow to left and right and finally to the
front we humbly acknowledge that it is G-d who unites and
resolves all conflicts and discrepancies within Nature and
mankind.

יהי רצון refers again to the ע"ש as a substitute for
the sacrificial service (cf. commentary p. 56).

תחנונים

On Mondays and Thursdays the following is added:

והוא רחום. *And he, being merciful, forgiveth iniquity
and destroyeth not: yea, many a time he turneth his anger
away, and doth not stir up all his wrath. Withhold not thou
thy tender mercies from us, O Lord, let thy lovingkindness
and thy truth continually preserve us. Save us, O Lord our
G-d, and gather us from amongst the nations, to give thanks
unto thy holy name, and to triumph in thy praise. If thou
shouldst mark iniquities, O Lord, who can stand? But there
is forgiveness with thee, that thou mayest be feared. Not
according to our sins wilt thou deal with us, nor requite us
according to our iniquities. If our iniquities testify against
us, work thou, O Lord, for thy name's sake. Remember, O
Lord, thy tender mercies and thy lovingkindness; for they
have been ever of old. May the Lord answer us in the day
of trouble, the name of the G-d of Jacob set us up on high.
Save, Lord: may the King answer us on the day when we call.
Our Father, our King, be gracious unto us ad answer us,
for we have no good works of our own; deal with us in charity
for thy name's sake. Our Lord, our G-d, hearken to the voice
of our supplications, and remember unto us the covenant of
our fathers, and save us for thy name's sake. And now, O
Lord our G-d, that hast brought thy people forth out of the
land of Egypt with a mighty hand, and hast made thee a name
as at this day; we have sinned, we have done wickedly. O
Lord, according to all thy righteous acts, let thine anger and
thy fury, I pray thee, be turned away from thy city Jerusalem,
thy holy mountain; because for our sins and for the iniquities
of our fathers, Jerusalem and thy people are become a reproach to all that are round about us. Now therefore, hearken,
O our G-d, unto the prayer of thy servant and to his supplications, and cause thy face to shine upon thy sanctuary that
is desolate, for the Lord's sake.*

הטה. *Incline thine ear, O my G-d, and hear; open
thine eyes, and behold our desolations, and the city which is*

called by thy name; for we do not lay our supplications before thee because of our righteous acts, but because of thine abundant mercies. O Lord, hear; O Lord, forgive; O Lord, hearken and do; defer not; for thine own sake, O my G-d, because thy city and thy people are called by thy name. O our Father, show us a sign for good, and gather our scattered ones from the four corners of the earth. Let all the nations perceive and know that thou art the Lord our G-d. And now, O Lord, thou art our Father; we are the clay, and thou art the potter, yea, we are all the work of thy hand. Save us for thy name's sake, our Rock, our King, and our Redeemer. Spare thy people, O Lord, and give not thine inheritance over to reproach, that the nations should make a by-word of them. Wherefore should they say among the peoples, Where is their G-d? We know that we have sinned, and there is none to stand for our defense in time of trouble. We know that we have no good works of our own; deal with us in charity for thy name's sake. As a father hath mercy upon his children, so, O Lord, have mercy upon us, and save us for thy name's sake. Have pity upon thy people; have mercy upon thine inheritance; spare, we pray thee, according to the abundance of thy tender mercies; be gracious unto us and answer us, for charity is thine, O Lord; thou doest wondrous things at all times.

הבט-נא. Look, we beseech thee, and speedily have mercy upon thy people for thy name's sake in thine abundant mercies. O Lord our G-d, spare and be merciful; save the sheep of thy pasture; let not wrath rule over us, for our eyes are bent upon thee; save us for thy name's sake. Have mercy upon us for the sake of thy covenant; look, and answer us in time of trouble, for salvation is thine, O Lord. Our hope is in thee, O G-d of forgiveness. We beseech thee, forgive, O good and forgiving G-d, for thou art a gracious and merciful G-d and King.

אנא מלך. We beseech thee, O gracious and merciful King, remember and give heed to the Covenant between the Pieces (with Abraham), and let the binding (upon the altar) of (Isaac) an only son appear before thee, to the welfare of Israel. Our Father, our King, be gracious unto us and answer us, for we are called by thy great name. Thou who doest wondrous things at all times, deal with us according to thy lovingkindness. O

gracious and merciful Being, look, and answer us in time
of trouble, for salvation is thine, O Lord. Our Father, our
King, our Refuge, deal not with us according to the evil
of our doings; remember, O Lord, thy tender mercies and
thy lovingkindness; save us according to thy abundant goodness, and have pity upon us, we beseech thee, for we have no
other G-d beside thee, our Rock. Forsake us not, O Lord our
G-d, be not far from us; for our soul is shrunken by reason
of the sword and captivity and pestilence and plague, and of
every trouble and sorrow. Deliver us, for we hope in thee;
put us not to shame, O Lord our G-d; make thy countenance
to shine upon us; remember unto us the covenant of our fathers
and save us for thy name's sake. Look upon our troubles,
and hear the voice of our prayer, for thou hearest the prayer
of every mouth.

אל רחום. *Merciful and gracious G-d! Have mercy upon
us and upon all thy works, for there is none like unto thee,
O Lord our G-d. We beseech thee, forgive our transgressions,
O our Father, our King, our Rock and our Redeemer, O living
and everlasting G-d, mighty in strength, loving and good to
all thy works; for thou art the Lord our G-d. O G-d, who
art slow to anger and full of mercy, deal with us according
to the abundance of thy tender mercies, and save us for thy
name's sake. Hear our prayer, O our King, and deliver us
from the hand of our enemies; hear our prayer, O our King,
and deliver us from all trouble and sorrow. Thou art our Father,
our King, and we are called by thy name; desert us not. Forsake us not, our Father, and cast us not off, O our Creator,
and forget us not, O our Maker, for thou art a gracious and
merciful G-d and King.*

אין כמוך. *There is none gracious and merciful like
thee, O Lord our G-d; there is none like thee, O G-d, slow
to anger and abounding in lovingkindness and truth. Save
us in thine abundant mercies; from fierceness and rage deliver
us. Remember thy servants, Abraham, Isaac and Jacob; look not
unto our stubbornness and our wickedness and our sin. Turn
from thy fierce anger, and repent of the evil against thy people.
Remove from us the stroke of death, for thou art merciful,
for such is thy way—showing lovingkindness freely throughout all generations. Spare thy people, O Lord, and deliver us*

from thy wrath, and remove from us the stroke of the plague, and harsh decrees, for thou art the Guardian of Israel. Unto thee, O Lord, belongeth the righteousness, but unto us confusion of face. How may we complain? What can we say, what can we speak, or how can we justify ourselves? We will search our ways and try them, and turn again to thee; for thy right hand is stretched out to receive the penitent. Save, we beseech thee, O Lord; we beseech thee, O Lord, send prosperity. We beseech thee, O Lord, answer us on the day when we call. For thee, O Lord, we wait; for thee, O Lord, we hope; in thee, O Lord, we trust; be not silent, nor let us be oppressed; for the nations say, their hope is lost. Let every knee and all that is lofty bow down to thee alone.

הפותח. O thou, who openest thy hand to repentance, to receive transgressors and sinners—our soul is sore vexed through the greatness of our grief; forget us not for ever; arise and save us, for we trust in thee. Our Father, our King, though we be without righteousness and good deeds, remember unto us the covenant of our fathers, and the testimony we bear every day that the Lord is One. Look upon our affliction, for many are our griefs and the sorrows of our heart. Have pity upon us, O Lord, in the land of our captivity, and pour not out thy wrath upon us, for we are thy people, the children of thy covenant. O G-d, look upon our sunken glory among the nations, and the abomination in which we are held as of utter defilement. How long shall thy strength remain in captivity, and thy glory in the hand of the foe? Arouse thy might and thy zeal against thine enemies, that they may be put to shame and broken down in their might. O let not our travail seem little in thy sight. Let thy tender mercies speedily come to meet us in the day of our trouble; and if not for our sake, do it for thine own sake, and destroy not the remembrance of our remnant; but be gracious unto a people, who in constant love proclaim the unity of thy name twice every day, saying, Hear, O Israel, the Lord our G-d, the Lord is One.

והוא רחום. The historic origin of this prayer is shrouded in mystery. In Gaonic responsa we find the following report. After the destruction of the Temple, Vespasian, the Roman Emperor, had a number of Jews set adrift in three rudderless ships. After many weeks of helpless drifting the vessel finally landed at the coast of France and the Jews came to Lyon, Arles and Bordeaux. They were, at first, well received. They settled in those towns and even grew quite prosperous. However when a new rule arose, they were deprived of their possessions and also oppressed in many ways.

Thereupon fast days were inaugurated, on which the והוא רחום prayer composed by two brothers Joseph and Benjamin and their cousin Samuel was recited for the first time. Subsequently the ruler died suddenly and the suffering of the Jews came to an end. When these happenings became known to other communities, they too introduced the והוא רחום prayer into the Monday and Thursday שחרית services.

It is customary to add supplicatory prayers to the regular service on these two days because they are "days of benevolence" (א"ח par. 134). Their character is actually an ambiguous one. They are, on the one hand, days of mercy, for Moses received the second and lasting two Tablets of the Covenant at Sinai on a Thursday and he returned from Mount Sinai to proclaim the message of mercy and forgiving to the people on a Monday. Since then these two days have always been considered days of benevolence, ימי רצון (B.K. 82a, Tosaphoth ibid.). On the other hand they are ימי הדין, days of judgment, the days on which according to the decree of Ezra the law courts were in session. At that time man's transgressions would be remembered before the heavenly throne (Sabbath 129a). This dualism in the nature of these two days expresses the idea, that it is just the severity of judgment which ultimately offers salvation, i.e. if man is able to pass through it cleansed and purified. Each Monday and Thursday therefore, calls the Jewish people to renewed תשובה. Hence these days were designated as days for the public reading of the Torah, and special תחנונים were included in the Service.

The והוא רחום is spoken immediately upon completion of the ש"ע, for like the ש"ע it is a supplicatory prayer and consists of 3 parts in each one of which the Divine Name is mentioned 18 times. Like the ש"ע it is, therefore, to be spoken in a low voice and standing up. (Orach Chaim, Par. 134.)

Bearing, on the other hand, the character of a penitential prayer just as the subsequent תחנון, it is omitted on days of festival joy as on days of deepest grief (e.g. in a house of mourning). Although born in an hour of acute and special need, the והוא רחום has lost none of its applicability for its recurrent motifs are the distress of Israel in exile, the awareness of our sinfulness and our pleas for redemption. The repetition and variation of similar phrases and ideas is due to the prayers' having been composed by three authors each of whom dealt with the same topic. Each part emphasizes the idea that Israel has been responsible for its dispersion among the nations by reason of its own religious and moral decay and that the plea for redemption has to be supported by a sincere resolve to repent.

ויאמר דוד. *And David said unto Gad, I am troubled exceedingly; let us fall, I pray thee, into the hand of the Lord, for his mercies are many; but let me not fall into the hand of man.*

רחום וחנון. *O thou who art merciful and gracious, I have sinned before thee. O Lord, full of mercy, have mercy upon me and receive my supplications.*

O Lord, rebuke me not in thine anger; neither chasten me in thy hot displeasure. Be gracious unto me, O Lord; for I am withered away; O Lord, heal me; for my bones are troubled. My soul is also sore troubled; and thou O Lord, how long? Return, O Lord, deliver my soul; save me for thy lovingkindness' sake. For in death there is no remembrance of thee; in the grave who shall give thee thanks? I am weary with my groaning; every night I make my bed to swim; I melt away my couch with my tears. Mine eye wasteth away because of grief; it waxeth old because of all mine adversaries. Depart from me, all ye workers of iniquity; for the Lord hath heard the voice of my weeping. The Lord hath heard my supplication; the Lord will receive my prayer. All mine enemies shall be ashamed and sore troubled; they shall turn back, they shall be ashamed suddenly.

ויאמר דוד. This prayer is called תחנון (based on Daniel 9, 18: אנחנו מפילים וכו'). The Zohar connects it with the report of the Torah, that Moses and Aaron fell down on their faces before G-d, whenever they prayed for the fulfillment of an urgent and intense need: ויפלו על פניהם (Num. 16, 22). Hence the prayer is also called נפילת אפים. It is, in fact, evident from the sources (cf. Tur. par. 131) that this act forms the most complete mode of prayer, thus connecting the תחנון with the preceding תפלה.

Hence it is linked directly to it; no interruption should intervene between ש"ע and תחנון. The קדיש following the ש"ע is accordingly deferred until after the תחנון. However, we do not actually prostrate ourselves while reciting the תחנון, but merely lower our heads and bury our faces in the bend of our arm. For only those who are worthy enough to expect fulfillment of their demands from G-d and not to be put to shame in public by a refusal, may use the extreme form of adoration. Where there is no Torah scroll present even the bowing down is omitted, "for following Joshua (7, verse 6) we want to demonstrate that our surrender to G-d means surrender to his law."

The text of the תחנון (according to our Minhag) consists chiefly of the 6th Psalm, which David suffering in body and soul uttered, after his transgression with בת שבע (cf. Malbim ibid.). It is a cry to G-d by a man worn down by the feeling of profound guilt and utter loneliness. Yet it shows us that there is a way to find mercy and help from on High even from the very depths of distress. "G-d has heard the voice of my crying." Everyone who speaks this Psalm may say this and be certain that G-d will answer his prayer, if it is a prayer issuing from a "broken and downtrodden heart which G-d never disdains." (Ps. 51, 19) (Kimchi).

ה' אלקי וכו'. Reader and Cong.—*O Lord G-d of Israel, turn from thy fierce wrath, and repent of the evil against thy people.*

Cong.—*Look from heaven and see how we have become a scorn and a derision among the nations; we are accounted as sheep brought to the slaughter, to be slain and destroyed, or to be smitten and reproached.*

Cong. and Reader.—*Yet, despite all this, we have not forgotten thy name; we beseech thee, forget us not.*

Cong.—*Strangers say, There is no hope or expectancy for you. Be gracious unto a people that trust in thy name. O thou who art most pure, bring our salvation near. We are weary, and no rest is granted us. Let thy tender mercies subdue thine anger from us.*

Cong. and Reader.—*We beseech thee, turn from thy wrath, and have mercy upon the treasured people whom thou hast chosen.*

Cong.—*O Lord, spare us in thy tender mercies, and give us not into the hands of the cruel. Wherefore should the nations say, Where now is their God? For thine own sake deal kindly with us, and delay not.*

Cong. and Reader.—*We beseech thee, turn from thy wrath, and have mercy upon the treasured people whom thou hast chosen.*

Cong.—*Hear our voice, and be gracious, and forsake us not in the hand of our enemies to blot out our name; remember what thou hast sworn to our fathers, I will multiply your seed as the stars of heavens—and now we are left a few out of many.*

Cong. and Reader.—*Yet, despite all this, we have not forgotten thy name: we beseech thee, forget us not.*

Cong.—*Help us, O God of our salvation, for the sake of the glory of thy name; and deliver us, and pardon our sins for thy name's sake.*

Cong. and Reader.—*O Lord God of Israel, turn from thy fierce wrath, and repent of the evil against thy people.*

אלקי 'ה. An ancient tradition reports that this piece was created by Hezekiah, King of Judah in hour of extreme danger, when Sancherib, King of Assyria was advancing against Jerusalem to conquer it. Hezekiah's name is said to be hidden in the acrostic of the verses, 'חוסה, זרים וכו.

From the highly personal tone of the תחנון, the prayer returns to the needs and problems of the entire nation. Its helplessness, its lowly position in a cruel and merciless world is contrasted with Israel's loyal adherence to the belief in the One G-d. Six times we appeal to His mercy, ה' אלקי ישראל וכו'. "begging forgiveness for disregarding the sixfold warning uttered in the תוכחה." (Lev. 26) (מטה משה par. 220).

שומר ישראל. *O Guardian of Israel, guard the remnant of Israel, and suffer not Israel to perish, who say, Hear, O Israel.*

O Guardian of an only nation, guard the remnant of an only nation, and suffer not an only nation to perish, who proclaim the unity of thy name, saying, The Lord our God, the Lord is One.

O Guardian of a holy nation, guard the remnant of a holy nation, and suffer not a holy nation to perish, who thrice repeat the three-fold sanctification unto the Holy One.

O Thou who art propitiated by prayers for mercy, and art conciliated by supplications, be thou propitious and reconciled to an afflicted generation; for there is none that helpeth.

Our Father, our King, be gracious unto us and answer us, for we have no good works of our own; deal with us in charity and lovingkindness, and save us.

שומר ישראל. This תחנה constructed in a form of a פיוט continues the trend of ideas of the preceding part. The protection of the "Watchman of Israel" (Guardian) is invoked for the pitiful remnants of Israel who faithfully proclaim His Glory שמע and קדושה.

ואנחנו לא נדע. *As for us, we know not what to do; but our eyes are upon thee. Remember, O Lord, thy tender mercies and thy lovingkindness; for they have been ever of old. Let thy lovingkindness, O Lord be upon us, according as we have waited for thee. Remember not against us the iniquities of our ancestors, let thy tender mercies speedily come to meet us; for we are brought very low. Be gracious unto us, O Lord, be gracious unto us; for we are sated to the full with contempt. In wrath remember to be merciful. For he knoweth our frame; he remembereth that we are dust. Help us, O God of our salvation, for the sake of the glory of thy name; and deliver us, and pardon our sins, for thy name's sake.*

ואנחנו לא נדע. We do not know what else to do after having offered our adoration, as once Moses did, while being seated, while standing and prostrate on our faces (cf. above).

This meaning of the sentence is brought out by our reciting its first half while seated, and rising while saying מה נעשה. The verse is taken from the prayer of King Joshaphat which he uttered to attain Divine aid in his battle against the hostile armies arrayed against his people. (II Chron. 20, 12).

Various sentences follow here which make the תחנון end on a note of faith and confidence in God.

The תחנון is recited at the Shacharis and Mincha Te-filla only, never at night. In the Temple, the assembled crowd fell on their knees only after the Tamid-sacrifices of the morning and afternoon (Tamid VII, 3). Following the practices of the sacrifice itself, the confession of sins too, never takes place at night. (Meg. 20b) For the night is the time when the spell of darkness and silence impresses upon mortal man the awareness of his dependency on a Higher Power; but the sombre reflections of the sins of the past are to be undertaken during the day only, when man with the free power of his free mind can make decisions to improve his behaviour and implement them as well. Similarly תחנון is not spoken on the 9th of Ab when all Israel is depressed by the impact of its great national disaster. On days of festive joy the תחנון is also omitted — whether it be a national holiday or the private שמחה of one of the worshippers e.g., a מילה or a wedding. For the congregation shares in the joys of each of its members, similarly the community also demonstrates its solidarity with the mourner by not reciting תחנון in his house.

קדיש. The fourth part of the Morning Service is concluded and the Kaddish is recited as it is after the conclusion of every other section (cf. comm. to ישתבח p. 88). However, not the complete קדיש is said here. It is deferred until after ובא לציון in order "not to let the subsequent prayers appear insignificant."

קריאת התורה The Reading of the Torah on Mondays and Thursdays.

The rule to read the Torah in public on Sabbath morning and on the two weekdays stems from Moses. Ezra instituted the reading on Sabbath afternoons. The Talmud (B.K. 82a) finds a reference to קריאת התורה on the two weekdays in the verse: (Ex. 15, 22) 'They travelled for three days in the desert and found no water. . . . then the people rebelled against Moses and said: what shalt we drink?" The interpreters of the Scripture explained: "Water" means the Torah which is compared to water, as it says: Everyone who is thirsty (for G-d) go to the water! (Is. 55, 1). When Israel had wandered for three days without the Torah they began to revolt. Hence the prophets arose and ordained that the Torah be read to them on Sabbath, Monday and Thursday so that they be never without Torah for three consecutive days.'

The basic thought of this aggadic interpretation seems to be this. Man can not forego the element of his physical life, water, for 3 days, without suffering serious harm. So too the Jewish people cannot last without the element of their spiritual life, the Torah, for more than three days.

There is an essential difference between the reading of the Torah and the other prayers. The latter are the call of Israel to its God — whereas the reading of the Torah represents the message of G-d to His people. Hence for the recital of the other prayers the שליח ציבור, the messenger of the congregation, stands in front of it, to submit the requests of the community to G-d. But the reading of the Torah is performed on the בימה in the midst of the congregation, from an elevated position, as if God had gathered the people in assembly around Himself to proclaim His will to them.

ארך אפים ל-א. *O G-d, slow to anger and abounding in lovingkindness and truth, rebuke us not in thine anger. Have pity upon thy people, O Lord, and save us from all evil. We have sinned against thee, O Lord; forgive, we beseech thee, according to the abundance of thy tender mercies. O G-d.*

O God, slow to anger and abounding in lovingkindness and truth, hide not thy face from us. Have pity upon Israel, thy people, and deliver us from all evil. We have sinned against thee, O Lord; forgive, we beseech thee, according to the abundance of thy tender mercies, O God.

ארך אפים ל-א. The opening of the Book of the Divine Law makes us aware of our insufficiency as compared with the standards of the Divine Will in the Torah.

ויהי בנסע. *And it came to pass, when the ark set forward, that Moses said, Rise up, O Lord, and thine enemies shall be scattered, and they that hate thee shall flee before thee. For out of Zion shall go forth the Law, and the word of the Lord from Jerusalem.*

Blessed be he who in his holiness gave the Law to his people Israel.

ויהי בנסע. As the Scroll of the Law is carried into our midst to speak to us, we recall the words which Moses uttered (Num. 10, 35) whenever the Holy Ark broke camp. They tell of the irresistible power of the Divine Word which will ultimately be victorious. For wherever the Torah goes, G-d goes, 'קומה ה. — כי מציון The Law will reign far beyond the circle of Judaism, and will bring justice and peace to all mankind. — ברוך. We, therefore, praise Him Who has chosen us to be heralds of His Truth.

בריך שמה. *Blessed be the name of the Sovereign of the universe. Blessed be thy crown and thy abiding-place. Let thy favour rest with thy people Israel for ever, show them the redemption of thy right hand in thy holy temple. Bestow upon us the benign gift of thy light, and in mercy accept our supplications. May it be thy will to prolong our life in well-being. Let me also be numbered among the righteous, so that thou mayest be mercifu unto me, and have me in thy keeping, with all that belong to me and to thy people Israel. Thou art he that feedeth and sustaineth all; thou art he that ruleth over all; thou art he that ruleth over kings, for dominion is thine. I am the servant of the Holy One, blessed be he, before whom and before whose glorious Law I prostrate myself at all times. not in man do I put my trust, nor upon any angel do I rely, but upon the God of heaven, who is the God of truth, and whose Law is truth, and whose prophets are prophets of truth, and who aboundeth in deeds of goodness and truth. In him I put my trust, and unto his holy and glorious name I utter praises. May it be thy will to open my heart unto thy Law, and to fulfil the wishes of my heart and of the hearts of all thy people Israel for good, for life, and for peace.*

בריך שמה follows the basic principle determining the choice of *all* the prayers and biblical quotations recited during

the taking of the Torah from the Ark and the restoring of
it to its place. The Zohar (פ' ויקהל) formulates this idea as
follows: "When the congregation takes the Torah from the
the Ark to read from it, the Gates of Mercy are opened in
Heaven and Love is awakened on High; therefore this prayer
should be spoken:" Thus this prayer makes use, as it were, of
a propitious hour to pray for the fulfillment of our hearts'
deepest desires. For a similar reason the אב הרחמים and the
יהי רצון are recited at this point of the service and the 13
attributes of mercy invoked on Holidays. The verse ואני תפלתי
alludes to this "hour of benevolence," עת רצון.

גדלו. *Magnify the Lord with me, and let us exalt his*
name together.

Thine, O Lord is the greatness, and the power, and
the glory, and the victory, and the majesty: for all that is
in the heaven and in the earth is thine; thine, O Lord, is the
kingdom, and the supremacy as head over all. Exalt ye the
Lord our G-d, and worship at his footstool: holy is he. Exalt
ye the Lord our G-d, and worship at his holy mount; for the
Lord our G-d is holy.

אב הרחמים. *May the Father of mercy have mercy upon*
a people that have been borne by him. May he remember the
covenant with the patriarchs, deliver our souls from evil hours,
check the evil inclination in them that have been carried by
him, grant us of his grace an everlasting deliverance, and in
the attribute of his goodness fulfil our desires by salvation and
mercy.

גדלו. Our rejoicing over the Torah manifests itself in
our rejoicing over the One Who gave it to us and in our admiration of His unattainable Greatness. To the call of the
reader, גדלו the congregation responds with verses praising His
Greatness and Power לך השם וכו'.

אב הרחמים, העמוסים, הנשואים, (cf. Isaiah 46, 3-4). We
are burdened with sufferings and tasks since the beginning of
our historical existence. Yet, at the same time we have been
sustained by His Grace and aid from the first day of our life.

ותגלה. *And may his kingdom be soon revealed and*
made visible unto us, and may he be gracious unto our rem-

nant and unto the remnant of his people, the house of Israel,
granting them grace, kindness, mercy and favour; and let us
say, Amen. Ascribe, all of you, greatness unto our God, and
render honour to the Law.

ותגלה forms the concluding sentence of the more elaborate piece על הכל, quoted in Soferim XIV, 12, which is not
spoken in its entirety on workdays, "in order not to prolong
the Service unduly for the working people." (לבוש). הכל
הבו גדל. . . etc. From this phrase with which Moses summoned the Jewish people to pay attention, our Sages deduced
the precept to speak a Bracha before the reading of the Torah:
"When I mention the Name of the Lord ascribe greatness to
our God, (i.e., bless Him)."

ברכו cf. p. 90 — ברוך אשר בחר cf. p. 45

ברוך אשר נתן. *Blessed art thou, O Lord our God, King*
of the universe, who hast given us the Law of truth, and hast
planted everlasting life in our midst. Blessed art thou, O Lord,
who givest the Law.

ברוך אשר נתן. In the Bracha recited before the reading
of the Torah, we proclaim that the sole aim of our election
is to fulfill the Torah in theory and practice. The Bracha
following the reading chiefly expresses our gratitude for having received along with the Torah, the gift of "Eternal Life."
The Talmud (Jer. Ber. VII, 1) deduces that Bracha from the
Biblical Command that we speak a blessing after having partaken from a meal (Deut. 8, 10). We are no less grateful
for satisfaction of our spiritual needs than for His providing
us with our daily bread. For the Torah is our spiritual life-
element. It is תורת אמת eternally immutable, the Truth, which
knows neither change nor evolution. This first part of the
Blessing refers to the Written Torah which is absolute and
unchanging (ח"א par. 139, 10). The second half points
to the Oral Laws. This, G-d has "planted in our midst" as
עץ החיים the Tree of Life, to grow and to thrive, to produce
from its roots, new knowledge and new ideas, and it itself
is kept alive by this activity. (cf. Chag. 3b). Through it we
too shall grow and develop and so gain "Eternal Life." For
this end God has planted the עץ החיים in our midst. — In the
Bracha before the reading we say את תורתו, *His* Torah; now

we speak of the Eternal Life planted in *our* midst. Indeed, when a man has learned Torah it has become his own, and only then does it bless him with Eternal Life. (Av. Z. 19a).

וזאת התורה. *And this is the Law which Moses set before the children of Israel, according to the commandment of the Lord by the hand of Moses. It is a tree of life to them that grasp it, and of them that uphold it every one is rendered happy. Its ways are ways of pleasantness, and all its paths are peace. Length of days is in its right hand; in its left hand are riches and honour. It pleased the Lord, for his righteousness' sake, to magnify the Law and to make it honourable.*

וזאת התורה. The Torah is lifted up high above the heads of the congregation, unrolled and shown to all. "It is raised far above the community, upheld and uplifted by man's endeavor." (cf. Ramban Deut. 27, 26). We recognize in it the same law which Moses brought to the בני ישראל. It is for us to keep and fulfill. But it is not a "Mosaic" law. It was proclaimed על פי השם, from the mouth of G-d. יד משה, Moses' hand merely wrote and carried it. The words על פי are attached to the verse וזאת התורה (Deut. 4, 44). They are taken from Num. 9,23, which tells how rest and departure of the Desert Camp depended on the direct command of God. (In the edition of a Siddur which was published in Jerusalem with the commentary of the Vilna Gaon the entire verse is quoted, . . . 'על פי ה' יחנו ועל פי ה' יסעו וכו. In our editions, by some error, only the end of the verse was retained).

יהי רצון. *May it be the will of our Father who is in heaven to establish the Temple, the house of our life, and to restore his divine presence in our midst, speedily in our days; and let us say, Amen.*

May it be the will of our Father who is in heaven to have mercy upon us and upon our remnant, and to keep destruction and the plague from us and from all his people, the house of Israel; and let us say: Amen.

May it be the will of our Father who is in heaven to preserve among us the wise men of Israel; them, their wives, their sons and daughters, their disciples and the disciples of their disciples in all places of their habitation; and let us say, Amen.

May it be the will of our Father who is in heaven that good tidings of salvation and comfort may be heard and published, and that he may gather our banished ones from the four corners of the earth; and let us say, Amen.

As for our brethren, the whole house of Israel, such of them as are given over to trouble or captivity, whether they abide on the sea or on the dry land,—may the All-present have mercy upon them, and bring them forth from trouble to enlargement, from darkness to light, and from subjection to redemption, now speedily and at a near time; and let us say, Amen.

יהי רצון belongs to the special supplications recited Monday and Thursday describing the typical sufferings of Israel in Exile.

יהללו*Let them praise the name of the Lord; for his his name alone is exalted:*

Cong. *His majesty is above the earth and heaven; and he hath lifted up a horn for his people, to the praise of all his loving ones, even of the children of Israel, the people near unto him. Praise ye the Lord.*

יהללו. (End of Ps. 148). Having extolled the Torah as the very element of our lives, reader and congregation now join in acclaiming God whose Glory far exceeds even that of His Torah, the work of His Hands. (מטה משה).

לדוד מזמור. *The earth is the Lord's and the fulness thereof; the world, and they that dwell therein. For it is he that hath founded it upon the seas, and established it upon the floods. Who may ascend the mountain of the Lord? And who may stand in his holy place? He that hath clean hands and a pure heart; who hath not set his desire upon vanity, and hath not sworn deceitfully. He shall receive a blessing from the Lord, and righteousness from the G-d of his salvation. This is the generation of them that seek after him, that seek thy face, (O G-d of) Jacob! (Selah.) Lift up your heads, O ye gates; and be ye lifted up, ye everlasting doors, that the King of glory may come in. Who, then, is the King of glory?*

The Lord strong and mighty, the Lord mighty in battle. Lift up your heads, O ye gates; yea, lift them up, ye everlasting doors, that the King of glory may come in. Who then, is the King of glory? The Lord of hosts, he is the King of glory. (Selah.)

לדוד מזמור. On workdays and Holy-days which occur on weekdays, Psalm 24 is sung while the Torah is restored to the Ark. The last verses of this Psalm were recited when the Holy Ark was carried into the Temple, שאו שערים ראשיכם. As we now open the doors of the Ark to receive His Law, thus in times to come the gates of the world will spring open for the triumphant entry of the King of glory. At first they will not open on their own, שאו והנשאו, they have to be opened. God, however, will conquer all that resist His will. Then, the Gates of humanity will open freely and voluntarily, שאו ושאו, and G-d will enter as השם צבאות, the G-d of Mankind.

ובנחה. *And when it rested, he said, Return, O Lord, unto the ten thousands of the thousands of Israel. Arise, O Lord, unto thy resting place; thou and the ark of thy strength. Let thy priests be clothed with righteousness; and let thy loving ones shout for joy. For the sake of David thy servant, turn not away the face of thine anointed. For I give you good doctrine; forsake ye not my Law. It is a tree of life to them that grasp it, and of them that uphold it every one is rendered happy. Its ways are ways of pleasantness, and all its paths are peace. Turn thou us unto thee, O Lord, and we shall return: renew our days as of old.*

ובנחה corresponds to the ויהי בנסע הארון which accompanied the taking of the Torah from the Ark. While Moses recited the ויהי when the Holy Ark broke camp, he spoke the ובנחה when it came to rest. When "the enemies of G-d will be scattered" — then the word of G-d can come to rest and dwell within the circle of men. Then the "thousands of Israel" will become "myriads" through natural increase from within and accretion from without.

אשרי. The Shacharis had, in ש"ע and תחנון, attained its climax. We had reached the "World of the Pure Spirit" (cf. p. 12). Now we descend again into the world of every-day life. This last part is opened by the 145th Psalm, because

it shows in impressive clarity how the omnipotent God, the
mighty King, to the recognition of whom the prayer has led
us in a gradual ascent, is also the Universal Provider, the
loving and just Providence, close to all those "who call to
Him in earnest." For the verse פותח את ידיך ומשביע לכל חי
רצון is the focal point of this psalm (Ber. 46), and we have
explained in our comment on the אשרי (p. 75) why the
Sages stressed the importance of this psalm, why they ordained
its threefold repetition every day. The Zohar (פ' פנחס)
further explains this point: "Why thrice? Because of the mention of sustenance and provision? But this occurs only twice
a day, as evident from Ex. 16,8: In the evening He will
give you meat to eat and in the morning bread to the full!
Hence it follows that אשרי is said twice a day as a prayer
for sustenance and once as a hymn to the "Hand of God"
which is always open. The first אשרי is the one of homage.
Its context is the other psalms of praise (the פסוקי דזמרה).
Only the second one, the one that follows upon the Tefilla
represents a prayer for sustenance; for only after we have
praised God and given Him his due (the Tefilla) is it be-
fitting to pray for ourselves."

"It is true, according to this, that in the Mincha too,
the אשרי should be said after the Tefilla. It precedes it, however, because the time after the Mincha Tefilla is considered
already belonging to the night, - - - at which time God grants
sustenance only with a "stern face," as the commentators
point out to Ex. 16, 7." — This explanation of the Zohar
shows also why the אשרי is not said at מעריב and why the
three recitals are distributed over שחרית and מנחה.

למנצח. *The Lord answer thee in the day of trouble;
the name of the God of Jacob set thee up on high; send thee
help from the sanctuary, and uphold thee out of Zion; remember all thy offerings, and accept thy burnt sacrifice
(Selah); grant thee thy heart's desire, and fulfil thy purpose.
We will exult in thy salvation, and in the name of our God
we will set up our banners: the Lord fulfil all thy petitions.
Now know I that the Lord saveth his anointed; he will answer him from his holy heaven with the mighty saving acts
of his right hand. Some trust in chariots and some in horses,
but we will make mention of the name of the Lord our God.*

*They are bowed down and fallen, but we are risen and stand
upright. Save, Lord: may the King answer us on the day
when we call.*

למנצח. This psalm was sung by David after the completion of 18 Psalms of praise (or 19 respectively, cf. Ber. 9b).
We recite it at this juncture of the Service to indicate that
only after we have praised God in the 18 Berachoth of the
ש"ע (. . . יענך), will God answer us on the day of distress.
Hence we recite this psalm after the ש"ע (Abudr.). This
psalm too develops the idea of the אשרי further, by pointing
out that when the danger is most acute we should set our hope
in אלקי יעקב the G-d who aided Jacob in all the dark hours of
his life. On days of festive character the psalm with its mention of the יום צרה, the day of distress is omitted. But the
psalm also possesses an inner connection with the following
ובא לציון, namely in its allusion to the ישועת ה', the future
salvation (Tur. par. 131). Daniel (12, 1) calls the period preceding the coming of the Messiah a period which will be darkened by heavy battles and profound upheavals, עת צרה. To
this the psalm refers and promises the help of God for His
Messiah כי הושיע ה' משיחו. Thus the ground is prepared for
the introductory phrase of the following ובא לציון גואל.

ובא לציון. *And a redeemer shall come to Zion and to
them that turn from transgression in Jacob, saith the Lord.
And as for me, this is my covenant with them, saith the
Lord: my spirit that is upon thee, and my words which I
have put in thy mouth, shall not depart out of thy mouth,
nor out of the mouth of thy seed, nor out of the mouth of
thy seed's seed, saith the Lord, from henceforth and forever.*

*But thou art holy, O thou that dwellest amid the
praises of Israel. And one cried unto another, and said, Holy,
holy, holy is the Lord of hosts; the whole earth is full of his
glory. And they receive sanction the one from the other, and
say, Holy in the highest heavens, the place of his divine
abode; holy upon earth, the work of his might; holy for
ever and to all eternity is the Lord of hosts; the whole earth
is full of the radiance of his glory. Then a wind lifted me
up, and I heard behind me the voice of a great rushing*

(saying), Blessed be the glory of the Lord from his place.
Then a wind lifted me up, and I heard behind me the voice
of a great rushing, of those who uttered praises, and said,
Blessed be the glory of the Lord from the region of his divine
abode. The Lord shall reign for ever and ever. The kingdom
of the Lord endureth for ever and to all eternity. O Lord,
the G-d of Abraham, of Isaac and of Israel, our fathers,
keep this for ever in the imagination of the thoughts of the
heart of thy people, and direct their heart unto thee. And
he, being merciful, forgiveth iniquity and destroyeth not; yea,
many a time he turneth his anger away, and doth not stir
up all his wrath. For thou, O Lord, art good and forgiving,
and abounding in lovingkindness to all them that call upon
thee. Thy righteousness is an everlasting righteousness, and
thy Law is truth. Thou wilt show truth to Jacob and lovingkindness to Abraham, according as thou hast sworn unto
our fathers from the days of old. Blessed be the Lord day by
day; if one burdeneth us, G-d is our salvation. (Selah).
The Lord of hosts is with us; the G-d of Jacob is our stronghold. (Selah.) O Lord of hosts, happy is the man who trusteth
in thee. Save, Lord: may the King answer us on the day when
we call.

      Blessed is our G-d, who hath created us for his
glory, and has separated us from them that go astray, and
hath given us the Law of truth and planted everlasting life
in our midst. May he open our heart unto his Law, and place
his love and fear within our hearts, that we may do his will
and serve him with a perfect heart, that we may not labour
in vain, nor bring forth for confusion. May it be thy will,
O Lord our G-d and G-d of our fathers, that we may keep
thy statutes in this world, and be worthy to live to witness
and inherit happiness and blessing in the days of the Messiah
and in the life of the world to come. To the end that my
glory may sing praise unto thee, and not be silent; O Lord
my G-d, I will give thanks unto thee for ever. Blessed is the
man that trusteth in the Lord, and whose trust the Lord is.
Trust ye in the Lord for ever; for in J-h the Lord is an
everlasting rock. And they that know thy name wil put
their trust in thee; for thou hast not forsaken them that seek
thee, Lord. It pleased the Lord, for his righteousness' sake,
to magnify the Law and to make it honourable.

וּבָא לְצִיוֹן. The core of this prayer is the קְדוּשָׁה and its Aramaic translation, the Targum Jonathan. It gave to the entire piece the name קְדוּשָׁה דְּסִדְרָא. It is the third time the קְדוּשָׁה is repeated in the Shacharis. The first recital in the בִּרְכַת יוֹצֵר led us into the lofty sphere of the עוֹלָם הַיְצִירָה, to listen into the chorus of the angels. The second קְדוּשָׁה is spoken at the very climax of Prayer in the motionless silence of the Tefilla. The קְדוּשָׁה דְּסִדְרָא finally, is pronounced in the concluding part of the Shacharis, which, as pointed out, leads us back into the regions of normal every-day life. According to S. R. Hirsch, the name קְדוּשָׁה דְּסִדְרָא itself indicates that its purpose is, to take us back into "the normal *order* of things." It calls for a Kedusha, a "Sanctification of G-d" in the very midst of a life of action, of working and suffering. Jonathan's translaton too points in this direction. It sees in the threefold קְדוּשׁוֹת not a threefold intensification of Holiness, but rather, the declaration that He is "Holy in the highest Heaven, the place of His abode — Holy on earth, the work of His might — Holy throughout the endless expanse of time." The concluding sentence "the whole *earth* is filled with His Glory" further emphasizes the idea. Finally the fact that the וּבָא לְצִיוֹן is, at this juncture of the Service, spoken on workdays only, also affirms that the "sanctification of everyday life" is its main function. We are to enter into the struggles of the day, suffused by the idea that He is with us at every moment of our earthly being and willing. It is an idea which touches the very foundations of our existence, inspiring us with awe and apprehension but also with profound pride and inner satisfaction.

There are varying accounts of the origin of this prayer. It is said to have been joined to the Shacharis in order to enable latecomers to recite the קְדוּשָׁה. This assumption is supported by the fact that the piece contains 19 Divine Names, as many as the שֶׁמַ"ע, and by its being omitted on Sabbath and Festivals when people are not prevented by their work from attending the entire Service. According to another opinion the Kedusha and its Aramaic translation is read in order to fulfill the duty to study Torah daily. (This would explain the frequent reference to the Torah in the וּבָא לְצִיוֹן.) However, the extraordinary emphasis placed on the Kedusha and the request that it be heard by everyone, can only be appreciated in the light of a view expressed in the Talmud (סוטה 49a). There it says: "Since the destruction of the Temple every day is more cursed than the preceding one; and the existence of the world is assured only by the קדושה דסדרא and the words אמן יהא שמה רבא וגו', spoken after the study of the Torah." Rashi comments that "this refers to the Kedusha in ובא לציון which was introduced in order that all Israel may study (Torah) every day. The translation, which is included in the Prayer, is considered as study. Since this piece is recited by all Israel, scholars and laymen alike and since its contents are the sanctification of the Divine Name as well as subject-matter for study, it has a special distinction."

The deeper meaning of this Talmudic saying is clarified by the following consideration. The Temple, as long as it existed, was the place whence the Holy Name was proclaimed to be sanctified over the whole world. Since the day of the destruction of the Temple the שכינה was banished from earth. Now a curse hovers over a godless world, a curse which can only be suspended, by proclaiming and promulgating His Name through the truth of the Torah. The Torah thus became a substitute for what the Temple was once to mankind — just as the Torah schools of Yavne once saved Judaism when the Sanctuary had fallen. Henceforth the supreme aim of Judaism was the "Sanctification of the Name," קידוש השם. This was fulfilled by the study and furtherance of the Torah. The Kedusha in ובא לציון as the proclamation of Divine Holiness rising from the midst of Torah-study, nay, being itself Torah-Study, became, as it were, the קידוש השם par excellence. It became קדושה דסדרא, the קדושה of Torah Study, as Rashi explains: סדרי פרשיות תורה. For the same reason all public Torah-Study is to be followed by the קדיש (containing as its central theme the אמן יהא שמה רבא), for it expresses the ultimate of Torah Study: קידוש השם.

Pursuing the trend of thoughts outlined here, the prayer begins with two verses from Isaiah (59, 20 and 21), ובא לציון and ואני. They point out that the redemption (promised in the preceding למנצח) shall be realized through the covenant of the Torah (and תשובה). For the Sanctification of G-d rests on the praises of Israel, ואתה קדוש. The wish for a speedy and universal recognition of the Kingdom of G-d

ה' ימלוך concludes the Kedusha. Then follows the entreaty that He strengthen us for our task (ה' אלקי וגו') and condone our weakness כי אתה, והוא רחום. Even in exile we recognize His perfect justice צדקתך צדק לעולם, תתן, and pray for the redemption promised to our fathers in love and truthfulness, for the protection and salvation which He so often granted to us in our past. ברוך — ביום קראנו.

Now follow some sentences (opening with ברוך אלקינו) which are attached here "to conclude the prayer with a homage to the Creator." They belong to the most beautiful passages of the prayer book. They combine the profound gratitude for our sublime destiny as Jews with the fervent prayer that with Divine aid we may always prove worthy of it and attain through Torah and Avodah to the highest plane of ethical perfection. May we then be chosen to see the era of the Messiah and the world to come. As we look down from this lofty plane upon the erratic course of human life, the call rings out, never to lose trust in G-d, whose help is the rock which never yields. — The final sentence השם חפץ למען צדקו is the one spoken at the conclusion of every Torah discourse, seeking "greatness and grandeur" for the Torah.

A brief remark has to be added on the historical background of this קדושה. According to ancient traditions — which we recounted in our commentary to לעולם יהא אדם (p. 38) — the recital of the קדושה was once prohibited. Guards were posted in the synagogues to supervise the observance of this decree. The קדושה was, therefore, postponed to the end of the Service when the informers had already left the Synagogues; and the Targum translation was added, so that as it were, two קדושות were recited to replace the two omitted in ברוך יוצר and the ש"ע. On Sabbath and Holy Days, however, there was an opportunity to insert the קדושה in the Mussaf. The קדושה דסדרא could therefore be dispensed with. As is customary in such cases, the קדושה דסדרא has been retained even after the decree had been revoked, "in order that the sin may not cause evil again" [i.e. the return of the decree].

And now, I pray thee, let the power of the Lord be great, according as thou hast spoken. Remember, O Lord, thy tender mercies and thy lovingkindness; for they have been ever of old.

יתגדל. *Magnified and sanctified be his great name in the world which he hath created according to his will. May he establish his kingdom during your life and during your days, and during the life of all the house of Israel, even speedily and at a near time, and say ye, Amen.*

Let his great name be blessed for ever and to all eternity.

Blessed, praised and glorified, exalted, extolled and honoured, magnified and lauded be the name of the Holy One, blessed be he; though he be high above all the blessings and hymns, praises and consolations, which are uttered in the world; and say ye, Amen.

Accept our prayers in mercy and in favour.

May the prayers and supplications of all Israel be accepted by their Father who is in heaven; and say ye, Amen.

Let the name of the Lord be blessed from this time forth and for evermore.

May there be abundant peace from heaven, and life for us and for all Israel; and say ye, Amen.

My help is from the Lord, who made heaven and earth.

He who maketh peace in his high places, may he make peace for us and for all Israel; and say ye, Amen.

קדיש. To conclude the Morning Service, the קדיש שלם. the Complete Kadish is recited here. It differs from the Half-Kadish spoken at various previous stages of the Service — in that it contains the added request for the favorable acceptance of our prayers תתקבל, for abundant peace and happiness (יהא), and in the end phrase, the customary blessing of peace, עושה שלום. The significance of the Kadish as an epilogue to the larger sections of the Service has (already) been commented upon (cf. pp. 88, 170). It proclaims that through all the changing conditions of times and places, the universal recognition of His Name in its undiminished grandeur שמיה רבה, shall be achieved; in a world which He has created, כרעותיה, according to His Will. All the apparent shortcomings and deficiencies of this world cannot prevent the goal from being attained, nay, they are in themselves but the means to attain it. For He could surely have created a different world if this would have better suited His purpose. The Kadish emphasizes at every turning point of the prayer, the unwavering faith of Israel in the ultimate realization of this aim of קידוש השם, בחייכון, in your lifetime and in the lifetime of all Israel as the reader proclaims. The congregation responds to it with Amen, making this ardent and confident faith their own. They add the wish and the hope יהא that the recognition of His Great Name be spread through all eternity and be brought to full realization on earth. To this praise the reader answers that the true greatness and splendor of His Glory extends לעלא far beyond all blessing, song, homage and praise that the mind of mortal man is capable of uttering. And to this confession too the congregation responds with "Amen." (Hirsch).

The language of the Kadish is Aramaic. One of the reasons for this, advanced in the Tur (Par. 56), is that it was customary to recite the Kadish after public Torah discourses and the majority of the people then present understood Aramaic only which was their vernacular. The Zohar, however, remarks that a profound idea intrinsically interwoven with the meaning of the Kadish itself finds expression in its idiom. We employ a secular language, to indicate that the secular has to be interpenetrated by the Holy in order to attain the supreme goal of the יתגדל ויתקדש "that His Great Name be magnified and sanctified on earth." — Thus the Kadish becomes a positive and creative act of sanctification. Its designation too as "Kadish" — the Aramaic translation of the masculine adjective "Kadosh" — expresses the identical idea. Here the maculine form, symbolizing active forming and constructing, prevails; whereas the "Kedusha," by its feminine form, symbolises the feminine way of paying homage, for the Kedusha is but the echo of the celestial chorus, perceived by Israel and returned heavenwards with renewed fervor.

The all-important position which the Kadish holds in Judaism is vividly illustrated by the following Talmudic account: R. Jose once entered one of the ruins of Jerusalem, to pray. When he had concluded, the prophet Eliyahu who had waited for him at the entrance, approached him and asked: "What did you hear in this ruin?" R. Jose answered: "I heard a voice crying mournfully like a dove: Woe unto

my children for whose transgressions I had to destroy My
House and burn My Temple, and exile them among the
nations." Then Eliyahu said: "My son! By your life! Not only
at this hour, but thrice daily does the voice repeat its lam-
entation. Moreover, whenever Israel enters its synagogues
and houses of Torah-study and proclaims the יהא שמה רבא,
He, as it were, nods with His head and says: "Happy the
King who is thus praised in His House." (Ber. 3a). This
story is a vivid illustration of the idea, that since the destruction
of the Sanctuary G-d has, so to speak, placed His hope for
universal recognition on the יהא שמה רבא, the unrestrained
praise which resounds time and again from Israel's places
of worship and learning. — "The gates of the Gan Eden
are opened for him who utters the אמן יהא שמה רבא with full
force," declares the Talmud (Sab. 119b). We, therefore,
pray before we recite the Kadish: ואתה יגדל נא כח (Num.
14, 17) that G-d may strengthen the *force* which utters the
Kadish. However, the words ואתה וכו' gain added significance
when regarded from a different angle. The unfolding of the
Divine *Force* is the theme of the entire Kadish and especially
of the יהא שמה רבא. This sentence contains 28 letters equalling
the numerical value of the word "כח" (Force). For 28 is
the symbol of the "full force;" typified by the 28 days of
the moon's complete cycle. This number is also obtained by
the sevenfold increase of the four-lettered Name of G-d, the
"שמה רבא." So this sentence comprised of seven words is
followed by seven expressions of praise (from וישתבח to ויתהלל)
and has to be spoken בכל כח. Finally the part from בעלמא
to יהא שמה also contains 28 words. (During the ten days
of תשובה therefore, when the word ולעלא is added, the two
words מן כל are contracted into one: מכל.) Some remarks on the
text of the Kadish have to be added: יתגדל according to Ex.
38, 23. The Kadish contains altogether 10 expressions of praise
corresponding to the 10 terms of homage employed in the
psalms, (Jer. Meg. I; cf. פר"ח) or to the 10 words of command
with which "He created the world to His Will" as the
Kadish mentions בחייכון — בעלמא די ברא cf. Malachi 3,
2 and Sanh. 98b. — לעלם cf. Daniel 7, 18 and Targum Ex.
15, 18, — There must be no pause or interruption between
עלמיא and יתברך for, out of the wish that His Name be

blessed grows immediately the demand that He be forever extolled. — "In the following expressions of praise the Aramaic form is identical with the Hebrew. Many have been led by this fact to the erroneous assumption that this part of the Kadish is written in Hebrew" (עכ״י). — בריך הוא refers to the foregoing as well as to the passage following it. — ונחמתא, may be understood as the Aramaic of מנחה (Targ. Joel 2, 14 a.o.), and means *praise* in the Arabic root חם. or else may finally express our hope for *consolation* (cf. נחמה) from on High.

In a Kadish recited after a discourse upon the Mishnah, Talmud, or Agadah the formula על ישראל is inserted here. It prays for the welfare of the students of the Torah and also of "all Israel," so that they be enabled to devote themselves unhindered to their sacred task. — צלותהון ובעותהון is the Targum for בחרבי ובקשתי (Gen. 48, 22), "my sword and my bow,"Israel's weapons are prayer and devotion. — יהא שלמא. The Kadish closes, in the same manner as the ש״ע, Grace after Meals and the Priest's Blessing, with a supplication for the quintessence of all blessings: peace. — עושה שלום cf. comm. at the end of the ש״ע. On the orphans' Kadish cf. comm. after עלינו.

עלינו. *It is our duty to praise the Lord of all things, to ascribe greatness to him who formed the world in the beginning, since he hath not made us like the nations of other lands, and hath not placed us like other families of the earth, since he hath not assigned unto us a portion as unto them, nor a lot as unto all their multitude. For we bend the knee and offer worship and thanks before the supreme King of kings, the Holy One, blessed be he, who stretched forth the heavens and laid the foundations of the earth, the seat of whose glory is in the heavens above, and the abode of whose might is in the loftiest heights. He is our G-d; there is none else; in truth he is our King; there is none besides him; as it is written in his Law. And thou shalt know this day, and lay it to thine heart, that the Lord he is G-d in heaven above and upon the earth beneath; there is none else.*

We therefore hope in thee, O Lord our G-d, that we may speedily behold the glory of thy might, when thou wilt remove

*the abominations from the earth, and the idols will be utterly
cut off, when the world will be perfected under the kingdom of
the Almighty, and all the children of flesh will call upon thy
name, when thou will turn unto thyself all the wicked of the
earth. Let all the inhabitants of the world perceive and know
that unto thee every knee must bow, every tongue must swear.
Before thee, O Lord our G-d, let them bow and fall; and unto
thy glorious name let them give honour; let them all accept
the yoke of thy kingdom, and do thou reign over them speedily,
and for ever and ever. For the kingdom is thine, and to all
eternity thou wilt reign in glory; as it is written in thy Law,
The Lord shall reign for ever and ever. And it is said, And
the Lord shall be king over all the earth; in that day shall
the Lord be One, and his name One.*

עלינו. From the Mussaf Service of Rosh Hashono,
where it opens the מלכיות section, this prayer has been taken
into the daily service at a comparatively late date (circa 1300
C.E.). No specific reason for this transfer can be found in
the sources. Later authors assume that the idea developed in
the Olenu, viz. the future harmony of all men in their recognition of the One G-d, was considered the most fitting finale
to prayer. Israel's parting request is not the wish for destruction
of its innumerable persecutors, but the hope that "all false idols
may disappear from the earth, to build a world in the dominion
of the Almighty."

The Olenu is among the most meaningful of our
prayers. In its first part it emphatically pronounces the
decisive difference between our belief in G-d and the belief
of the rest of mankind; while the second part with equal emphasis utters our confident hope (which is part of even that belief)
that ultimately all men will return to G-d. A return to G-d,
according to the Jewish view does not imply the acceptance of
the Jewish faith at all, but rather the recognition of the One
G-d as the Immutable Source of Truth and lovingkindness, and
the decision to serve Him, each one in the way willed by
Him (cf. our comm. to שלא עשני נכרי p. 27).

שלא עשנו. G-d has fashioned us into a nation in a unique
manner, ולא שמנו and gave us a special position among the
families of the earth.

כרעים expresses the submission, משתחוים the complete surrender to the fulfillment of the Divine command — ומודים. The object is שהוא נוטה שמים וגו'. The present tense conveys that He not only *created* Heaven and Earth but that they are also kept in existence by His will. — אפס זולתו. Everything, from the smallest particle of matter to the vast expanse of the cosmos, only exists because of Him. והשבת אל לבבך. If ever this conviction should grow dim and vague in your conscience, "restore it to your heart" and make it dominate your mind with renewed vigor. — לראות מהרה. That He will attain His ultimate aim to be universally recognised, we are certain; but we pray that it may happen "soon," that we may witness it.

The עלינו is said to have been composed by Joshua upon his entrance into the Holy Land (R. Hai Gaon and Kol Bo). He desired to impress upon Israel the ideas of their distinction and of their direct dependence on the One G-d, in the hour when they were about to enter personal contact with the pagan peoples of Palestine. הושע is supposed to have hidden his original name (Hoshea) in the acrostics of the first sentence read backward: עלינו, שלא, ואנחנו, הוא. Others attribute the authorship of the עלינו to the Babylonian Amora Rav, who is mentioned as the author of the other Piutim of the Mussaf of ראש השנה (Jer. R. H. I 5). His literary style seems apparent in the עלינו. It is not impossible, however, that the ideas expressed originally by Joshua formed the basis for a later arrangement by Rav.

With the עלינו prayer on their lips many of the saintly martyrs of the Middle Ages went to their death by sword and fire. For no other prayer expresses so powerfully the unshakable faith of Israel in the Eternal G-d. Later, when the עלינו was accepted in the daily liturgy one of its sentences caused repeated attacks against the Jewish religion.

In Germany, this did not cease for centuries after. The passage in which we thank G-d, "that He has not made us like unto the other families of the earth nor our lot like theirs," was followed by the words: שהם וכו' "for they bow to void and vanity and pray to a god who does not help." These words are taken from the prophecies of Isaiah (30, 7 and 45, 20). In the year 1400 a baptised Jew spread the calumny that these words referred to the founder of Christianity. He "proved" it by pointing out that "וריק" as well as "יקרו" had the same numerical value as Yeshu, 316. Although Menasse ben Israel in his "Salvation of Israel" and others thoroughly refuted the accusation, it was raised time and again. Finally the entire phrase was dropped from the Ashkenazic prayer book.

קדיש יתום, the orphan's Kadish. The Kadish after עלינו belongs to the number of the prescribed seven daily קדשים. (ט"ז. Par. 55, 1). However, the Minhag has been generally adopted that it is recited by those who are mourning for their parents.

Jewish tradition holds that the souls of the deceased parents are redeemed by the Kadish that their children recite in public. The following story — recounted in various versions — is pertinent to this. Rabbi Akiba once saw a man burdened with a heavy load of wood wandering about a cemetery. He asked the man: "Are you man or demon?" "I am a dead man" was the answer, "who has to gather wood every day to prepare a funeral pyre for myself." "What was your occupation while you were alive?" demanded Rabbi Akiba. "I was a tax-collecter who favored the wealthy and oppressed the poor, and committed acts of despicable immorality." "Have you heard from your superiors, whether there is any means of saving you?" asked Rabbi Akiba. "Do not delay me any longer," was the answer, "lest I contact the wrath of my superiors. There is no way to redeem me unless my wife, whom I left pregnant, should bear a son, and he should recite in public ברכו את השם המבורך or say the Kadish. But who would teach him?" R. Akiba did not rest until he had found the woman and her son. With great effort he succeeded in teaching him to pray, and to recite the Kadish and ברכו in public. Then the father appeared to R. Akiba in a dream and said: "You have redeemed me from the punishment of the Gehinnom, may your spirit, therefore, rest in Gan Eden." (Cf. מנורת המאור, נר א' כלל א' חלק ב').

It is clearly evident from this story, that the Kadish in itself is by no means — as has been claimed — a prayer for the salvation of the soul of the deceased. Nor does the text of the Kadish contain one single word which could be interpreted to that effect.

The public recital of the Kadish, with its summons to the congregation to join in the praise of G-d, is rather a manifestation of the fact that the parental root of the child is not without merit, that the parent's life was not lived without furthering the cause of the Good, the promulgation of G-d's name on earth. The *actions* of the children thus influence the judgment passed on the parents on High. For their lives do not end with their physical death but are continued in the actions of the sons. (cf. Higayon Nefesh p. 32). — This Kadish is recited for eleven months only. By continuing to say the Kadish through the entire year of mourning, the son would, as it were, brand his father as a sinner whose judgment lasts for a full year. (י"ד 376, 4). On the anniversary of the death, the "Jahrzeit," the Kadish is recited also, for on this day the memory of the deceased appears before the Heavenly Throne. — In its text the Orphan's Kadish differs from the regular complete Kadish insofar as the phrase תתקבל is omitted, which is spoken only after the ש"ע.

שיר של יום. It was customary in the Temple after the performance of the Daily Tamid sacrifice for the Levites to chant certain psalms which varied in accordance with the day of the week. (Tamid VII). In remembrance of this usage the psalms have been retained in our Morning service. They are introduced with the formula היום וגו' counting the days of the week from the preceding Sabbath. Thus we comply with the Biblical injunction "Remember the day of Sabbath" every day by not calling the days of the week by names of their own (like Sunday, Monday etc.) but "by counting them with relation to the Sabbath: the first from Sabbath, the second, etc.."

The selection of the daily psalms was made with a view on the events that took place on the corresponding seven days of Creation (R. H. 31a). On the first day Heaven and Earth were created. This is alluded to in the psalm for the

first day of the week (XXIV), לה' הארץ ומלואה, "The earth
is the Lord's......For He has founded it on the oceans...."

On the second day the division between the "upper and the
lower waters" took place, and although G-d made His Residence
in the Upper Spheres, He left the knowledge of His glory
on earth. This is recounted in the 48th psalm chosen for the
second day. For the third day on which "the dry land became
visible," the 82nd psalm was selected. It points out that
without the observance of law and justice "the very foundations
of the earth tremble." G-d is acclaimed as the Lord of vengeance
in the 94th psalm, said on the fourth day; for the celestial
bodies created on this day were idolised by misguided mankind. The colorful world of fish and fowl appearing in the
profusion of its forms on the fifth day evokes in us the
admiring acclaim of the Creator and His work and strengthens
our faith in His omniscient guidance of the world as is
manifested in every minute creature. (Ps. 81). On the sixth
day the creation was completed. Then He covered Himself
with the splendid raiment of beautiful nature. "The world
is set on an unshakable foundation never to yield," as the
psalm of the Friday proclaims. (Ps. 93). (This psalm numbers
45 words, the numerical value of "Adam," who was created on
this day.) Finally the 92nd psalm, the one which, according
to tradition, the first man sung when he beheld the dawn
of his first day of life, the Sabbath, is the Sabbath-Psalm.
It sees in the Sabbath a reflection of the coming eternal Sabbath
of the future world, יום שכולו שבת. It points to the perfect
harmony and justice to be realized in that future era. Only
them at the dawn of that future day can G-d's love be
proclaimed, whereas his faithfulness is manifest even in this
dark world, להגיד בבקר חסדך.

The Minhag has spread in many communities to
recite the "Song of Unity," the שיר היחוד, after the Daily
Psalm. However various objections have been raised against
this practice. Already at a rather early date certain passages
in this Song as for example: סובב את כל ואתה בכל were
criticised for their naturalistic undertones. Others pointed
out that on weekdays, when the time is limited, the sublime
ideas of the שיר היחוד are in danger of being profaned by a

hurried recital. (נתיבות עולם, הגר"א, יעב"ץ). The same applies
to the אנעים זמירות, the Song of Glory שיר הכבוד which,
therefore, in many communities is chanted on Sabbaths and
Holidays only; while still other communities defer both songs
to Kol Nidre Eve. — Cf. comm. for Sabbath Morning.

Another objection put forward against the שיר היחוד,
namely, that it contains an excessive accumulation of Divine
attributes, (which is inadmissible cf. p. 131) was raised also
against the יגדל prayer. Although these criticisms were countered
by יעב"ץ (cf. א"ח par. 113, 9), the Minhag to recite the
יגדל every day has not taken root. Of unknown origin, the
Yigdal is a poetical arrangement of the 13 Principles of Faith
of Maimonides. Many recite these principles after Shacharis
in the original form given by Maimonides himself at the end
of his Mishnah Commentary (on the 10th Perek of Sanhedrin).
They begin with the recurrent phrase אני מאמין באמונה שלמה.
— Others say, at the end of the Service, the Ten Commandments. These were originally an integral part of the morning
prayer. They were omitted later on so as to repudiate the
contention of early reformers who claimed that only the
Ten Commandments were the essentials in Judaism, while
everything else was of secondary importance (Ber. 12a; O.
Ch. par. 15).

אין כאלקינו with the adjoining פטום הקטורת are —
according to Maimonides and Tur (par. 132) — parts of the
regular Shacharis. However, the רמ"א objects to the recital
of the פטום הקטורת on workdays. The פטום הקטורת as well
as the אין כאלקינו which is connected with it, are therefore,
both omitted. The Minhag to say them, which is still observed
by the Sefardim, dates back to times of epidemics, when
the פטום הקטורת was recited in remembrance of Aaron who
halted the plague by the offering of incense (Num. 17, 12).
The שלחן ערוך (par. 1, 9) on the other hand recommends the
recital of biblical passages concerning the incense offering
and the corresponding parts of the Talmud (Ex. 30, 34-36
and 7-8; כריתות 6a and ירושלמי יומא IV, 5) every day after
the paragraph on the Tamid (the Daily Sacrifice). This would
emulate the routine in the Temple.

The זכירות printed in many editions of the Prayer Book
are to keep alive the most important marks of our early history
in our minds (cf. מגן אברהם par. 60, 3).

Numerous other additions to the regular Shacharis are
mentioned in the sources; as for instance, the portion of the
עקדה, of the Manna etc.. They are, according to יעב״ץ, reserved for those alone who have the leisure to say them with
devotion. The Prayer of the Community, however, ends with
the Daily Psalms and the Kadish following them.

THE MINCHA PRAYER

On the origin and significance of the Mincha cf.
our introduction p. 9. There are two periods of time provided for this prayer corresponding to the Daily Afternoon
Sacrifice (Tamid) which it replaces: מנחה גדולה beginning
½ hour after mid-day and מנחה קטנה beginning 3½ hours
after mid-day (cf. Pes. V, 1 and Ber. 26b). However, the later
period is the perferred one, as the "Hour of Mercy," in
which, as the Talmud states, Eliyahu's prayer at Mt. Carmel
found acceptance. (I Kings 18, 36). This also coincides with
the time at which Isaac's prayer was said, לפנות ערב, towards
evening. His prayer as we have pointed out was the Mincha.
(Ber. 26b). Thus, the morning prayer is to be said under
the sign of the ascending sun, the Mincha under the sign of
its descent, as once David sang: "They shall revere you with
the sun's rise and before the moon (rises) for all generations."
(Ps. 72, 5; cf. Ber. 9b, Rashi).

We already have pointed out in our introductory remarks
that a special distinction is accorded to the Mincha prayer.
The Tur (Par. 232) offers this reason for its importance.
Whereas the morning service takes place before the beginning
of the day's work, and the evening prayer after its conclusion,
the Mincha is placed right in the middle of one's professional
activities, and a special effort is required to tear oneself away
from them to pray. There are, therefore, numerous injunctions
lest the prayer be omitted through preoccupation with undertakings that require time and concentration. The מנחה — being a
substitute for the Afternoon תמיד — consists essentially
of the ש"ע. The Shema (and its Berachoth) is confined by
the Torah itself to the hours, "when you lie down and when
you arise." (Deut. 6, 7). We also do not, at the Mincha
time, offer the פסוקי דזמרה hymns which formed such an
important part of the Morning Service. For the time of the
Mincha already foreshadows the night, when we no longer
praise G-d's lovingkindness, but implore His faithful protection for the hours of darkness. The Kabbalists make the keen

psychological observation that, as soon as the sun passes its Zenith and turns downward, man's soul is no longer moved by the feeling of joyous gratitude as it is in the morning. It is the desire for security and protection in the approaching darkness which now pervades the soul. To these changing states of mind the prayers closely correspond. Of all the praise hymns of the morning, only the אשרי remains in the Mincha, and even this is said before the ש"ע for reasons explained above (p. 178). The אשרי at Mincha is the third and last of the three אשרי to be recited daily. According to Rashi, it also serves to lift the worshipper out of his mood of sorrow and dejection, of distraction or talkativeness, into that spirit of joyous devotion, שמחה של מצוה, which is a prerequisite for prayer (Ber. 31a). For the concluding verses of the אשרי,— קרוב, רצון, שומר are eminently suited to evoke this feeling of joyous and confident faith. The אשרי thus forms the prelude for the ש"ע which, being the most sacred of our prayers, should never be recited without proper inner preparation. Before אשרי the section of the Tamid is recited (Num. 28, 1) as at the corresponding place of the Shacharis. Some also add the paragraph on the קטורת which according to the Jerusalem Talmud was offered during Mincha time (Ber. III).

On the תחנון and עלינו cf. our commentary to the Morning Service (pp. 166, 188).

On public Fast Days the portion ויחל is read from the Torah at Mincha and at Shacharis. It expresses our fervent hope that G-d pardon the sins of the fathers, which have caused the institution of the fast-days, as He has pardoned the sin of the Golden Calf. The הפטרה is read at Mincha only. For this practice Tosafoth (Meg. 21a ד"ה הקורא) advances a reason which strikingly illuminates the indissoluble unity of the duties towards G-d and those towards our fellow men in Judaism. For the words "safeguard Justice and practice Charity" which are set off prominently in this הפטרה, are, according to תוספות, to remind us of our duty to support the poor just at the end of the Fast Day, so that those unfortunate will not be prolong their fast-day involuntarily for lack of food (cf. Rashi Sanh. 35a ד"ה כל תענית).

THE EVENING PRAYER

The evening prayer, the basic significance of which has already been explained in the introduction, consists essentially of two parts: The שמע ישראל with its accompanying four ברכות and the ש"ע. The Torah ordains that we proclaim the Shema, the fundamental teaching of Monotheism twice a day: "when thou liest down and when thou risest up." (Deut. 6, 7). The time for the Shema of the evening begins with the appearance of the stars and ends with dawn, although it should as a rule be spoken before midnight. The ש"ע on the other hand may be recited before night fall, for it is considered as a substitute for the burning of the remnants of the sacrifices which, beginning 1¼ hours before nightfall continued throughout the night (Ber. 26b; Aruch Hash. par. 235, 3).

From the Minhag to recite the Tefilla early, the custom has developed in many places to say the entire מעריב, including the Shema before nightfall. To justify this practice three arguments are adduced in טור א"ח par. 235. According to Rashi the Shema of the Maariv is to be considered as an introduction to the ש"ע similar to the אשרי in Mincha. Another motive given is, that it would be difficult for the community to assemble again at night to recite the Shema with its Berachoth (R. Asher ben Yechiel). According to these two opinions we have to comply with the Mitzvah of קריאת שמע at night by saying it again after nightfall. Finally there is the view which holds that the time of the ending of the sacrificial service (i.e. 1¼ hours before nightfall) in this respect, marks the beginning of the night. (Rabbenu Tam). However, even according to this opinion at least the first two paragraphs of the שמע should be said again after darkness. מג"א. ad loc.).

There are four Brachoth surrounding the Shema at night as opposed to the three of the Morning. They make up a total of seven blessings. This complies with David's declaration: "Seven times daily I shall praise Thee for Thy just laws" (i.e. the Shema which these Berachoth embrace) (Ps. 119, 164).

שיר המעלות. *Behold, bless ye the Lord, all ye servants of the Lord, who stand in the house of the Lord in the night seasons. Lift up your hands towards the sanctuary, and bless ye the Lord. The Lord bless thee out of Zion; even he that made heaven and earth.*

The Lord of hosts is with us; the G-d of Jacob is our stronghold. (Selah.)

O Lord of hosts, happy is the man that trusteth in thee.

Save, Lord: may the King answer us on the day when we call.

שיר המעלות. (Ps. 134) serves as a transition from the professional occupation to the evening prayer, as does the אשרי at Mincha. For "When you return at night from your work in the fields, go to the house of worship and, according to your habit, read (the Scriptures) or study (the Talmud) and then say the Shema and the Tefilla." (Ber. 4b). Hence if Mincha and Maariv are recited in succession, this introduction is omitted at Maariv. The choice of this particular psalm was made with a view on the "servants of G-d, who stand in the House of G-d *at night*," mentioned in it. The Kabbalists added the three following verses of which the Talmud says (Jer. Ber. V, 1) that they "should never cease from your mouth." Therefore they are said three times in order to impress them indelibly in our minds. Their contents make them especially suited to form a transition to the night, the time of human weakness and dependency.

והוא רחום.*And he being merciful, forgiveth iniquity, and destroyeth not: yea, many a time he turneth his anger away, and doth not stir up all his wrath. Save, Lord: may the King answer us on the day when we call.*

והוא רחום (Ps. 78, 38). This verse may well be called the motto of the Evening Service. Whereas in the Shacharis we acclaimed the lovingkindness of G-d renewed every morning להגיד בבקר חסדך, and at Mincha, the time of the waning daylight, we approached G-d without hymn or song to render account in prayer, now, when darkness descends, it is His mercy which we invoke, ואמונתך בלילות. Thus the words והוא רחום give the entire significance of the Evening prayer. From among the numerous verses treating of His abundant mercy, this one was selected because it contains thirteen words alluding to the "Thirteen Attributes of Divine Mercy" and their conquest of the three messengers of wrath: משחית, אף, וחימה. This verse thus outlines the workings of His mercy. The reader proclaims it aloud, and the congregation responds with השם הושיעה calling for G-d's merciful aid to be revealed without delay (Ps. 26, 10). ברכו. cf. comm. p. 90.

ברוך. *Blessed art thou, O Lord our G-d, King of the universe, who at thy word bringest on the evening twilight, with wisdom openest the gates of the heavens, and with understanding changest times and variest the seasons, and arrangest the stars in their watches in the sky, according to thy will. Thou createst day ad night; thou rollest away the light from before the darkness, and the darkness from before the light; thou makest the day to pass and the night to approach, and dividest the day from the night, the Lord of hosts is thy name; a G-d living and enduring continually, mayest thou reign over us for ever and ever. Blessed art thou, O Lord, who bringest on the evening twilight.*

ברוך. The structure, significance and ideas of the Brachoth surrounding the Shema are essentially like those of the morning prayer, and we refer to our commentary there. The *variations* result from the different perceptions and notions of the evening. We are especially struck by the omission of the Kedusha of the angels from the first Bracha. This might be explained on the basis of numerous passages in the Midrash (Gen. R. Ch. 78) which state that the angels proclaim their Kedusha only in the daytime. This would mean that the tribute which the forces of Nature pay to G-d is perceptible only during daytime. It is the day which leads man towards the recognition of G-d. Abraham once saw the work of the Creator revealed in the steady course of the Sun, ruling all terrestrial activity. (Gen. R. Ch. 39). The order of cosmic happening visible to all has been the mightiest proof of G-d's rule ever since. The קדושה as the highest pronouncement of the Divine Glory should, therefore, be spoken only during the day, when our senses are able to perceive Nature in its full activity and splendor. It is omitted at night when the world of Nature is hidden from the grasp of our senses.

This, according to the Kabbalists, also explains the omission of the repetition of the ש״ע at Maariv, for the Kedusha should not be recited at night.

בדברו. The creative word which called forth the rhythm of day and night continues working at night also. — ערבים, זמנים, עתים. "עת לכל" (Eccl. 3, 1) "To everything is a season and a time to every purpose." This sentence indicates that זמן means "time" in general, whereas "עת" implies a certain limited span of time, an hour, a moment. The division into day and night causes each single moment of day and night to differ from the next, for each one is but a transitory link in the change from day to night, from night to day. Day and night are complete contrasts, but the Creator's providence makes the day fade gradually into night and darkness yield slowly to light through the unceasing minute changes of time's "particles": He is משנה עתים and thus מחליף את הזמנים. — ומסדר. He directs each star to its predetermined position cf. Neh. 7, 3: איש במשמרו. G-d has ordered their courses too into an harmonious system, כרצונו, according to a plan known only to Him. We might see their positions and calculate their courses, but their nature and purpose are unknown to us.

בורא יום ולילה. Just as we do in the morning (יוצר אור), we testify at night to the basic truth of the unity of G-d in a world replete with contrasts. He is the Creator of both Light and Darkness and He made both serve His purpose. This "creation" of day and night is effected, גולל, by the gradual retreat of the light before the growing shadows of the night, and by the darkness slowly yielding to the Dawn. ומעביר יום And when the day has done its duty, He makes it go; then the night enters upon its duty. ומבדיל, He lets neither of these contrasts intrude upon the other. Therefore His name is ה' צבאות, He who unites the countless variety of opposing forces into one cosmic harmony. (cf. Amos 4, 13. עושה שחר, also Chullin 87a).

א-ל חי וקים. Among all that is mortal, He alone is alive forever. Among all that perishes He alone is Eternal. He rules, תמיד, perpetually, לעולם ועד, in all eternity, day and night. This concluding sentence has been objected to by some authorities, because it introduces a different train of ideas

and hence contradicts the rule of מעין חתימה סמוך לחתימה.
It must be pointed out, however, that at the corresponding
place of the morning prayer also, in the words אור חדש we
turn towards the future salvation, the time "known only to
Him, neither day nor night, and it shall come to pass towards
evening: there will be light . . . Then the Lord shall be King
over the whole earth." (Zach. 14, 7).

אהבת עולם. cf. commentary to אהבה רבה (p. 107).
All the other goods which G-d has granted to nation and individual have no lasting value. The most precious gift, however,
the Torah with its laws and teachings for our enlightenment
and practicing, they are the eternal gift of eternal Divine love.
They persist through the dark hours and centuries of our
individual and national existence. They are the imperishable
blissful heritage not only of עמך, our national commonwealth,
but also of בית ישראל all the individuals great or small, who
form the House of Israel, who were born and brought up
to serve Israel's destiny. — תורה ומצות. after Deut. 6, 1. —
בשכבנו. after Deut. 6, 7 and Proverbs 6, 22. Though Israel's
physical existence may seem to have sunk into darkness, just
as nature has fallen into the silent clasp of night when no sign
of life or activity is evident,—yet in slumbering Israel as in
slumbering nature, the undying spirit is awake. So it is indeed
the night which should be devoted to the study of the Torah, for
that is the breath of life which alone is awake in Israel's night
(Chag. 12b). בדברי תורתך the study of the Torah Law, ובמצותך
its practice. — כי הם, after Deut. 32, 47. — ובהם וכו', after
Joshua 1, 8.

שמע. Cf. comm. p. 112. Regarding the third paragraph ויאמר, Maimonides explains that: "Although the precept of ציצית is not observed at night, this paragraph is
read also in the evening because it mentions the Exodus from
Egypt. This remembrance is a Mitzvah for the day as well as
for the night, and is derived from the verse "that thou remember the day of thy going out from Egypt all the days
of thy life" (Deut. 16,3; Rambam הל' קריאת שמע I, 3 —
Ber. 12b). The fact of the precept has to be *derived* from
Scripture, and is not taken as following from the explicit
statement of the Torah "led God thee from Egypt *at night*"
which places the essential events of the liberation into the

night, seems significant. A superficial view would primarily
derive from the Egyptian Exodus faith for the night times
of life. It would conceive the precept of זכירת יציאת מצרים
as applying primarily to the night. Judaism, however, knows,
that it is quite easy to show trust in God during the nights
of distress. It is more difficult to remain faithful to our appointed task during the rush and activity of the day, and this
consciousness of an active Judaism is the far more important result of יציאת מצרים. The duty to remember it during the
day was, therefore, always considered foremost and it was
for the night that one had to look for special reference in
Scripture (Hirsch, Deut. 16, 3). — The selection of just this
paragraph from among the many others mentioning יציאת
מצרים is explained by תוספות יום טוב by the observation that
"everybody is familiar with it, because it is recited regularly
during the day time." (Ber. I, 5).

אמת ואמונה. *True and trustworthy is all this, and it
is established with us that he is the Lord our G-d, and there
is none beside him, and that we, Israel, are his people. It is
he who redeemed us from the hand of kings, even our King,
who delivered us from the grasp of all the terrible ones; the
G-d, who on our behalf dealt out punishment to our adversaries, and requited all the enemies of our soul; who doeth
great things past finding out, yea, and wonders without number; who holdeth our soul in life, and hath not suffered
our feet to be moved; who made us tread upon the high places
of our enemies, and exalted our horn over all them that hated
us; who wrought for us miracles and vengeance upon Pharaoh, signs and wonders in the land of the children of Ham;
who in his wrath smote all the first-born of Egypt, and
brought forth his people Israel from among them to everlasting freedom; who made his children pass between the
divisions of the Red Sea, but sank their pursuers and their
enemies in the depths. Then his children beheld his might;
they praised and gave thanks unto his name, and willingly
accepted his sovereignty. Moses and the children of Israel
sang a song unto thee with great joy, saying, all of them,*

*Who is like unto thee, O Lord, among the mighty
ones? Who is like unto thee, glorious in holiness, revered
in praises, doing wonders?*

Thy children beheld the sovereign power, as thou didst cleave the sea before Moses: they exclaimed, This is my God! and said, The Lord shall reign for ever and ever.

And it is said, For the Lord hath delivered Jacob, and redeemed him from the hand of him that was stronger than he. Blessed art thou, O Lord, who hast redeemed Israel.

אמת ואמונה. "Truth and Trust" are the two ideas which for us grow out of the remembrance of the redemption from Egypt. "Truth" when God revealed himself in signs and miracles to liberate us. He thereby planted in our hearts the seed of undying "trust" in Him. The Bracha, גאל ישראל, therefore, praises Him as the Redeemer in the past, whereas the Bracha שומר עמו ישראל לעד proclaims our trust in Him as the Guardian of Israel in the present and, לעד in the future. This latter Bracha might be called the specific night Bracha in its reaffirmation of God's faithful watch over Israel; (characteristically there is no corresponding Bracha in the Shacharis). Both Berachoth are however, considered as one in the Talmud. Together they are גאולה אריכתא a "lengthened blessing of redemption." The preservation of Israel in Exile (שומר עמו etc.) is after all no lesser a miracle than the actual redemption (גאל) (Ber. 4b).

There is a significant textual difference between the paragraph אמת ואמונה and the parallel piece of the morning service, אמת ויציב. There, the events of the Exodus are recounted in the past tense גאלתנו, פדיתנו whereas here, in the Maariv they are described in the participial form employing a constant and continuing action (הגואלנו, הפודנו etc.). In the morning we are filled with gratitude for having overcome the hours of darkness and despondency. At night we seek to find reassurance in the recounting of His ever-present protection and watchfulness. Hence the past tense, the tense of gratitude, חסד, was chosen for the morning. For the evening the present, the tense of hope (אמונה) was adopted. Rashi and Tos. (Ber. 12a) hint at this implication in reference to the verse: להגיד בבקר חסדך which, as we have repeatedly pointed out, gives the Leitmotif for both Shacharis and Maariv.

A similar idea might have caused the variance in the Bracha at the conclusion of these paragraphs. In the morning the Bracha ends with the appeal to צור ישראל calling Jacob by the name signifying victory and conquest; the parallel phrase of the Maariv, however, reads כי פדה ה' את יעקב. It alludes to Jacob in his period of weakness, when he hoped for redemption from "the hand of one who was stronger than he." — השם נפשנו בחיים. "Who gives our soul a hold on life." Without God Israel would have disappeared from the stage of history long ago. — ולא נתן. Taken from Ps. 66,9, this phrase alludes to Ps. 121,3: Even when all living beings are asleep your Guardian watches over you. — המדריכנו. He lets us attain the heights to which our enemies have aspired in vain (after Deut. 33, 29). — גורי. after Ps. 136, 13. — וראו בניו. cf. Rashi Ex. 14,31. Two sentences from the Song of Moses are quoted verbatim: מי כמכה proclaims the assurance gained at the Red Sea of the Omnipotence of G-d and the concluding phrase ה' ימלוך, His Everlasting Kingship.

השכיבנו.*Cause us, O Lord our G-d, to lie down in peace, and raise us up, O our King, unto life. Spread over us the tabernacle of thy peace; direct us aright through thine own good counsel; save us for thy name's sake; be thou a shield about us; remove from us every enemy, pestilence, sword, famine and sorrow; remove also the adversary from before us and from behind us. O shelter us beneath the shadow of thy wings; for thou, O G-d, art our Guardian and our Deliverer; yea, thou, O G-d, art a gracious and merciful King; and guard our going out and our coming in unto life and unto peace from this time forth and for evermore. Blessed art thou, O Lord, who guardest thy people Israel for ever.*

השכיבנו. It has already been mentioned that this Bracha is considered merely an extension of the preceding one, גאולה אריכתא. Hence it does not constitute an interruption between גאולה and תפילה (cf. p. 119). The Midrash (to Ps. 6), however, finds an additional cause for the introduction of this Bracha. During the night, it is explained there, when the Mitzvah of ציצית is not practised, a substitute for it is found in the words ופרוש עלינו סכת שלומך. When we wear the ציצית, we feel sheltered in "The shadow of His Wings;"

a feeling which we express by reciting the verse: . . . מה יקר
. . . ובצל כנפיך. (Ps. 36,8), when we don the Tallis in the
morning. At night, when the ציצית, these admonitions to
refrain from "turning after your hearts and your eyes after
which you go astray," are missing, we pray for "the shadow of
His Wings," "His Tabernacle of Peace," to protect us from
the powers of evil and corruption.

שלום, undisturbed rest leads to העמידנו לחיים restored vigor for the tasks of the next day. — ותקננו. Just
as the day is the time for active accomplishment, so the night
is the period for quiet planning. The tranquillity of the night,
the relaxation of restful sleep refreshes the mind and allows
it to view everything with greater clarity and to judge more
soundly (Rabbi S. R. Hirsch). On שטן cf. comm. p. 36;
the word comprises all powers of evil (B.B. 16a). Keep the
hindrance of the שטן away מלפנינו, from the road ahead of
us, when יורד ומתעה Satan descends to seduce us — and
מאחרינו, when he ascends עולה ומרגיז, to accuse for what
we have done (ibid.). — ישמור צאתנו after Ps. 121, 8. —
שומר עמו ibid. V. 4.

ברוך ה' לעולם או"א. *Blessed be the Lord for evermore.
Amen, and Amen. Blessed be the Lord out of Zion, who dwelleth in Jerusalem. Praise ye the Lord. Blessed be the Lord G-d,
the G-d of Israel, who alone doeth wondrous things; and blessed be his glorious name for ever; and let the whole earth be
filled with his glory. Amen, and Amen. Let the glory of the
Lord endure for ever; let the Lord rejoice in his works. Let
the name of the Lord be blessed from this time forth and for
evermore. For the Lord will not forsake his people for his great
name's sake; because it hath pleased him to make you a people
unto himself. And when all the people saw it, they fell on
their faces: and they said, The Lord, he is God; the Lord
he is God. And the Lord shall be King over all the earth:
in that day shall the Lord be One, and his name One. Let
thy lovingkindness, O Lord, be upon us, according as we
have hoped for thee. Save us, O God of our salvation, and
gather us and deliver us from the nations, to give thanks
unto thy holy name, and to triumph in thy praise. All nations
whom thou hast made shall come and worship before thee,
O Lord; and they shall glorify thy name: for thou art great*

and doest marvellous things; thou art God alone. But we are thy people and the sheep of thy pasture; we will give thanks unto thee for ever: we will recount thy praise to all generations.

Blessed be the Lord by day; blessed be the Lord by night; blessed be the Lord when we lie down; blessed be the Lord when we rise up. For in thy hand are the souls of the living and the dead, as it is said, In his hand is the soul of every living thing, and the spirit of all human flesh. Into thy hand I commend my spirit; thou hast redeemed me, O Lord G-d of Truth. Our G-d who art in heaven, assert the unity of thy name, and establish thy kingdom continually, and reign over us for ever and ever.

יראו עינינו. May our eyes behold, our hearts rejoice, and our souls be glad in thy true salvation, when it shall be said unto Zion, Thy G-d reigneth. The Lord reigneth, the Lord hath reigned; the Lord shall reign for ever and ever: for the kingdom is thine, and to everlasting thou wilt reign in glory; for we have no king but thee. Blessed art thou, O Lord, the King, who constantly in his glory will reign over us and over all his works for ever and ever.

ברוך ה' לעולם או"א. An ancient tradition sets the origin of this piece at a time when the synagogues were situated outside the boundaries of towns and villages. In order to enable the worshippers to reach the safety of the city-walls before darkness this shorter prayer containing 18 Divine Names was introduced instead of the ש"ע. According to a slightly varying version the ברוך ה' was *added* in order to enable late-comers to catch up with the congregation. For our Houses of G-d are not only Houses of Worship בתי תפלה, but also Houses of Assembly, בתי כנסיות. There we meet *with* G-d, but also, in brotherly association with our friends, *before* G-d, so that a bond of communal responsibility unites all members of the community.

However, both explanations for the ברוך השם are based on the halachic decision תפלת ערבית רשות, that the ש"ע of the evening is a voluntary prayer. Otherwise it could not have been replaced by a different prayer (according to the first explanation) nor could the repetition of the ש"ע have been omitted, which, according to the second explanation, necessitated the introduction of the ברוך ה'.

Considered historically the ruling תפלת ערבית רשות, follows from the fact that the Maariv has no corresponding sacrifice, as the Morning and Afternoon Prayer have in the Tamid. The Maariv was instituted as a replacement for the burning of certain members of the sacrifices. This ritual was deferred to the night only when it could not be concluded during the day. Today, however, disregarding its historical background the Maariv has acquired the character of a תפלת חוב (רי"ף ורא"ש, Ber. IV). (On the inner motivation underlying the decision תפלת ערבית רשות, cf. our commentary below on the ש"ע). We further refer the reader to the account in the Talmud of the memorable conflict between R. Gamliel and R. Joshua on this question of תפלת ערבית רשות which only after a long and grave controversy led to the acceptance of the latter's opinion (Ber. 27b). For the selection of Biblical passages for the ברוך ה' לעולם the guiding principle was, on the one hand, that this piece should come under the heading of גאולה, as an extension of the ברכת גאל ישראל, and on the other hand to achieve an eighteen-fold repetition of the Holy Name. — In most Siddurim the version given in I. Chron. 16, 35 of the verse הושיענו (containing only one "שם") has been accepted, whereas others chose the version of Psalms 106,47 (containing two Divine Names), thus arriving at 19 שמות, the number contained in the present, final form of the ש"ע.

יראו עינינו. This short prayer is, according to Rashi (Ber. 31a) the transition to the ש"ע which should not be recited in a sombre mood but with a feeling of joyous elevation.

The prayer ברוך ה' לעולם is recited on work-days only, when the ש"ע of 18 Berachoth, which it was to replace, is said. It is, therefore, omitted on Sabbath and Holy Days.

ש"ע. The Service in the Temple עבודת המקדש was essentially restricted to the daytime. Thus prayer, the "service of the heart," עבודה שבלב is also essentially confined to the daytime. The recital of the Shema, it is true, even at night is considered a precept of the Torah; for its principal sub-

jects, קבלת עול מלכות שמים ועול מצות, the acceptance of the
"yokes of the Divine Kingdom and of our duties" is the
great challenge all through the days *and* nights of life; and
the Berachoth of the Shema express our willingness to follow the call.

The Tefilla however, voicing our pleas for a vigorous
development of all the potentialities of the individual and the
nation, is specifically the prayer of the day. For the Jew,
the daytime above all, when his senses are awake and his
thoughts are clear calls on him to create and to work. This
is the time for prayer. With this view, Judaism places itself in direct contrast to pagan feeling and thinking. The
night which makes man sink back into the clasp of physical
bondage may bring the pagan mind closest to his gods; man
senses the power of his gods, when, like all other creatures,
he too is deprived of vision and consciousness. And the day,
when man feels free and enters the struggle to master the
material world, is to the pagan mind the time of the battle
of man against the gods, the battle to tame the hostile and
independent forces of Nature. Judaism, in contrast to this
view, teaches, that we do not only find G-d in the helpless
passivity of the night, nor even primarily in it. We find G-d
in broad daylight, when man's searching spirit is burning
within him, when the energy of his free will and the creative
achievements of his hands bring his personality to its full
flowering, when he shapes his life and his surroundings according to the will of his Creator. The accomplishments of
the day's work attained by his free and creative endeavor,
and furthered by G-d, are offered by the Jew to G-d. The
day, in pagan concept, is a battle of man against the power
of the gods. The Jew's day is accomplishment in the service
and to the satisfaction of his Creator.

However, the night, and the dark hours of life are not
to be considered as areas beyond the control of G-d. Not
only the day, and the bright periods of life are associated
with G-d. For "His is the night as is the day." He is "the
Fashioner of light" just as He is "the Creator of darkness."
It is the absurd view, which turns just during the night-
times of life towards the godhead and seeks G-d only in the
dark hours of life, which was to be negated. Only when

man, through the free, active exercise of his faculties has
found G-d in the midst of the day's activity — only when
he has surrendered his whole being to Him and His Law,
then does the night too lie beneath the afterglow of a hal-
lowed day, for "הלילה הלך אחר היום." From such a life the
sun never disappears completely. Such a life forever remains
close to G-d. The aims, the aspirations and the achievements
which during the day have found their way to Him, will remain "burning upon the altar all night until the morning,"
as an offering to G-d (cf. Hirsch, Lev. 6, 2). As the fire
on the altar did not die out even during the night, thus in
prayer too, the Jew approaches his God at night also and lays
his hopes and wishes, his aims and expectations upon His
altar. In contrast to the prayer of the day, however, the
prayer of the night retains the subordinate character of a
voluntary prayer, תפלת ערבית רשות. Yet through constant
observance it later acquired the status of an obligatory prayer,
ועכשיו קבעוה חובה.

קדיש תתקבל, עלינו (cf. p. 184) form the conclusion
of the סדר התפלה, as in Shacharis and Mincha. On the
omission of Tachanun from the Maariv prayer cf. p. 170.
The addition of various psalms to the Maariv serves to provide an opportunity for additional Kadeshim for the mourn-
ers. (כלבו par. 28). However objections are raised against
an undue accumulation of such additions.

GRACE AFTER MEALS

Before the Grace after Meals we recite the 137th psalm על נהרות בבל. This psalm expresses our mourning for the destruction of the Sanctuary, an event which (acc. to B.B. 60a) we are not to forget, even during our meals (של״ה). On Sabbath and Holidays, however, the 126th psalm is recited instead. Its optimistic vision of the future re-union in ארץ ישראל fits the festival spirit of these days better. The recital of these Psalms, at the same time fulfills the purpose of providing some spiritual nourishment for the unlearned who is unable "to occupy himself with the words of the Torah." Thus, according to a saying of R. Shimon (Aboth III, 4), the table is ennobled and becomes one that "stands before the Lord." It does not merely serve the satisfaction of the body.

"Three who have eaten together must have זמון (i.e., recite the ברכת המזון in unison)." For this rule of the Mishna (Ber. VII, 3), Samson Raphael Hirsch gives the following reason: "Nothing is more likely to turn a man into a egoist, and make him view everyone else as a competitor on the road to fortune, than the struggle for one's daily bread. The Rabbis, in their endeavor to educate through the precepts, therefore, placed great emphasis on communal meals. They ordained that whenever three or more have eaten bread together, one of them must summon the others to say grace together with him. Thus the idea is impressed upon them and clearly proclaimed to all, that it is the One G-d, common to all, through Whose bounty they all live, and Whose loving-kindness is the impartial source and sustainer of life. This common praise of G-d as the One who is equally close to all as their Father, Sustainer and Supporter makes any thought of jealous competition vanish, and implants, in its stead, the feeling of brotherhood. We no longer see a lessening of our own fortune, through our neighbour's prosperity. We know that the Father of all has sufficient power and love to give at all times everyone what is good and beneficial for him."

210

The Grace after Meals is the only one among all blessings which is expressly ordained in the Torah. "When Thou hast eaten and art satisfied, then praise the Lord, Thy G-d, for the good Land which He has given to thee" (Deut. 8, 10). The *purpose* of this blessing is clearly defined in the subsequent verses: "Beware, lest thou forget the Lord, Thy G-d . . . when thou hast eaten and art satisfied' . . . and all that thou hast is multiplied; lest thy heart be lifted up and thou forget the Lord, Thy G-d, Which brought thee forth from Egypt, from the house of bondage, Who fed thee manna in the wilderness . . . ."

The Grace after Meals thus introduces into the very midst of the "every-day" process of eating the awareness of G-d's special Providence which was so dramatically demonstrated in the miracle of the manna. Every piece of bread eaten is considered as much a direct gift from on High as the manna sent to the wanderers in the desert. (R.S.R. Hirsch).

The wording of the Biblical command furnishes the basis for the various ברכות of the Grace after Meals. (Ber. 48b). ואכלת ושבעת וברכת is the source for the blessing for the food ב' הזן; על הארץ for the ensuing Bracha for the Land ברכת הארץ, and the adjective הטובה, "the good," alludes to Jerusalem and Zion, through which the Land receives its "Goodness" בונה ירושלים. The fourth Bracha הטוב והמטיב was added at a later date. Though the various parts of the Grace were already thus predetermined in the Torah, their final formulas were only fixed after Israel had received the particular benefits alluded to. "When the manna descended, Moses recited the first Bracha, הזן. (This is the oldest prayer in our possession). When Israel entered the Holy Land, Joshua recited the second blessing, ברכת הארץ. David and Solomon composed בונה ירושלים, David spoke the words על ישראל עמך and Solomon ועל הבית הגדול ועל ירושלים עירך וכו'. Later, after the destruction of the Temple the text was changed to accord with the changed circumstances. The last Bracha was introduced in Yavne." (Ber. ibid.).

The elaboration of the ב' המזון into a rendition of thanks for "The Land," for Jerusalem and for Zion, made the "Grace after Meals" into something far greater than "a dutiful expression of thanks for the gift of a meal." To the Jew the satisfaction of his physical needs shall never become an ultimate aim or foremost necessity. His life must not be degraded into sheer selfishness and unmitigated materialism. We have pointed out, how, in the ע"ש, the first requests voiced are not those for material prosperity and success, but for spiritual guidance and freedom from sin. Similarly here too, when the Jew, after having partaken from a meal, proceeds to thanks his G-d, he does not restrict himself to a mere expression of gratitude for the satisfaction of his physical needs. He also gives thanks for "the good and spacious land," for "the Torah that Thou has taught us" and for "Zion, the abode of Thy Glory." Thus our ב' המזון resolves our materialistic urge for food into a broader offering of gratitude, encompassing the physical Providence ב' הזן as well as the national blessings, the Land, the Covenant and the Torah ב' הארץ, as finally the spiritual possessions of Judaism ב' ירושלים. These are essentially all the benefits which we receive from on High.

ברוך. *Blessed art thou, O Lord our G-d, King of the universe, who feedest the whole world with thy goodness, with grace, with lovingkindness and tender mercy; thou givest food to all flesh, for thy lovingkindness endureth forever. Through thy great goodness food hath never failed us; O may it not fail us for ever and ever for thy great name's sake, since thou nourishest and sustainest all beings, and doest good unto all, and providest food for all thy creatures whom thou hast created. Blessed art thou, O Lord, who givest food unto all.*

ברוך וכו' הזן. The Grace after Meals begins with the thanks for our nourishment. G-d's Providence appears to the world in two aspects: as השגחה כללית, His general Providence, acclaimed in this Bracha in the words הזן את העולם כלו and the Special Providence, granting the needs of every individual creature, הוא נותן לחם לכל בשר. Both are the efflux of the boundless love of the Creator, taking effect, in accordance with the desires and needs of the individual, as חן, חסד or רחמים, — as an act of grace, of lovingkindness or of mercy. The knowledge of His ever present love gives us confidence in the future. The concluding sentence of this paragraph, כי הוא זן וכו'

forms a transition, in accordance with the established rule, to the idea expressed in the concluding Bracha (מעין חתימה סמוך לחתימה. Pes. 105a). It emphasizes that it is He alone who "prepares sustenance for all." "While all His creatures are asleep, G-d causes the wind to blow. This in turn causes the clouds to gather. Then rain falls causing the fruit to grow. Thus G-d prepares the meals for all living beings." (Lev. R. 14; Ber. 58a).

נודה לך. *We thank thee, O Lord our G-d, because thou didst give an heritage unto our fathers a desirable, good and ample land, and because thou didst bring us forth, O Lord our G-d, from the land of Egypt, and didst deliver us from the house of bondage; as well as for thy covenant which thou hast sealed in our flesh, thy Law which thou hast taught us, thy statutes which thou hast made known unto us, the life, grace and lovingkindness which thou hast bestowed upon us, and for the food wherewith thou dost constantly feed and sustain us on every day, in every season, at every hour.*

For all this, O Lord our G-d, we thank and bless thee, blessed be thy name by the mouth of all living continually and for ever, even as it is written, And thou shalt eat and be satisfied, and thou shalt bless the Lord thy G-d for the good land which he hath given thee. Blessed art thou, O Lord, for the land and for the food.

נודה לך. This second Bracha of the Grace, ב' הארץ. which recalls the memory of our Homeland at each meal, was first spoken by Joshua upon entering the Holy Land. In its words still vibrates the gratitude for the fulfillment of a deep nostalgic longing: "We thank Thee, Lord, our G-d, that Thou hast caused our fathers to inherit a precious, good and spacious land, and that thou hast led us from the land of Egypt, and redeemed us from the house of bondage." However, besides the blessing for Land, this Bracha mentions other matters too which, according to Ber. 48b, are essential to it, e.g. Milah and Torah. For the possession of the Land is conditional upon the observance of the Milah-Covenant, while the ultimate purpose of our ownership of the land is the realization of the Torah in the Jewish State.

ועל הכל. After the enumeration of all the spiritual and physical, national and individual benefits, which G-d confers upon us always, every day, and every hour, the following paragraph ועל הכל summarises them once more in a concluding expression of gratitude quoting the scriptural passage on which the ברכת המזון is based, ואכלת ושבעת וברכת וכו' (Deut. 8, 10). This repeated rendition of thanks at the beginning and end of the benediction is specifically enjoined by the Talmud (Ber. 49a): צריך שיאמר בה הודאה תחלה וסוף. This seems to imply that, not only after having received a gift from on high, are we to thank for it, but even before we have benefited from it and without knowing its nature. For כל מה דעביד רחמנא לטב עביד, whatever G-d's mercy does, is for the best. In this paragraph the על הנסים is inserted, on Chanukah and Purim, which tells of the miraculous deliverance from the enemy. The concluding Bracha על הארץ ועל המזון is to be interpreted according to the Talmud, "the land which yields the nourishment." It formally complies with the scriptural precept ואכלת ושבעת וברכת וכו'.

רחם. *Have mercy, O Lord our G-d, upon Israel thy people, upon Jerusalem thy city, upon Zion the abiding place of thy glory, upon the kingdom of the house of David thine anointed, and upon the great and holy house that was called by thy name. O our G-d, our Father, feed us, nourish us, sustain, support and relieve us, and speedily O Lord our G-d, grant us relief from all our troubles. We beseech thee, O Lord our G-d, let us not be in need either of the gifts of mortals or of their loans, but only of thy helping hand, which is full, open, holy and ample, so that we may not be ashamed nor confounded for ever and ever.*

And rebuild Jerusalem the holy city speedily in our days. Blessed art thou, O Lord, who in thy compassion rebuildest Jerusalem. Amen.

רחם. Just as the first Bracha הזן acknowledged the events of the *present* as completely dependent on G-d, and the second Bracha traced all happenings of the *past* to His activity, thus the third Bracha, called for short בונה ירושלים, points out that the *future,* the distant as well as the immediate restoration and maintenance of our national and personal existence, is to be expected only from G-d. Hence this Bracha is kept in the form of a supplication, רחם נא.

This prayer for a future blessed by G-d was, in the course of historical developments, adapted to the specific conditions prevailing at different periods. In the Davidic era, prayer was offered for the Divine blessing upon Israel and Jerusalem. At the time of Solomon the "Great and Holy House" of G-d was included, and a prayer for the endurance of the rule of the House of David was added. (טור par. 188). This explains the order of petitions at the beginning of the Bracha: For Israel, Jerusalem, Zion, the House of David and the House of G-d. When, in later times, Israel was exiled and the Temple destroyed, these entreaties for preservation were changed into prayers for restoration. Thus the Bracha acquired the form of a prayer for consolation, and is briefly called נחמה. (Ber. 49a). One of its essential constituents is the mention of the מלכות בית דוד (ibid.); "for there is no true consolation without the restitution of the Davidic Kingdom" (Maimon. הלכות תפלה). We pray especially for the House of David, for "at the time of Rehoboam, disaster overtook Israel, because they held three things in disrespect: The Kingdom of G-d, the Kingdom of David, and the Sanctuary. The people will only be redeemed therefore, when they shall pray in earnest for the restoration of these three things." (הושע III, 5, רש"י). Hence we pray in this Bracha for the restoration of Sanctuary and Davidic rule. The plea for the return of the Kingdom of G-d is postponed to the following Bracha. It would be improper to place a prayer for a human ruler next to the supplication for the restoration of the Rule of G-d. The version אלקינו אבינו מלכנו רענו is, therefore, erroneous. The word מלך is also omitted at the end of the יעלה ויבא (א"ח. par. 188, 3).

However, in all the various versions which this Bracha acquired during the course of history, it always contained the plea for Divine succour for the individual. Nothing is more suited to ennoble and elevate the lowly urge for satisfaction of the requirements of our body, than to associate them with the highest, holiest matters of the Jewish commenweal. And if through the exaggerated valuation of material pleasures and

possessions, we have lost our national independence, land and
sanctuary, we atone for this failing, through all the millennia,
by never permitting ourselves an enjoyment, by never rising
satisfied from the table, without remembering those spiritual
ideals and praying for their return. As a rule, the person whose
needs are satisfied is apt to forget those of others, and even
more so those of the community. The ברכת המזון however,
awakens in us, at the time of the satisfaction of our bodily
needs the plea for Divine mercy for Israel, G-d's nation and
its most precious possessions.

The personal requests beginning with אלקינו, אבינו,
רענו, occupy the center of the Bracha and then flow into
the prayer for Jerusalem: ובנה ירושלים. They contain inter alia
the wish that G-d sustain us with His "full, open, holy and
generous Hand." This is to distinguish the gift from on
High, from the gift of human hand. The latter is often
insufficient. It may be granted through favoritism. Moreover, the goods themselves may have been acquired by un-
ethical means.

The concluding Bracha emphasizes that G-d will rebuild "ברחמים" ירושלים in mercy. Indeed the Bracha also
began with the appeal to His mercy, רחם, for the rebuilding
of ירושלים will be the result of a special act of mercy and
love: שבתי לירושלים ברחמים (Zach. I, 16); cf. also in the
תפלה: ולירושלים עירך ברחמים תשוב. — "At the end of this
Bracha, we answer "Amen," even though we say the Bracha
ourselves, (an exception to the general rule), since this is
the last of the Berachoth prescribed in the Torah" (א"ח par.
188, 1).

In this Bracha of "consolation" the רצה is inserted
on Sabbaths (Ber. 49a). This does not, however, indicate,
that we are in greater need of consolation on the Sabbath.
Instead, as Abudraham remarks, it shows that the Sabbath
should be connected with the memory of Jerusalem. For, as
the Psalmist demands, the thought of Jerusalem should always
"precede all enjoyment." (Ps. 137, 6).

רצה. *Be pleased, O Lord our G-d, to fortify us by thy
commandments, and especially by the commandment of the
seventh day, this great and holy Sabbath, since this day is*

great and holy before thee, that we may rest and repose thereon in love in accordance with the precept of thy will. In thy favour, O Lord our G-d, grant us such repose that there be no trouble, grief or lamenting on the day of our rest. Let us, O Lord our G-d, behold the consolation of Zion thy city, and the rebuilding of Jerusalem thy holy city, for thou art the Lord of salvation and of consolation.

יעלה ויבא. cf. p. 149.

רצה. In the text of this interpolated prayer the word והחליציגו is significant. Referring to the scriptural passage ועצמותיך יחליץ (Is. LVIII, 13), the Midrash finds a fourfold meaning in the root חלץ (Lev. R. ch. 34): To take of, to arm, to save and to give rest. The use of this word here then was to indicate that Israel shall be saved through the observance of the Sabbath, achieve restfulness and shall return girded with strength to the Promised Land. Another Midrashic passage also (commenting on Ps. LX, 7: למען יחלצון וכו') predicts that the tranquility which Israel's enemies now enjoy, shall in the days to come, be granted to the Jewish people as a reward for their observance of the Sabbath. (ילקוט ibid.) To us the Sabbath means rest, and at the same time regeneration. It grants rest and relaxation to the spirit and gives to the body and soul the chance to recover and to prepare. These are the ideas expressed in the רצה.

On Rosh Chodesh and Holidays, the יעלה ויבא is added here, "because it voices pleas and prayers similar to the Bracha בונה ירושלים," not praises, as the preceding sections (Tos. Sab. 24a).

ברוך אתה וגו' הא-ל אבינו וכו'.*Blessed art thou, O Lord our G-d, King of the universe, O G-d, our Father, our King, our Mighty One, our Creator, our Redeemer, our Maker, our Holy One, the Holy One of Jacob, our Shepherd, the Shepherd of Israel, O King, who art kind and dealest kindly with all, day by day thou hast dealt kindly, dost deal kindly, and wilt deal kindly with us; thou hast bestowed, thou dost bestow, thou wilt ever bestow benefits upon us, yielding us grace, lovingkindness, mercy and relief, deliverance and prosperity, blessing and salvation, consolation, sustenance and support, mercy, life, peace and all good; of no manner of good let us be in want.*

ברוך אתה וגו' הא-ל אבינו וכו'. The fourth Bracha of the
Grace was introduced by R. Gamliel in Yavne. The occasion
was the permission granted by the Romans to bury the "Slain
of Bethar." In the heroic but futile revolt of Bar Kochba,
thousands were massacred at the fortress of Bethar. Hadrian.
the Roman Emperor, prohibited them to be buried. Thus their
corpses were left lying in the fields around Bethar for years.
When permission was granted at long last to inter them,
the sages uttered the blessing: הטוב והמטיב, "Blessed be He
Who in His goodness did not let the corpses decay (הטוב) and
Who let them be buried (המטיב)" (Ber. 48a). The Rabbis
joined this blessing to the Grace after Meals because this is
a prayer which is spoken in joyous gratitude (אבודרהם).
Others give the following reason for its inclusion at this
particular place: When Bethar was destroyed, the glory of
Israel had sank to its lowest point, nor will it rise again,
till the descendant of David come. Therefore we connect this
Bracha with the preceding בונה ירושלים in which we pray for
his coming." This connection will for all times remind us
that the future of our national destiny ultimately depends
upon G-d alone.

However, the fact that the events of Bethar gave rise
to the introduction of this ברכת הטוב והמטיב, which to-day
we recite at all joyful occasions, demands further explanation.
There was a time, it seems to say, when Israel was so utterly
downcast and helpless, that even the mere permission to bury
the dead, appeared as a "twofold mercy" הטוב והמטיב, and
this in our own land. The remembrance of this disastrous period
was perpetuated in the typical prayer of thanksgiving, the
ב' המזון, for there might be times when we do not feel at all
that we should render thanks to G-d, times when we feel
disgruntled and bitter because our wishes have not been fulfilled immediately. Then this Bracha reminds that our fathers
were at times so utterly dejected that the mere permission to
bury their dead elicited their fervent thanks.

The threefold mention of G-d's Kingship שלש מלכיות in
אבינו מלכנו ,אלקינו מלך העולם, and המלך הטוב is an essential
part of this Bracha. It declares Him the absolute ruler over
the world and over all mankind. This idea of the Kingdom
of Heaven is like a motif interwoven through all the ברכת

המזון, it is emphasized in this last Bracha. It accentuates the basic idea of the ברכת המזון, the concept of the solicitude of the King of Kings for all His subjects.

In this entire Bracha the blessing of G-d is kept in the third, indirect person הא-ל, הוא הטיב וכו' exactly as in the first Bracha הזן. In the intervening second and third Bracha, however, we address G-d in the direct form נודה לך; רחם נא וכו'. Here G-d appears as the proximate "Thou," there as the invisible "He." To explain this apparent inconsistency, Rabbi J. L. Oppenheim, in his מטה יהודה, offers a brilliant explanation based on the Talmudic parable which compares the relationship between G-d and Israel to the relationship between husband and wife. The periods of the journey through the desert, the possession of the Holy Land and the exile, are compared to the times of courtship, when the bride shows modest restraint towards her lover, of married life, when this restraint is overcome, and finally to the time of separation when the earlier feeling returns. (Yoma 54a). Thus the first Bracha composed by Moses during the journey through the desert — reflects, in its indirect form of address, the chaste restraint of the bride. The second and third Bracha, however, both originating in the Holy Land, discard this modest reserve and approach G-d as "Thou." The fourth Bracha finally, added during the period of destruction and impending exile, agains returns to the more indirect, remote form of address.

הרחמן. *The All-merciful shall reign over us for ever and ever. The All-merciful shall be blessed in heaven and on earth. The All-merciful shall be praised throughout all generations, glorified amongst us to all etrnity, and honoured amongst us for everlasting. May the All-merciful grant us an honourable livelihood. May the All-merciful break the yoke off our neck, and lead us upright to our land. May the All-merciful send a plentiful blessing upon this house, and upon this table at which we have eaten. May the All-merciful send us Elijah the prophet (let him be remembered for good,) who shall give us good tidings, salvation and consolation. May the All-merciful bless (my honoured father) the master of this house, and (my honoured mother) the mistress of this house, them, their household, their children, and all that is theirs; us and all that is ours, as our fathers Abraham, Isaac and Jacob were blessed each with his own comprehensive blessing; even thus may he bless all of us together with a perfect blessing, and let us say, Amen.*

Both on their and our behalf may there be such advocacy on high as shall lead to enduring peace; and may we receive a blessing from the Lord, and righteousness from the G-d of our salvation; and may we find grace and good understanding in the sight of G-d and man.

On Sabbath: *May the All-merciful let us inherit the day which shall be wholly a Sabbath and rest in the life everlasting.*

On New Moon: *May the All-merciful renew unto us this month for good and for blessing.*

On Festivals: *May the All-merciful let us inherit the day which is altogether good.*

On New Year: *May the All-merciful renew unto us this year for good and for blessing.*

On Chol-Hamoed Succoth: *May the All-merciful raise up for us the fallen Tabernacle of David*

May the All-merciful make us worthy of the days of the Messiah, and of the life of the world to come.

On Week-days: *Great salvation giveth he to his king.*

On Sabbath, Festivals and New Moons: *He is a tower of salvation to his king; and showeth lovingkindness to his anointed, to David and to his seed, for evermore. He who maketh peace in his high places, may he make peace for us and for all Israel, and say ye, Amen.*

O fear the Lord, ye his holy ones; for there is no want to them that fear him. Young lions do lack and suffer hunger; but they that seek the Lord shall not want any good. O give thanks unto the Lord, for he is good: for his lovingkindess endureth for ever. Thou openest thine hand, and satisfiest every living thing with favour. Blessed is the man that trusteth in the Lord, and whose trust the Lord is. I have been young and now I am old; yet have I not seen the righteous for-

*saken, nor his seed begging for bread. The Lord will give
strength unto his people; the Lord will bless his people
with peace.*

הרחמן. The following short entreaties added to the
Grace, during the period of the Gaonim, contain special personal
requests and may be varied in their number and content. They
are a direct logical continuation of the idea expressed in
ב' הטוב והמטיב viz. that G-d is the ultimate source of all
that we receive (טור par. 189). The text of these sentences,
varies widely in the different Siddurim. All of them, however,
contain the "blessing for the Master of the House" mentioned
already in the Talmud (Ber. 46a). Between the הרחמן praying
for "abundant blessing for this house and this table at which
we have eaten" and the one for the בעל הבית the entreaty
for the coming of Elijah, the Prophet, is inserted. He is the
one who will bring us "good tidings of זכור לטוב and consolation." For Elijah is the prophet who will bring peace
into the homes by overcoming the divergences between the
generations," restoring the hearts of the parents to the children,
and the hearts of the children to their parents." - בכל מכל כל
cf. B.B. 17a and Gen. Rabbah ch. 43. To be as contented with
our lot as the Patriarchs were with theirs, is the greatest blessing
which we could ever hope for. Here, prior to the concluding
sentences, special prayers are inserted on Sabbaths, Festivals
and on R. Chodesh, in accordance with the Talmudic interpretation of the verse ברוך ה' יום יום, בכל יום תן לו מעין ברכותיו
(Ps. 68, 14; Ber. 40a).

הרחמן הוא יזכנו. The conclusion of this as of so many
other prayers is formed by the contemplation of the Messianic era — מגדיל - מגדול. This verse begins in Ps. 18, 51
with מגדיל and in II Sam, 22, 51 with מגדול. The difference
is explained in the Yalkut in this way: Salvation for Israel
will not come suddenly and abruptly, but will grow gradually
to fruition מגדיל. At that time, the Messianic King will be
established as strongly and powerfully as a tower, מגדול.
Hence we say מגדיל on workdays when G-d, as it were,
works on the coming of salvation. On the Sabbaths and
Holidays, however, which are in themselves a reflection of
the future bliss, מעין עולם הבא, we say מגדול. The sentence
עשה שלום forms here, as in the Tefilla, the conclusion.

"Peace on us and all Israel" is always the quintessence and climax of our wishes. However, in the ברכת המזון, this sentence acquires a special significance. It alludes to Lev. XXVI, 6, where after enumeration of all material blessing it says: "And I shall give peace in the Land." For, as the Midrash explains, "What good is an abundance of food and drink without peace? Therefore all blessings end with peace." (תורת כהנים ibid.). The appended sentences are, as in many others of our prayers, compiled to express in informal sequence the ideas of G-d's solicitious mercy, of our gratitude and trust, and our prayer for peace. They are spoken in a subdued voice since they are not part of the ברכת המזון in the strict sense (which ends with עושה שלום), just as the אלקי נצור at the end of the ש"ע.

PRAYERS BEFORE RETIRING TO SLEEP

Gratitude for the benefit of sleep, and prayer for protection from the dangers of the darkness — out of these two affections of the human soul grew the "Prayer before Retiring." The relaxation offered by restful sleep is accounted by our sages among the great benefits granted to man by the Creator.

"And behold it was very good"; this refers — according to R. Shimon ben Eleazar — to nothing else but sleep, which, even in a short time, restores to the mind the ability to absorb anew the light of knowledge. (Gen. R. ch. 9). For this blessing we recite a special Bracha and say it immediately before going to sleep. But with this Blessing we combine the prayer for protection from the twofold perils of the darkness, the dangers to our physical and spiritual welfare. For the night is the time when the powers threaten the helpless. Terror grips him "of the trap set down and of the death that lurks in the darkness." However, the soul no less than the body faces perils at night, those evoked by "bad dreams and evil phantasies," חלומות רעים והרהורים רעים. They menace the purity of our thoughts and feelings. The Rabbis of the Talmud stated emphatically that the only protection against the "terrors of the night" is a clear conscience, created by the harmony of mind and soul with the will of the Creator. However as protection from the dangers of the soul, they recommend two weapons.

The one is the reading of the שמע. The שמע impresses on our minds with unequalled clarity the precept to love G-d "with all thy heart, and all thy soul and with all thy might." Spoken with proper concentration and devotion, these words cannot fail to have a profound effect on anyone willing to listen to their call. This protective weapon against sinful thought is accessible to each and everyone. For the educated Jew, a second protection measure is available, no less effective than the first: The occupation with Torah-study, considered a substitute equivalent to the reading of the שמע. (Ber. 5a).

It testifies to the admirable psychological insight of our sages when thy urge us, either to repeat the שמע over and over again or to keep the mind occupied with a subject of Torah-study, until we yield to sleep (א"ח par. 239, 1). For, whoever falls asleep in so pure a mood or so pure an activity of the mind is, within limits attainable to man, protected from the defiling and humiliating "accidents of the night," which overcome man in his sleep.

Thus, on the one hand the ברכת המפיל, which combines the thanks for the blessing of sleep with the prayer for protection, and the שמע on the other, form the core of the Prayer for the night.

ברוך. *Blessed art thou, O Lord our G-d, King of the universe, who makest the bands of sleep to fall upon mine eyes, and slumber upon mine eyelids. May it be thy will, O Lord my G-d and G-d of my fathers, to suffer me to lie down in peace and to let me rise up again in peace. Let not my thoughts trouble me, nor evil dreams, nor evil fancies, but let my rest be perfect before thee. O lighten mine eyes, lest I sleep the sleep of death, for it is thou who givest light to the apple of the eye. Blessed art thou, O Lord, who givest light to the whole world in thy glory.*

ברוך וגו' המפיל. This Bracha recorded in varying versions in the Talmud (Ber. 60b) and elsewhere, corresponds to the Bracha המעביר שנה מעיני spoken in the morning. There we thank G-d for the removal of the bonds of slumber, here for the gift of sleep. The Bracha then refers first to protection from physical danger, שתשכיבנו לשלום וגו', next the thoughts menacing our peace of mind and soul ואל יבהלוני וכו'. — רעיוני. The "thoughts" which we nurse in our wakeful hours produce dreams and phantasies during the sleep. — והאר עיני וגו' according to Ps. 13, 4 cf. Ber. 57b: שינה אחד מששים ממיתה. — Similarly to the corresponding Bracha of the morning this Bracha too is kept in the first person singular, because it is concerned with personal physical and mental wellbeing, and is not prescribed for the communal service (cf. however מ"א Par. 46, 4). — For שמע cf. p. 211.

ויהי נעם, יושב בסתר עליון וגו'. R. Joshua ben Levi used to recite (Ps. XCI) יושב and (Ps. III) ה' מה רבו before

66666

retiring (Sheb. 15b). Both were, therefore, included in the Prayer before Retiring. Their contents, in fact, are none else than pleas for protection from all hurtful forces and influences. Ps. XCI, especially, one of the Psalms attributed to Moses, forms a comprehensive prayer for safeguarding us from all sorts of perils. (Hence it is also spoken at the end of the Sabbath when the Sabbath, the "Tabernacle of Peace" is withdrawn.) However, the Talmud states most emphatically that the recital of these Psalms is by no means to be understood as an (actual) panacea for all suffering and distress. The question is raised: How could R. Joshua ben Levi want to protect himself for the night by reading those psalms? Did not he himself forbid the use of scriptural verses as curative measures? The answer is given: "For preventative purposes it is allowed." This reply Maimonides explains further: "To seek healing through the words of the Scripture is forbidden. The Holy Scripture is destined, not for the healing of the body, but of the soul. However a healthy man may read scriptural passages and Psalms in order that the merit of this reading be with him and protect him from danger and hurtful influences." (הלכות עכו"ם XI, 12; cf. Ber. 54b. "Three need special protection.") ה' מה רבו צרי. In the hour of his deepest despair, David found new hope and strength in the simple fact that he laid down, slept and awoke. In this, he saw the assurance that G-d had not forsaken him. And he inspires all those who have sunk into guilt and suffering with the eternal hope: Whomsoever G-d allows to awake to a new day, He has assured for His help to re-gain a pure and serene life (Rabbi S. R. Hirsch).

ברוך ה' ביום, יראו cf. 206. These two השכיבנו cf. p. 204. parts of Maariv are repeated here, although without their Brachoth. The verse בידך אפקיד (Ps. XXXI, 6) is already mentioned in the Talmud as part of the Prayer before Retiring. There is on the other hand no mention in any of the sources of the inclusion of the paragraph beginning יראו.

המלאך. *The angel who hath redeemed me from all evil bless the lads; and let my name be named on them, and the name of my fathers Abraham and Isaac; and let them grow into a multitude in the midst of the earth. — And he said, If thou wilt diligently hearken to the voice of the Lord thy G-d,*

*and wilt do that which is right in his eyes, and wilt give ear
to his commandments, and keep all his statutes, I will put none
of the diseases upon thee, which I have put upon the Egyptians; for I am the Lord that healeth thee.* — *And the Lord
said unto the adversary, The Lord rebuke thee, O adversary;
yea, the Lord that hath chosen Jerusalem rebuke thee. Is not
this a brand plucked out of the fire?* — *Behold the bed of
Solomon: threescore mighty men are about it, of the mighty men
of Israel: they all handle the sword, expert in war: every man
hath his sword upon his thigh, because of fear in the night.*
— *The Lord bless thee, and keep thee: the Lord make his face
to shine upon thee, and be gracious unto thee: the Lord turn
his face unto thee, and give thee peace.*

הנה לא ינום. *Behold, he that guardeth Israel will neither
slumber nor sleep.*

לישועתך. *For thy salvation I hope, O Lord. I hope, O
Lord, for thy salvation. O Lord, for thy salvation I hope.*

בשם ה'. *In the name of the Lord, the G-d of Israel,
may Michael be at my right hand; Gabriel at my left; before
me, Uriel; behind me, Raphael; and above my head the
Divine presence of G-d.*

המלאך. Now follows a number of verses called by
the Talmud פסוקי דרחמי, verses of Divine Mercy. They are
recommended for recital before retiring (Ber. 5a). The first
is the invocation with which Jacob blessed his grandsons,
המלאך הגאל. (Gen. 48, 16). The Zohar remarks that the text
does not read אשר גאל "Who has redeemed me," but הגאל,
the present form. This refers to the accompanying Angel of
Protection who is "forever redeeming," the worthy. — ויאמר
אם שמע Ex. XV, 26. This verse forms the basis for the
Talmudic statement, that Torah-study no less than the reading
of the שמע protects man from danger (Ber. ibid.). — ויאמר ה'
אל השטן. The Satan, embodiment of all those obstacles and
forces which counteract progress, and which are active at
night, is on no account an independent power. He is subject
to the Divine Will as much as any other being (Zach. III, 2).
— הנה מטתו (Cant. III, 7). Before surrendering to sleep,
our prayer draws our eyes to Solomon's bed, as if to say:
"Behold, the wealthy, mighty, wise King Solomon, at a time

of moral weakness and aberration, sixty armed warriors
had to surround his bed with drawn swords to protect him
from the terror of the night." "Before man sins," remarks the
Midrash to this verse, "his fellow-men regard him with awe
and respect; after he has sinned, fear and terror of others overcome him. But you, who are not a king, not wealthy nor
powerful, yet if only you have a clear conscience, you need
no sword-carrying warriors to save you from the terrors
of the night: "G-d blesses and protects you, brightens your
path and bestows grace upon you, turns to you with His
countenance and gives you peace. יברכך, יאר, ישא וגו' שלום."
(Rabbi S R Hirsch). הנה לא ינום. You may sleep in peace;
for He who neither slumbers nor sleeps, guards over you.

לישועתך קויתי ה'. For the help of no one else but G-d
himself do we hope. ה' לישועתך קויתי . It is the Allmerciful
Source of all for whose help we hope. (Rabbi S R. Hirsch).

בשם ה' אלקי ישראל. In Num. Rabba ch. 2, this description
is given of the position of the angels surrounding the Divine
throne. To His right is Michael, performer of miracles,
to His left Gabriel, messenger of His Omnipotence; Uriel
in front carrying the Divine light; and finally Raphael,
healer of the sick. Man however, בשם ה', with the permission
from Above, places himself in the center of the assembly
of angels, the Divine Presence above His head (Rabbi S.
R. Hirsch). For the pious is always suffused by the inner
certainty that "an angel of G-d encamps around those that
fear G-d, and delivers them." (Ps. 34, 8).

שיר המעלות. (Ps. CXXVIII). This Psalm is spoken
in the Night-Prayer, because, according to the Talmud (Ber.
57a), the two images depicted in it are a good omen for those
to whom they appear in a dream. (מטה משה 401). A further
reason is its mention of Zion and Jerusalem.

רגזו. *Stand in awe, and sin not: commune with your own
heart upon your bed, and be still. (Selah.)*

רגזו ואל תחטאו. We should know one fear only, the fear
of sin. To avoid it should be our silent, and earnest vow voiced
only in solitude and heard by G-d alone (Rabbi S. R. Hirsch).
Cf. מ"א Par. 239, 7: "Before retiring one should take account
of oneself, meditate upon one's actions during the day, and

repent of all injustice and sins, especially of those transgressions which one commits frequently, e.g. flattery, untruthfulness, mockery and slander."

אדון עולם cf. p. 27. The concluding verses of this song indicate that its proper place is here in the Prayer before Retiring. It is the song that expresses the quiet, serene and steadfast trust in G-d. The Jew ends his day with the confession of his profound faith in G-d and as soon as he awakens he immediately greets the new day with the same, serene declaration. This, as all other additions to the original, basic Prayer before Retiring, (consisting of שמע and ברכת המפיל), accentuate the purpose of this prayer, viz. to elevate the worshipper to a mood of serene faith in G-d, of a purified activity of the mind, and of peace of soul. Together they create the ideal basis for an undisturbed and restful enjoyment of blissful sleep.

GLOSSARY OF AUTHORS AND WORKS QUOTED

אבודרהם. Abudraham — R. David ben Josef from Toledo (Spain). His work includes explanations on the Prayer Book, portions of the scriptures, customs and laws. The work was written in 1341. The author was a friend of the טור.

אבוהב. Aboab, R. Isaac. Author of מנורת המאור "The Candelabrum of Light." Little is known of his life. His work discusses in 7 parts, (corresponding to the seven arms of the candelabrum) moral and ethical precepts of Judaism. One of the most popular works of its kind.

אברבנל. Don Yitzchak Abarbanel born in Lisbon 1437, died in Venice 1508. His father was state treasurer of Portugal, but R. Yitzchak had in 1483 to flee and settled first in Toledo, later, in the first expulsion from Spain (1492) emigrated to Italy. His comprehensive commentary on the Bible is very systematic and provides an introduction to every book discussing its historical background and basic teachings. Malbim (cf. ibid.) frequently refers to his explanation.

ר' שמשון רפאל הירש, Hirsch, Rabbi Samson Raphael, 1818-1889. Leading figure in German Orthodoxy in the 19th century. His influence extended through all spheres of Jewish life. Foremost fighter against Reform Judaism. Founder of the famous Orthodox Community of Frankfort on Main, and of the first modern Jewish school. His literary output is amazing in size and unique in its kind. It combines strict adherence to traditional sources with a highly original method of interpretation. His works comprise a translation and very comprehensive commentary to the Five Books of The Torah (The Pentateuch), to the Psalms and to the Prayer Book, (frequently quoted in the present commentary). In a large number of essays and articles, first published in the Monthly "Jeshurun" which he edited for years, S. R. H. laid down his views on the problems of Judaism in a modern world and on

fundamentals of theory and practice of Judaism. His
"Nineteen Letters on Judaism" by "Ben Uziel," first of
his books published, became the clarion-call of traditional
Judaism rallying it to combat the disastrous effects of
the Reform movement. In his Choreb Essays on Israel's
Duties in Exile, R. Hirsch revealed the ideas underlying
the practices of the Mitzvoth. Throughout his writings
R. Hirsch aimed for an integration of the valuable ele-
ments of modern culture into the structure of Judaism
(Torah im Derech Eretz).

טור (ארבע טורים). "The Four Rows." Early Codifi-
cation of the Jewish Law as applicable in the Disapora,
eventually became the Shulchan Aruch. (cf. ibid.). By R.
Jacob ben Asher (His father R. Asher ben Yechiel is
known for his extracts of halachic decisions from the Talmud ("רא"ש"). The title "The Four Rows" refers to the
four rows of jewels on the breastplate worn by the High
priest. The work comprises:

טור אורח חיים (Way of life) containing the laws
of daily life, of Sabbath and festivals.

טור יורה דעה (Teacher of Knowledge) comprises
dietary laws, ritual cleanliness, idolatry, superstition, busi-
ness ethics, Torah study etc.

טור אבן העזר (Stone of Help) deals with marriage.

טור חושן משפט (Shield of Justice) is concerned
with civil and criminal law.

ילקוט. Collection of Midrashic interpretations of the
Bible.

יעב"ץ (Yaakov ben Zvi) Yaabetz — R. Jacob (Israel) Emden son of R. Zebi Hirsch Ashkenazi the Chacham
Zvi. Born in Altona 1697, died 1776. Here his widely-used
commentary on the Prayer-Book is quoted. R. Jacob Emden is popularly known for his involvement in
the controversy with R. JonathanEybeshutz which was
an aftermath of the great upheaval caused in European
Jewry by the appearance of Sabbatai Zevi, the self-styled
Messiah. Other works of R. J. Emden include Responsa,
a commentary on the Zohar, on the Mishnah and on the
Seder Olam.

כל-בו. An ancient compilation of ritual regulations especially as concerning prayers and holidays. Author unknown. Frequently quoted by R. Yosef Caro, the author of the Shulchan Aruch (cf. ibid.).

לבוש, Levush ("Raiment") R. Mordechai ben Abraham Jaffe. Of the ten sections it has, the first five parts of the Levush outline the entire Jewish law, parallel to the Sh. Aruch, while the second half treats various special subjects. R. Mordechai succeeded the great Rabbi Loew Betzalel as Rabbi of Prague (1592).

מהרש"א ("Maharsho") R. Samuel Eliezer ben Judah, born Posen 1555 died Ostrog 1631. From 1585 to 1609 head of a Yeshivah founded by his wife's parents for him. His mother-in-law Edel supported hte students out of her own money. His "Chiddushim" to the halachic and haggadic parts of the Talmud are contained in most editions of the Talmud.

מחזור ויטרי. Machsor Vitry. An ancient and comprehensive prayer book compiled by Simcha ben Samuel of Vitry around 1100. It contains the text of prayers and Piyutim, and explanations and regulations relating to these.

מטה משה by R. Moses ben Abraham of Premiszla. Laws concerning Prayer, Blessings, Sabbaths and Festivals.

מלבים. Malbim. Abbreviation of the Hebrew name Meir Loeb ben Iechiel Michael, "The Kempner." 1809-1879. In spite of a life embittered by persecution and wanderings caused by Malbim's vigorous and uncompromising stand against the German Reformers, he produced a number of unique works. Chief among them is his great commentary on the entire Bible. This includes an introduction to the 3rd book ויקרא called "Ayeles Hashachar," in which the Malbim by means of a most subtle and sensitive analysis of the Holy Language shows how the interpretations of the Oral Law result directly from distinctions and peculiarities of the Written Text. His detailed commentary (often referring to Abarbanel's work) reveals an unfailing sense of style and language of the Bible and thus frequently opens new and surprising insights.

נתיבות עולם by R. Leow Judah ben Betzalel (Maharal of Prague — "Der hohe Rabbi Loew"). Born Posen about 1525 died Prague 1609. Held in highest esteem by his distinguished contemporaries, the Maharshal, R. Meir of Lublin etc., contemporary and friend of the great astronomers Tycho Brahe and Kepler who flourished in Prague. His works abound in profound and original ideas which always keep to the basic and essential trend of thought, never losing themselves in vague homily. His person is associated with the Golem story.

ס' הגיון נפש (also called ס' המוסר) by R. Abraham ben Chasdai Halevi. Treats of man's origin and destiny, on the relation of matter and form, on man's task on earth, on Teshuvah and the meaning of life.

ספר הלכות גדולות. One of the earliest compilations of decisions extracted from the Talmud and arranged in accordance with the order of the Mishna.

סידור הגר"א by R. Elijah of Vilna, 1720-1798. Outstanding genius in all branches of religious law and lore as well as general sciences. Author of many works, among them a prayer book with notes and explanations.

ספר חסידים. Sefer Chassidim by R. Jehuda Ha-Chassid ("The Pious") one of the תוס'. Parts of it by his father R. Samuel ha-Navi ("The Prophet").

עטרת זקנים R. Menachem Mendel of Krotoshin. Addenda to the laws as codified in the שולחן ערוך (cf. ibid.).

קדושת לוי, Kedushath Levi by R. Levi Yitzchak of Berditchev, the "Berditchever" one of the leaders of early Chassidism, 1740-1809. Pupil of R. Baer of Meseritz and son-in-law of R. Shneur Zalman of Ladi. R. Levi became known as the most ardent intercessor for his people. Numerous stories tell of his pleading with G-d for mercy and forgiveness for his brothers.

רד"ק, (ר' דוד קמחי) R. David Kimchi (known as ReDaK) 1160-1235, lived in Narbonne, S. France. Grammarian and exegete his commentary on the books of

prophets, psalms and Chronicles are widely studied. (Parts
of his commentary on Genesis are also preserved). His
commentaries are highly valued by Jews and Christians.
They were translated into Latin by the latter and profoundly affected later Bible translations such as the King
James version.

רמב״ם. R. Moses Ben Maimon (Maimonides). Born
in Cordova, Spain on Nison 14, 1135; died in Fostat,
Egypt on Tebet 20, 1204. First systematic codifier of the
entire Jewish law, in the Mishne Torah, also called יד
החזקה, under which name the work is generally known.
Leading Jewish philosopher of the Middle Ages. His
philosophical ideas are expounded: 1. In the שמונה
פרקים, that part of his Commentary to the Mishnah which
forms the introduction to Aboth. 2. In an excursus to the
Commentary on the 10th פרק of Sanhedrin, where he
collected the י״ג עיקרים, the 13 "roots" articles of faith.
3. In various portions of the יד החזקה such as the הלכות
דעות and הלכות יסודי התורה. 4. In his philosophical treatise
Moreh Nevuchim, "The Guide of the Perplexed." The
influences of Rambam's works on life, thinking and development of Judaism can hardly be overestimated. The
clarity of his thoughts, the classical simplicity of his exposition, the magnificent sweep of his concept have attracted
the devoted study of Jewish scholars throughout the ages.

רש״י, Rashi — R. Shlomoh bar Yitzchak. Lived in
Troyes, France 1040 - 1105. The standard commentator
of Bible and Talmud. With its unrivalled combination
of brevity and lucidity of exposition, Rashi guides the
student through the most difficult passages of Torah and
Talmud. His commentary on the Torah was the first Hebrew work to be printed (1475). The Talmud-commentary
was, by his successors, simply called Kuntres, "The Commentary." The pedagogic genius of Rashi instinctively
recognizes what the questions and objections of the
students will be, and he answers these with touchingly
modest brevity, often by a single word. Yet despite
the bewildering completeness of his knowledge, Rashi
uses almost exclusively interpretation received from his
teachers, very rarely his own.

שבולי לקט by R. Zilkiah ben Abraham ha-Rofe ("The Physician"). Glosses on the first part of the טור.

שני לוחות הברית) של"ה) by R. Jesaiah Horwitz (Intro. by his son R. Sheftel H.). Lived in the early 17th century. Famous Kabbalist.

שלחן ערוך) ש"ע) "The Prepared Table." The authoritative Code of Jewish law. Author R. Joseph Caro. First printed 1565. Its four parts correspond to those of the טור (cf. ibid.).

תוספות (תוס'). Tosafoth — Additions. Notes on the Talmud discussing difficult passages, extracting halachic decisions, establishing correct versions etc.. They were composed in the centuries after Rashi (cf. ibid.). Among their authors were Rashi's grandsons. The Tosafists have greatly influenced the formation of Halacha.